3650

CLIENT

SERVER

dBASE

PROGRAMMING

Building Mission-Critical dBase Systems

Martin L. Rinehart

Addison-Wesley Publishing Company
Reading, Massachusetts • Menlo Park, California • New York
Don Mills, Ontario • Wokingham, England • Amsterdam
Bonn • Sydney • Singapore • Tokyo • Madrid • San Juan
Paris • Seoul • Milan • Mexico City • Taipei

Many of the designations used by manufacturers and sellers to distinguish their products are claimed as trademarks. Where those designations appear in this book, and Addison-Wesley was aware of a trademark claim, the designations have been printed in initial capital letters or all capital letters.

The authors and publishers have taken care in preparation of this book, but make no expressed or implied warranty of any kind and assume no responsibility for errors or omissions. No liability is assumed for incidental or consequential damages in connection with or arising out of the use of the information or programs contained herein.

Library of Congress Cataloging-in-Publication Data

Rinehart, Martin L.
    Client-server dBase programming : building mission-critical dBase
systems / Martin L. Rinehart.
      p.   cm.
    Includes index.
    ISBN 0-201-40640-3
    1. Client/server computing.   2. dBase IV (Computer file)
    I. Title
QA76.9.C55R56   1994
005.75′8—dc20   94-8467
                                                      CIP

Sponsoring Editor: Philip Sutherland
Project Editor: Elizabeth Rogalin
Production Coordinator: Lora L. Ryan
Cover design: Barbara T. Atkinson
Set in 10 point Times Roman by G & S Typesetters, Inc.

1 2 3 4 5 6 7 8 9 -MA- 9897969594
First printing, April 1994

Addison-Wesley books are available for bulk purchases by corporations, institutions, and other organizations. For more information please contact the Corporate, Government and Special Sales Department at (800) 238-9682.

This book is dedicated to Wayne Ratliff, the mother of dBASE.

Acknowledgments

In the late 1970s, Wayne Ratliff wanted to keep track of the office football pool. Wayne didn't think he should use the mainframe, so he decided to implement the mainframe's fourth-generation database language on his personal, 8-bit microcomputer.

If Wayne had an ounce of sense, he would have realized that you can't fit an operating system, a fourth-generation language, a user program, and data into just 48K of RAM. But sometimes it helps not to know that something is "impossible."

Working in assembler, Wayne did the impossible, and NASA'S 4GL, JPLDIS, was reborn as "Vulcan" on a Z-80 micro.

George Tate and Hal Lashlee, with marketing help from Hal Pawluk, turned Vulcan into dBASE II, growing it from an obscure language into an industry standard.

Without these pioneers we wouldn't have dBASE today.

Without the crew at Addison-Wesley you wouldn't have this book.

My thanks to all.

Contents

Chapter 1

Client-Server dBASE Systems

I've been helping clients build client-server dBASE systems for years. These systems have ranged from simple, departmental information systems to auditable, mission-critical accounting systems. In every case, using a client-server system has saved at least 80% of the hardware costs of a traditional minicomputer or mainframe system. *Average* savings have been around 90%.

In this book, I'll help you build client-server dBASE systems that can handle even the toughest, mission-critical, auditable requirements. I assume that you already know dBASE programming and have either developed personal systems in dBASE, or have come from a minicomputer or mainframe background. Whether you are coming from the PC side, or the "glass house" side (minicomputers and mainframes), there is a knowledge base presented here that will let you build successful client-server dBASE systems, starting with your first one.

The Future of Client-Server

Client-server systems hardware costs an average of 90% less than the systems it replaces. This has made client-server systems very popular with management. PC-based systems hardware has become cheap while the power of inexpensive servers has increased dramatically, and there is no end to this trend in sight. Applications that required a mainframe a few years ago are now within the capabilities of an inexpensive server.

As this trend continues to accelerate, small, mass-produced servers are receiving more and more of the computer industry's research and development budget. The transfer of development funds from mainframes into PCs guarantees that the small computers will become as powerful as today's largest mainframes in the near future, ensuring the explosive growth of client-server computing.

Still I hear and read that you can't do real client-server systems in dBASE. And those same pundits say you definitely cannot build auditable, mission-critical systems in dBASE. Well, I guess there are still people who believe that the earth is flat, and who let no contrary facts confuse their opinions.

There is some legitimate confusion, so let's dispense with that, first. The term "client-server" is itself undefined. In general, it refers to the use of multiple computers on a network. One or more of these computers act as "servers," providing data to the others, the "clients," as they request it.

Data Servers and DBMS Servers

But if you try to pin down the term "server," it starts getting elusive. Exactly what constitutes a server? Is it a server if it simply stores the data? Or is it a server when it provides other services, such as checking data updates against business rules?

Data Servers

To avoid confusion, we'll use the terms "data server" and "DBMS server." A data server is a central repository for data files, providing access to these files on request. The data server has no intelligence with one exception: It will cooperate with the network operating system to check that the requesting client has permission to access the data. With appropriate permission, it will allow reads and/or writes to the data.

Centralizing data on a server makes network administration much simpler. The network managers make sure that frequent data backups are performed, that user names and passwords are validated, and so on. This way, the data is isolated from the habits (some good, and some not so good) of individual users.

Otherwise, the data server does not have any intelligence.

DBMS Servers

The DBMS server, unlike the data server, provides a wealth of intelligent services. It makes sure that data updates conform to business rules (no six-figure salaries for the Junior Assistants, please!). It enforces other data integrity rules, such as not deleting customers who have outstanding invoices.

Those who said that dBASE could not "do" client-server systems were referring to DBMS servers, not data servers. dBASE has been capable of doing client-server work with data servers for years. Today, you can use dBASE in either its native, data-server configuration, or you can use it along with a DBMS server from any of the most popular DBMS software providers.

Through the magic of Borland's IDAPI (Independent Database Application Programming Interface), the same program that addresses native .DBF-format data files on a data server can also address other RDBMS (Relational Database Management System) data on true DBMS servers. As you will see in Chapter 2, you should base your choice of back-end configuration (.DBF files or RDBMS system) on performance considerations.

Mission-Critical, Auditable Systems

What is a mission-critical system? Any system your enterprise depends on to meet its basic objective(s) is correctly called mission-critical. For example, almost every system that controls the collection and disbursement of funds is mission-critical if the amounts involved are substantial (relative to the size of the organization).

Almost every system that deals with an enterprise's customers is mission-critical. For an airline, the reservation system is mission-critical. For a hospital, the admissions system is mission-critical. For a lending institution, the loan qualification system is mission-critical. For a sales organization, the prospect and customer-tracking systems may be mission-critical.

Auditable systems are those that are of vital importance to an organizations' auditors. They are a subset of the organization's mission-critical systems. These are generally the systems that deal with collection and disbursement of funds and other important assets and liabilities. Auditable systems must meet the highest standards for accurate data that is consistently maintained and well-protected from both casual and deliberate misuse.

The essence of dBASE, some contend, runs contrary to the needs of mission-critical, auditable data. Any user can simply go to the dBASE Control Center and start to mess around with the data in ways no one can control. The very nature of *ad hoc* data use seems to oppose the needs of mission-critical, auditable data systems.

As always, there's a kernel of truth, and a huge misunderstanding behind this misconception.

The truth is that *ad hoc*, end-user access to data is not compatible with the requirements for mission-critical, auditable systems. However, this does not mean that the underlying data files need to be available for *ad hoc*, end-user access.

For example, every employee in an organization has a legitimate interest in certain types of personnel information, such as names, titles, telephone numbers, and mail addresses. The Personnel Department can extract a file containing this public information and place it on readily available servers. Other confidential information, such as compensation, can be kept separately, usually on a single machine or on a network with access limited to the personnel department.

More generally, files containing public information can be extracted from the auditable files as required. Certainly, the Marketing Department will make extensive use of a business's sales data, but this does not imply that Marketing is permitted *ad hoc* entry into accounts receivable data. What it does require is that the

Accounting staff makes copies of this data available, probably in summary form, for the needs of the analysts in Marketing.

Native dBASE data (tables in .DBF-format files) is more widely readable than the proprietary formats used in RDBMS systems. Most popular spreadsheet and word processing software can read .DBF files directly. So data in this format should be tightly controlled if it is sensitive.

With the advent of "middle-ware" packages such as Borland's IDAPI and Microsoft's ODBC, data in RDBMS packages is becoming as widely readable as the .DBF format. The ready availability of .DBF-format data should be counted only a minor and temporary difference between this format and the proprietary RDBMS formats. RDBMS data also requires strong controls if its use is to be restricted to those who are duly authorized.

To summarize, dBASE systems can do client-server work directly using .DBF-format data on servers, or can do the client portion of the work cooperating with a wide variety of RDBMS software packages running on DBMS servers. One of these alternatives, or a combination of both, may be selected to optimize your system performance, as discussed in Chapter 2.

While dBASE does provide ad hoc analysis, it is up to the system's designers and administrators to see that data is provided where it is needed, but that ad hoc access is not permitted in the auditable files. The same types of precautions that are required for .DBF-format data also must be taken for other data sources.

Client-Server Operations

The one thing that everyone agrees is needed for client-server computing is a server computer, one or more client computers, and a network to connect them. From our point of view, client-server operations are dBASE operations carried out over a network.

Installing and maintaining even a modest Local Area Network (LAN) is a major undertaking, one outside the scope of this book. Most large organizations already have multiple LANs, linked through routers and bridges into Wide Area Networks (WANs)— a subject of considerable complexity that will not be addressed here.

For the purpose of this book, I assume that you have at least a LAN and a server, probably a dedicated server, available with enough disk space to accommodate your application.

If you have never accessed data from a remote server in a dBASE program, the good news is that it's trivially simple. The drive(s) on the server are given a drive letter by the network operating system, and your software just uses that identifier as it would any local drive. For example, if your network server is drive N:, you access the data via a simple USE command:

```
USE N:<tablename>
```

This is no more complex than accessing local data. Of course, if that were all there were to mission-critical, auditable client-server programming, this would be a very short book! As you'll see, there are many issues you'll need to understand and address as you build your system. However, using the network to access remote data is not one of them.

If you choose to install an RDBMS on your server, you can still bring a table on a remote server into use with the same command:

```
USE N:<tablename>
```

In general, the dBASE commands for RDBMS work are the same as those you use for local .DBF access, mapped to appropriate calls by Borland's IDAPI interface. In this book, I will explain the use of native .DBF files, as these place the most demands on you as analyst, designer, and programmer. If you have an RDBMS system, some of these considerations will already be taken care of for you.

But just using an RDBMS does *not* build a client-server system for you. If we look at the job in terms of this book, if you build a system with an RDBMS server you can skip over Chapters 8 and 9, some of 10 and 11, and a bit of some others. An RDBMS will not simplify the design job, and will simplify only some of the server portion of the programming job.

Is it easier to use an RDBMS? It depends. If you install an RDBMS, someone will still have to master whichever package you choose. That is a significant job—perhaps three to six months' work to become highly skilled. Once your organization is over that hurdle, the RDBMS can simplify the other programming.

Building a back-end subsystem as explained here is somewhat simpler than mastering an RDBMS package. It also provides fewer features. In general, if you have a large programming staff an RDBMS will pay dividends in reduced programming effort. For a small staff, an RDBMS will not save time. Chapter 2 addresses the performance trade-offs.

In this book, you will learn to build client-server software without the benefit of an RDBMS. If you have already decided to use an RDBMS for your next job, this means you can skim over the chapters mentioned above. You will find, however, that knowing how to do this work without an RDBMS will give you a better appreciation of what the RDBMS is doing, and it will let you build your next .DBF-based system.

Summary

Client-server computing can use mass-produced PCs for most or all of the computing power needed in a system. This saves up to 90% of the hardware cost that would be needed for a traditional mainframe or minicomputer system. The hardware cost differential will continue to increase.

Along with the cost differential, the power of PC-based systems will continue to increase exponentially until it exceeds the power of mainframe systems. This will happen in the foreseeable future as hardware vendors continue to move their R&D budgets out of the older computers and into PC-based computers.

These factors guarantee that the future of data processing is in client-server systems, even though these systems may be more demanding to properly design and program than the older "glass house" systems.

Servers can be either data servers, which basically store and provide access to files, or RDBMS servers, which provide relational database services to the client computers. Some people have argued that dBASE could not do client-server computing since it was not an RDBMS.

While RDBMS back-ends may be desirable in some situations, dBASE provides an excellent environment for programming the client portion of all client-server solutions. Through IDAPI, it accesses RDBMS systems as easily as it accesses .DBF files.

In this book we will look at using .DBF-based systems, since the programming effort of these is a superset of the effort required for RDBMS-based systems. You will see that RDBMS-type services, such as maintaining secure database access and referential integrity, are definitely possible with only native dBASE tools. .DBF-based systems running on data servers can meet the most demanding requirements for mission-critical, auditable systems.

Mission-critical systems are those that your enterprise depends on for its fundamental requirements. This could be the manufacture and sale of products, the treatment of hospital patients, or the delivery of government services. Almost all systems dealing with the enterprise's finances, including control of assets and liabilities, are mission-critical.

Auditors are employed by the enterprise, or mandated by oversight organizations, to review the quality of mission-critical systems. We call a system "auditable" if it meets the auditor's standards. These systems must meet the highest standards for accurate, consistently maintained data.

Client-server operations imply data access over a network. These operations are no more complex than accessing data on a local drive, thanks to the network operating system and, if you use an RDBMS, the services of Borland's IDAPI. In this regard, client-server programs only differ from simple, personal programs in the drive letter specified in the USE command.

However, client-server programs are more demanding than single-user systems. Multi-user systems have an additional set of requirements, and the need for auditable systems imposes other requirements. Using an RDBMS saves some of the programming effort required to meet these additional requirements, but you still need an additional skill set to master client-server programs.

In the following chapters, we'll go over the additional tools you'll need to produce your own mission-critical, auditable client-server systems.

Chapter 2

Client-Server System Design

Systems are built from four key components: hardware, people, data, and software. This book is mainly about the software component, but we will consider the other three in brief.

This does *not* imply that your consideration of the other components should be brief. It simply reflects the fact that no one book can cover more than a portion of this vast subject.

In some cases, design failures are relatively rare and correctable, assuming that you use a little common sense. For example, you may choose one type of client computer, only to later discover that it is not a suitable choice. If you bought two or three for use during development, you will have spent only a very small amount of a typical hardware budget. (And the hardware budget will usually be only a small part of the total budget.)

On the other hand, if you ignore the people issues at the outset, you may very well be undertaking a system that will eventually be a failure, no matter how successfully you build the software.

You should, of course, stay flexible in your design. Picking today's best server, for example, will certainly give you a choice that is far more expensive and far less powerful than what will be available in a few months. The same is true of RDBMS software, if your system is going to use an RDBMS.

Hardware

Hardware can be considered in three parts: clients, servers, and networks. Generally speaking, contemporary PCs make fine client computers. For text-mode systems, client computers can be considerably less than state-of-the-art, which means inexpensive. Graphical User Interface (GUI) clients require more computing horsepower, but can still provide excellent performance with only middle-of-the-road capabilities.

Servers can be PC-based or larger. Current off-the-shelf, PC-based servers accommodate a few gigabytes of data. As a rule of thumb, get three times the disk space required to accommodate your target application. As another rule of thumb, if an off-the-shelf server is large enough, your application will run nicely.

If your data requirements lead you into custom servers, using the latest multi-gigabyte drives, you will need to look at performance issues very closely. If the network traffic and CPU utilization considerations as detailed below suggest an RDBMS-based solution, you will be able to use a variety of more powerful UNIX-based computers for the server, so an acceptable solution is at hand. If the same calculations lead you to choose a .DBF-based solution, you will be pushing the state-of-the-art in PC-based systems.

Of course, any system that pushes the state-of-the-art today is going to be within range of off-the-shelf hardware in only a year or two. So you should carefully consider the growth of your system, in areas such as database size and number of simultaneous users. If your system is too large for PC-based client-server solutions today, will it be too large tomorrow? In many instances, the power of off-the-shelf components will expand quickly enough that your system will fit nicely even before it is fully operational.

Except as a design factor in the .DBF- or RDBMS-based system decision, this book will not cover networks. From the dBASE software point of view, networks just mean that the data is on a drive such as N: instead of on C:. As a designer, however, you must constantly keep network throughput in mind.

You can easily build a .DBF-based system that your server will support, even under the load of hundreds of users. On the other hand, the same system may be disastrously slow because there is too much traffic for your network. (Or your system may be performing faultlessly as you designed it, but the unexpected boom in email traffic over your network still leads to the system slowing to a crawl.)

Networks are generally outside the scope of this book, but they are not outside of your concerns as a system designer.

People

Over the years, I have been involved with many successful systems, and a few failures. In every case, the failures happened when the people involved were not committed to the project's success. If the people involved are behind the system effort, you can always fix the technical problems.

If the people affected feel threatened by your system, or are not behind it for political reasons, technical brilliance will be wasted. If your potential users are not with you, nothing in this book will help.

People are your first priority.

Stop right now and think through your people situation. Do you have eager users, anxious to get their work automated? Are they willing to sit with you and look at screen designs? Are they standing by to help in any way they can? Good! Go forward.

But maybe your users are worried that your system will automate them right out of a job. Maybe senior management wants to cut staff and thinks that your system will help. Don't kid yourself that the folks "in the trenches" can't sense this. They know it and under these conditions you will probably *never* get your system to work.

If this is your situation, go back to management immediately. Tell them that there is no way to build a successful system without the support of the employees. Suggest that there are two ways to deal with this problem.

If the employees are valuable, management must first find their post-implementation career paths and lay them out. There is nothing like an employee who gets a promotion as soon as your system is up and running! You will get all the help you could want.

The other solution is brutal. If the people affected are slated to become unemployed as soon as your system is up and running, fire them today. Your system will never get going with an entrenched base of employees who are doing everything possible to make it fail.

Fire them, and divide their work over the survivors. Hire temps if you must. The survivors will be eager to get your system installed, since they will be hopelessly overworked without it. (Make sure that hopelessly overworked doesn't mean earning fat overtime bonuses, or you will have done nothing to improve your system's chances.)

Data

Presumably, you are reading this book because you have decided to use dBASE, or are considering it as an option. This means you have already made the first decision: you will be using a relational database.

Relational v. Other Databases

E.F. Codd, the father of relational databases, first wrote about their benefits in the late '60s and early '70s. During the '70s, most commercial databases were hierarchical ones.

Hierarchical databases work well for tree-structured data. For example, you have multiple customers. Each customer can have multiple invoices. Each invoice has multiple line-items.

Of course, the invoice's line item involves a product or service. The product or service file is outside the simple customer/ invoice/line item hierarchy. In practice, a lot of data is hierarchical, but very few databases are entirely hierarchical. Systems built with hierarchical databases tend to start clean and then get messy as soon as the non-hierarchical components are grafted on.

To address the problem, the network data model was invented. Network databases were intended to replace hierarchical ones, eliminating the requirement that data relationships be tree-structured. The network model allowed data connections in unlimited ways.

Other database technology was also developed. Many of the older structures are no longer with us. In many cases, this is fortunate. One of the structures that has survived and is very important today is the inverted database.

In an inverted database, some or all of the fields in the file are stored in a sorted order, with a complex system of pointers tying the entire record together. For example, names might be stored in alphabetical order, and addresses might be stored by metropolitan region. This technology makes access to the data very rapid.

It is not really correct to compare the network model to the inverted model, of course, since a network database could use inverted technology at the implementation level. To clean up this discussion, we can separate the database into logical and physical components.

The logical model is the one that the user sees and the programmer addresses. The physical model is another, lower layer. The database system programmers can choose many different physical structures to implement a logical model.

Codd proposed the use of tables (in mathematics, "relations" are the name given to tables) as the single, unifying logical model. He showed that tables could hold all of the data in a database. By using a very small number of operations on tables, we could get whatever data we needed, in whatever form we needed it. For instance, a "join" operation would let us tie customer name and address data to data in an invoice table.

The elegant simplicity of the relational model led to its acceptance as the model of choice. By the late '70s, all database vendors sold systems that were called "relational." However, many critics, led by Codd himself, pointed out that the relational capabilities of those databases were often features built by the marketing staffs, not the development staffs.

Frequently, the marketers simply put the word "relational" into the name of an existing hierarchical or other database. The original dBASE was dBASE II, shipped in 1981 by a company subsequently acquired by Borland. It was marketed as a relational database management system, when the truth was that it was and still is a programming language that could manipulate data in tables.

Having all the data in tables naturally led dBASE programmers into a relational view of their data. But there was no underlying database system, unless the programmer created one. dBASE was typical of the systems that were marketed as relational without giving serious consideration to the implementation of true RDBMS capabilities.

In this book, we will discuss the techniques needed to use dBASE's table manipulation capabilities as the foundation for an integrated, relational database.

Data Accuracy

Our system, whether .DBF-based or built around an RDBMS, will be no better than the data that is entered. Maintaining bullet-proof referential integrity, for example, means that each invoice will be for one and only one customer, and that there will be no way to delete that customer while an invoice record refers to that customer.

This is desirable, of course. On the other hand, it is useless if the invoice was assigned to the wrong customer in the first place.

The data accuracy problem may be another manifestation of the people problem. Are your people providing accurate data, or just data that fits into the system? Your system can be programmed to do a fine job of helping its users in entering accurate data, but it will ultimately fail if the users are not motivated to collect and enter accurate data.

Data accuracy may extend beyond your boundaries, even if your people are totally dedicated to the system. You have to examine the sources of data to be sure that it is reliable before it arrives in your enterprise.

You may be surprised that, when you first meet with an auditor, he or she gives a rather quick look at the audit trails and rollback recovery subsystems of which you are so proud. Instead, you'll get all sorts of questions about your source documents—who prepares them, who checks them, and so on.

Before you start to question your auditor's technical competence, think about the order of things. What good is the world's best system if it does not have reliable data? Until you have a clean (or, at least, the cleanest possible) source of data you can't really start worrying about the system that processes the data.

As with the people problem, the data accuracy problem (or Garbage In, Garbage Out—GIGO) is beyond the scope of this book. GIGO problems are usually easy to solve as long as you do not also have fundamental people problems. People problems inevitably surface as GIGO issues.

Software

There are many ways of creating client-server software. You can work with dBASE, or one of the other Xbase flavors, or with other languages such as BASIC or C. There is no single "best" language for software development. Any of these could work successfully for almost any client-server software system.

The Xbase dialects, including dBASE, were developed specifically for data processing system development. Since they all interface with routines written in lower-level languages, such as C or assembler, there is no fundamental limit on the work that can be done in Xbase.

dBASE is the grandfather of all the Xbase flavors. For a time it was the market leader, but remained a great deal slower than its competitors. When Borland took over, however, dBASE closed the speed gap, then opened a lead over its competitors in many areas. With the release of version 2.0 of the dBASE Compiler for DOS, Borland set a new standard. dBASE is an excellent choice for client-server software development.

System Look and Feel

In general, I recommend using a CUA-compatible design (IBM's Common User Access specification) whenever possible. This makes it easy to train users who have any experience with other CUA-compatible programs, such as most Microsoft Windows applications.

Unfortunately, one of the most common of the CUA specifications does not work very well for database applications. The Files option is the option on the left of a CUA-compliant main menu. Having a single Files option is generally inapplicable for database work since the whole application is based on files.

Generally, we will have two classes of users: those entering and maintaining the data, and those using the data. We'll call them "data collectors" and "data consumers."

Data Consumers' Systems

Data consumers will be running reports, entering queries, and building spreadsheets. *Ad hoc* query capability is seldom provided in the core client-server system. *Ad hoc* updating ability must never be available.

Generally, the system administrator runs a batch process (at a regularly scheduled time, usually in the evenings or on weekends when system load is otherwise light) that will create subsets of data, summarized in ways that your data consumers want.

Multiple summary data sets are generally made available for querying, use in spreadsheets, or analysis via tools such as the dBASE Control Center and other personal computing tools. As almost all end-user tools have the ability to read .DBF-format data, preparing useful sets of .DBFs is straightforward.

These data consumers are doing personal computing jobs outside the scope of this book. An auditable, mission-critical client-server system must provide data for these users, but must not permit *ad hoc* updates of the source data files. Your analytical users will consider the system successful if they have open access to lots of data summarized in useful ways. It's our job as system architects and implementors to ensure not only that the data they need is available to them, but to control access to the source data as well.

In open environments (open political environments, not necessarily open computer systems) the simplest and most complete *ad hoc* capability is provided by simply copying the entire database onto a publicly available server. (Of course, some sensitive data, such as salaries, will not be handled this way.) If you can possibly do this, I recommend it, because two things will happen.

First, some users will make a mess of the data. Other users will be unable to do their jobs, at least temporarily. Both groups of users will then begin to appreciate the need for data controls. Most PC users are not accustomed to, nor will they be comfortable with, read-only access to the data. (Though read-only access is, of course, exactly what they need). Let them tell you to make their access read-only—don't do it until they ask you to.

Second, most users will find that joining data from multiple tables into a usable form is a non-trivial job. Even tools such as QBE begin to hit usability limits when your users need to join many files to get useful results. Processes such as totaling transactions into a useful form are at best slow, and at worst beyond the scope of personal computing tools.

I have *never* been able to convince any PC-literate user community that this would be the case by telling them so in advance. The need for summary data prepared by a central authority (MIS or otherwise) always makes users suspicious that they are marching backwards to the bad old days when only those in the "glass house" had access to the data, and user requirements could go unmet for years.

The only technique I have found to be reliable is to let the user communities discover for themselves that they need regularly updated, controlled summary data. If you let them come to you and request this service, they will understand that you are working for them. If you provide this service without letting them discover the need, they will never trust you.

This book will not further cover the needs of data consumers. If you provide them with a generous supply of summarized data, they will be able to do their personal computing work. We are mainly concerned with the organizational, client-server computing portion of the task.

Menus for Data Collectors

For our core client-server system, our users are the data collectors who enter and maintain the source data. Generally, they will need direct access to each Object and Event table, and indirect access to the Detail and Relationship files.

Your data collection system will typically include a direct menu selection for each Object and Event in your system. If there are a small number of these tables, simply place them on the main menu, in the center area that CUA reserves for application-specific menu items.

If there are more Objects and Events than conveniently fit, create reasonable categories and group them accordingly. The categories may hold Objects and Events separately, or they may group Objects with related Events—this should grow out of your application. Again, the categories should go in the center area of the main menu.

The categories will then have associated pull-down mcnus to go directly to the individual Objects and Events. You should not normally need a second level of pull-downs to accommodate a reasonable number of Object and Event tables.

The CUA specification places the Print and Exit items in the pull-down from the Files menu selection on the left. If you have ancillary files that are separate from the main tables, you can group these together with the Print and Exit options under the Files menu. In their absence, you can still group the non-Files options, Print and Exit, under the left-most menu option.

What about the Detail and Relationship tables? These normally are accessed through the Object and Event maintenance routines.

Scrolling Maintenance

I do all my Object and Event maintenance through Scrollers. Each Object or Event is given a "natural" order index—one that puts the data into an order that the user finds understandable.

With Object tables, ordering the table alphabetically in ascending order on name (last name for people) generally provides a natural order. With Event tables, you usually want to organize in date (or date/time) order, in descending sequence. Within a time, you may wish a sub-sort criteria if you have many events for a single time.

The scroller responds to the normal navigation keys (arrows, PgUp/Dn, Home/End) and responds to one or more alpha-numeric keystrokes (pressing "smi" to get to the first "Smith").

I supplement the scroller with "information" boxes. These are windows that show additional data on the highlighted record. The scroller might just have a person's last name, for example. The information box could have full name, address and telephone data. This leads the users' eyes from the scroller for coarse searching (finding the first "Smith") to the information box for fine-grained searching (finding "Josephine Q. Smith").

One keystroke pops up a data-entry screen for the highlighted scroll record. Another keystroke provides the ability to add new Objects or Events, and a third deletes the highlighted record (usually with a dialog box popping up that asks, "Do you really want to delete this record?"). I use Enter, Ins, and Del for these functions, but any other consistently used set could work as well.

Many-to-One (M:1) Scrolling Lookup

Being able to scroll through any Object or Event implies the existence of scrolling subroutines for each of these table types. This makes many-to-one (M:1) scrolling lookup very simple to code. (Relationships such as M:1 are the subject of Chapter 5.)

For example, in entering a sale Event, the customer table scroller should pop up. The data collector can then point at the correct customer and press a confirming key (normally Enter). On editing the sale Event record, the customer table scroller will pop up with the previously selected customer highlighted.

If Enter is used as the confirming keystroke, this means that the data collector can press Enter to leave the prior selection intact, as can be done for any character string or numeric field.

By enabling multiple keystroke lookups (again, typing "smi" to get to the first "Smith") the scrolling lookup method is guaranteed to never require more keystrokes than typing in a name or other identifier. You will see that this is critical when we discuss relational integrity.

One-to-Many (1:M) Scrolling

The scrolling lookup in the M:1 context has become standard fare. Less standard, but equally straightforward, is the activity in the 1:M direction. Generally, the M:1 direction is automatically travelled at the appropriate point in the data-entry screen.

The 1:M* (zero or more) is available from the 1-side data-entry screen via a question. The customer data screen might ask "View invoices?," for example. The 1:M+ (one or more) relationship may automatically be triggered at the appropriate point in the data-entry screen. For example, the invoice details might come up after choosing the invoice and customer.

Whether entry to the M side is user-selected or automatic, the same scroller activity occurs. The M-side data is restricted to those data participating in the relationship. Only invoices for the selected customer are shown, only invoice detail lines for the particular invoice are shown, and so on.

The scroller on the M side effectively eliminates all entries except those tied to the 1 side.

Note that the behavior described here applies to almost all Detail tables. An employee's dependents can be accessed from the entry panel that handles the employee Object. In most cases, this is exactly the access you want. From the point of view of the data collector, details are just that: details about an Object or Event (or, less commonly, about other Details).

This does not mean that Detail tables should not be directly accessible from a menu selection. For example, in an insurance claims system it might be helpful to have direct access to the employees' dependents table. (Your clerk is working on a claim for Mary Smith, a dependent of one of your employees. Without direct access to the dependents, it might be difficult to find the "Smith" to whom Mary is related.)

If you provide direct access to a dependent's Detail table, the access to the employee Object table is just the same as the other M:1 lookups discussed above. Note that the information boxes displayed as the user scrolls through a table may include data from the 1 side of an M:1 relationship. Scrolling through the dependents may show the employee's name and other data.

Many-to-Many (M:M) Scrolling

A many-to-many (M:M) relationship table may be entered from either side. The 1:M and M:1 handlers discussed above also handle M:M Relationship tables. Consider a set of consultants and a set of clients. Each consultant handles assignments from multiple clients; each client engages multiple consultants. A relationship table holds the M:M consultant:client relationship.

Let's consider the client side first. From the client side, the relationship is 1:M*. The client can employ zero or more consultants. The client's data-entry screen presents an option such as "View consultant engagements?." On a Yes answer, the data collector sees the list of consultants that have been engaged by that client.

Actually, the system is showing the entries in the M:M Relationship table, restricted to those pertaining to a particular client. Scrolling through the engagement table, the information panels show parent table data from the M:1 relationship between engagements and consultants. In this case, that would be data in the consultant table, such as name, address, phone, and specialties.

An interesting fact about this M:M treatment is that it does not require any software beyond that which you create to handle 1:M and M:1 relationships. You would have guessed this to be the case if you remembered that the relational model does not have a separate M:M relationship facility—it handles M:M relationships via a table with two or more M:1 relationships.

Queries and Reports

There will be less need in the data collector software for queries and reports than you might first assume. These can be handled in the same manner as data consumer queries and reports—separate, personal computing tasks that can be performed with standard personal computing tools accessing a generated summary data set.

You must take the same precautions with the data collectors that you take with the data consumers. If the data collector is given *ad hoc* update access to the source .DBFs, all your other efforts to maintain auditable, mission-critical data are defeated.

This is not to suggest that your data collectors will act with anything other than the best intentions (although other intentions are certainly a possibility to be kept in mind). If your data collector can use the dot prompt to DELETE a record, your referential integrity is defeated.

Remember that your data administrators can get around all restrictions. My clients all report the same problem: the software has bullet-proof integrity (it's not difficult, as you'll discover in Chap-ter 15), but everyone has at one time or another caused a referential integrity failure by doing manual data edits.

These data administrators are highly-trained people doing their best to maintain a solid system. (If any were doing otherwise, they didn't report that fact to me!) Data collectors presumably are less skilled and much more likely to cause inadvertent damage.

Summary

While this book is about software, in particular dBASE software, the client-server system is a collection of parts that must work together for the system to succeed.

A dBASE client-server system can be built with inexpensive PCs as clients. The servers can also be PC-based if the system will be using no more than a few gigabytes of data. For a larger system, UNIX-based servers can be used with dBASE clients.

Hardware choices are relatively simple. You should keep in mind the rapid rate of growth in PC-based hardware capacity. If today's PC solutions are somewhat low in capacity, you should remember that tomorrow's PCs will be faster and larger. If you build and deploy a system over a year, you will be able to use PCs with much more capacity than are available today.

People issues, while outside the scope of this book, are critical to your success. If your potential users are not with you, nothing in this book will help. People problems can undermine any system.

The most common prescription for failure is to attempt to build a system that will eventually displace the people you're depending on to get the system up and running. You must make sure that management has provided clear benefits, such as promotions for the people involved, or you must bite the bullet and downsize the staff before, not after, you build the system.

Data problems are also outside the scope of this book, but are just as important as people problems. If you do not have clean data, the most bulletproof referential integrity, for example, is wasted.

Data problems are frequently the manifestation of underlying people problems. If your people do not want your system to succeed, it is unlikely that your system will ever become populated with clean data. Even with motivated people, outside data sources can still cause serious problems.

Software, our subject, is the last of the design considerations. dBASE is an excellent choice for most client software and for many systems' server software, as well.

Using a CUA-compatible user interface simplifies design, and simplifies training. You cannot slavishly follow the CUA specifications, however, as they will not be entirely appropriate for your system.

Using a scroller-based design allows you to support all the common user requirements in a simple, smooth system. One-to-many relationships, many-to-one relationships, and many-to-many relationships can all be handled smoothly using a scroller-based system.

We'll cover database design first. Then we'll move on to the internals of mission-critical, auditable client-server systems, using the database design tools for the back end and the scroller-based design for the front end. But first, we'll take a detour.

In the next chapter, we'll get ready to work by looking at a powerful programmer's workbench. You'll pick up a tool that you can customize to your own needs as you build your own systems. You'll also see the tricks of event-driven, mousable front-end programming.

Chapter 3

dBASE Programmer's Workbench

In this chapter we'll put my highly personal, event-driven programmer's workbench into use. When I say "personal," I don't mean in relation to me; rather, I mean that it's personalized by everyone who uses it. Data files store its personality information so you can have a different version in each of your working directories.

It's event-driven in responding to regular keystrokes, special keystrokes, and mouse clicks. The regular keystrokes are for normal data cntry. Special keystrokes let you control it, doing tasks such as switching windows. Mouse input provides similar controls to special keystrokes.

While the rest of this book discusses back-end, database programming, in this chapter you will meet all the techniques of event-driven programming. If you decide that your client software should support a mouse-operable, event-driven front-end (and I think it should) this chapter will show you how to program these front-ends.

While we are at it, you will explore the internals of a tool that you'll probably want to use in all of your dBASE programming.

The Basics

dBASE lets you assign keystroke sequences to the PC's special function keys, or F keys. This is very handy for setting your routine programming tasks into a single keystroke. I generally use the odd-numbered keys for editing .PRGs and the even-numbered keys for running them.

As handy as this capability is, I ran into a problem—if I assigned more than three or four keys, I started to forget which did what. To get around this human limit, I wrote a program that showed little boxes for each F key, and then did GETs into fields lined up next to these boxes. I picked F2 as the key that invoked this program.

From then on, I could tap F2 and see the assignments for F3 through F10. I could also type in new assignments. That was so handy that I soon used it continuously. dBASE automatically locks F1 onto HELP and I locked F2 onto my program FKEYS. That gave me 8 assignable keys. Since the program showed all the commands, remembering them was no longer a problem.

Of course, that also made me want to have more keystrokes. So I added Ctrl-F1 (^F1) through Ctrl-F10 (^F10) in a second panel, and Shift-F1 (SF1) through Shift-F9 (SF9) in a third. (dBASE reserves Shift-F10 for keyboard macros, and ignores higher-numbered F keys if you have them.) FKEYS2 was born when I added these keys, and big, clickable pads to choose them with the mouse.

Right now, I pressed ^F3 to start editing this chapter. Shift-F3 would have started editing Chapter 13. I use the regular F keys for editing and running the programs presented throughout this book.

I found this so handy that I also wanted the DOS and dot prompt environments accessible. This took a little work, but you'll see that the results were well worth it.

A Full Tour

The code listings are all on your diskette. If you haven't already done so, bring FKEYS2.PRG into any directory where you have dBASE work in process. Bring up dBASE and get to the dot prompt. Then DO FKEYS2.

This section will take you on a guided tour of the workbench. You'll see event-driven operations at work and be able to put FKEYS2 to use for your own work. In the following sections, you'll see exactly how it's built, so you can add similar capabilities to your own programs.

F2 through F10

The first time you DO FKEYS, you are shown the dBASE default assignments. I never could remember these, since I didn't find them terribly useful. You probably have your own ideas of what *should* be assigned and I doubt that any two of you would actually agree on the best assignments.

This is not a problem with FKEYS2. For starters, let's make the F2 key invoke FKEYS2. The text cursor should be blinking in the start of the F2 field. (Click there with the mouse if you've moved it elsewhere.) Delete the word ASSIST and replace it with DO FKEYS2. Don't use any punctuation (such as the semi-colon line terminator that dBASE uses). FKEYS2 will supply this for you.

Once you've typed this command in F2, click on the Exit pad. At the dot prompt, press F2 and FKEYS2 pops right back up. Only this time, it shows "DO FKEYS2" in the F2 field. How does it know this?

FKEYS2 creates a file called FKEYS.DAT in your working directory. This is a simple ASCII file, with one line per F key. You could also assign new F keys by editing this file. Let's invoke your editor from F3 to examine this file.

I'm going to pretend that the DOS command you use to edit a file is "EDIT <filename>". I'm pretty sure that this is not true, since we all have a favorite editor. Substitute whatever works for you.

In FKEYS2, click on the first character of the F3 field. (Or use any other combination of regular field-navigation keystrokes—these

F key values are just GET fields under a regular dBASE READ.) Change this to say "!EDIT FKEYS.DAT". The "!" is needed to invoke a DOS command, of course. ("RUN EDIT FKEYS.DAT" would work, too.)

Click on the F3 box. (If you prefer, press the F3 key—either works.) You should now be in your editor, looking at the FKEYS.DAT file. Go to any line in the first 10 and type your own command right over the dBASE default. Then save and exit your editor.

You should be right back in FKEYS2, looking at the old commands you had before. Your change was ignored because FKEYS2 makes the sensible assumption that you will edit your commands in FKEYS2, not in your editor. Press Esc or ^Q to leave FKEYS2. (Pressing ^W or Enter in the last field is the same as clicking on Exit. You want to leave without saving.)

Now press F3 to check that your change is still in the FKEYS.DAT file. Make another change if you need to. Save and exit from your editor. Press F2 and you are back in FKEYS2 with the new command showing.

Ctrl and Shift F Keys

You now know how to manipulate the F keys, how they are stored, and how FKEYS2 reads your commands. Let's add the rest. Click on the Shift pad, and then on the Ctrl pad. You see the rest of the F keys displayed (they are all empty to start).

As the regular F keys were, the Shift and Ctrl F keys are each just another data-entry screen, with GETs being processed by a READ. Add some commands to test these out.

Click back on Normal, and you return to the plain F keys. From the Normal display, press ^F8 (or whatever). You see the F keys switch to ^F keys, the Ctrl pad highlighted, and your text cursor in the start of the ^F8 field. (If you had a command in ^F8, the command would have been executed. Again, pressing ^F8 is the same as clicking on ^F8—it either executes the command assigned or puts the cursor into the field waiting for you to assign a command.)

DOS and the Dot Prompt

Now let's get on to the last two boxes. First, click on the DOS box. (No mouse? Press ^O, for Operating system.) You are looking at a DOS prompt at the bottom of a nearly clear screen. At the top of the screen, a single line shows simulated System and Down buttons. Click on either of these buttons and the DOS window returns to its location on the right of the screen. (Pressing Esc works, too.)

Click on the DOS window (or ^O) again. Now try some DOS commands. When you are convinced that you're in DOS (you're *not*, of course) click on the top line. (Those little buttons are really just decorative: Clicking anywhere on the top line works.)

How does that work? There's no mouse ability in DOS, and you certainly aren't reloading dBASE every time, so what's up? Simple, it's not DOS at all. It's a dBASE program that looks like DOS. As you'll see when you get to the code, it's pretty simple to trick it.

For instance, if you use "cd" or "d:" commands to change directories, the dBASE program is smart about handling them. But if you have a batch or other program that changes directories, dBASE won't know it, so its simulated DOS prompt won't change.

Now let's go to the dot prompt. Esc or click on the top line to get out of our pseudo-DOS, back into FKEYS2. Click on the dot prompt box (or press ^P for Prompt) and you are in a small dot prompt window. Try a couple of dBASE commands to convince yourself that this is really a dot prompt running in a window under control of a dBASE program.

Again, it's *not* the dot prompt. It's a dBASE subroutine pretending to be the dot prompt. Try making a deliberate error to see the difference. (The comment in the FKEYS2 code says "world's dumbest error handler," which summarizes it nicely.)

If you want the real dBASE dot prompt, just click on Exit, or press Esc or any other READ exit keystroke. FKEYS2 is available by pressing F2, so you don't really need this imitation dot prompt. But it's handy, and takes very little code.

Back in FKEYS2, click up the dot prompt window again. Now click on the "resize" button on the upper-right corner. You get a large dot prompt. Click on "resize" again and you're back to the small window. Click it back to large and "LIST MEMORY" in the big dot prompt window.

Click on the pseudo-system button on the top left and you exit back to FKEYS2. (The actual responding click area is the button and one character to either side, so you don't have to be too precise for either the system button or the resize button.) The system button is just a nicety, since you can click anywhere outside the dot prompt window or press Esc to exit.

There is no keystroke access to the resize command. If you will be running without a mouse, you'll need to correct this. The code is explained in a little while, so you'll have no problem getting this done.

Before getting to the code, though, let's do a better installation of FKEYS2.

Another Install

FKEYS2 makes a very nice workbench. As opposed to a general purpose IDE (Integrated Development Environment), you turn it into a dedicated, personal IDE. The F key assignments in the directory I'm in right now make sense for writing this book.

In other directories, I've got completely different assignments that make sense for other projects. There is no way that anyone could remember all the different F key assignments I've made, but with FKEYS2 the screen politely displays them.

One thing is consistent in my setup: FKEYS2 is always available on the F2 key. Any other key would work just as well, but consistency pays off.

To run FKEYS2 in multiple directories, you have to be a little smarter about your installation. We just copied FKEYS2 into a working directory and began using it. Now you should move FKEYS2 (both the .PRG and .DBO files) into the directory that holds your DBASE.EXE.

I've changed my "COMMAND =" line in CONFIG.DB to:

```
COMMAND = DO \DBASE2\FKEYS2
```

(I've got multiple \DBASEx directories, with different dBASE versions.)

Remember: FKEYS2 reads FKEYS.DAT in the current directory. That way, the single copy of FKEYS2 gets a custom set of commands from each directory. (If it doesn't find FKEYS.DAT, it uses the dBASE default commands.)

Now we'll look at the code, piece by piece, so you can see how this works. Even if event-driven programming is a mystery to you right now, it will be just another coding technique you've learned by the time you get to the end of this chapter.

Startup Code

As we go through this code, you'll find a great deal that you can skim quickly. Other places you will want to read the code line-by-line to thoroughly understand it. I will suggest the appropriate treatment in the text, so you won't miss key parts but I won't waste time on the obvious.

As with any other program, event-driven or otherwise, the first item of business is the startup process. I begin with comments.

Header Comments

Header comments are a matter of style and managed by every experienced programmer in a different fashion. Mine, as shown in Listing 3–01, include an alphabetic listing of the routines in the file. The routines are included in the file in alphabetic order, too.

Code Listing 3–01

```
* FKEYS2.PRG — dBASE IV F-key set up program
* Copyright 1993, Martin L. Rinehart

* Hereby licensed to ALL for personal use.
* May be distributed for free, only.
* Not legal for sale.

* includes:
    * ctrl_o      — handle ^O call to DOS
    * ctrl_p      — handle ^P call to dot prompt
```

```
* dborder   — draw dot prompt border
* dmickey   — dot prompt mouse handler
* dos       — simulated DOS session
* dos_mick  — handle mouse click in DOS window
* dos_top   — display top line over DOS screen
* dot       — do a simulated dot prompt
* dot_error — dot prompt error handler
* dot_prmpt — simulated dot prompt
* dsize     — dot prompt size setting
* dsp_boxes — display the F key boxes
* dsp_ctrl  — display the CTRL button
* dsp_dos   — display DOS prompt box
* dsp_dot   — display dot prompt box
* dsp_esc   — display the ESC button
* dsp_norm  — display the NORMAL button
* dsp_shft  — display the SHIFT button
* dsp_stat  — display the F key shift/ctrl status
* get_fkvs  — get F-Key ValueS
* fkey      — process F-key presses
* fkey_act  — process Fkey-directed action
* init_fkvs — initialize FKEYS.DAT
* mickey    — handle mouse input
* mouse_act — process mouse-directed action
* mky_inbx  — which box is mouse in?
* not_a_dir — handles invalid directory
* not_a_drv — handles invalid drive
* on_keys   — set up F keys
* re_color  — restores color settings
* re_set    — restores all settings
* re_re_set — resumes FKEYS settings
* read_fkvs — get F-Key ValueS from disk
* say_gets  — say all the GET fields
* set_fkvs  — set the new keystroke commands
* str_pad   — pad string to length
* writ_fkvs — write FKEYS.DAT
```

Although the routines are stored alphabetically, I will present them in functional order, working more or less from the top down.

Preparation

The initial code, shown in Listing 3–02, does the preparation work. Similar code is found in every dBASE program.

Code Listing 3–02

```
* preparation:
  save_talk = SET( 'TALK' )
  SET TALK OFF

  save_colo = SET( 'ATTRIBUTES' )
  save_curs = SET( 'CURSOR' )
  save_scor = SET( 'SCOREBOARD' )
  save_row = ROW()
  save_col = COL()

  IF ISMOUSE()
    save_mous = SET( 'MOUSE' )
    SET MOUSE ON
  ENDIF

  SAVE SCREEN TO scrn_buf
  SET CURSOR ON

  IF ISCOLOR()
     fkey_clr = 'N/W'
     stat_clr = '+W/W'
     scrn_clr = 'W/B'
     hilt_clr = '+W/B'
     lolt_clr = 'N/B'
   ELSE
     fkey_clr = 'N/W'
     stat_clr = '+W/W'
     scrn_clr = 'W/N'
     hilt_clr = '+W/N'
     lolt_clr = '+N/N'
  ENDIF

  wind_clr = 'W/N'
  dw_out_clr = '+W/N'
  dw_con_clr = 'W/N'

  fkey_len = 40
  DECLARE fkey_vals[ 29 ]   && No Shift-F10

  tl_row =  1
  tl_col =  2

  box_lft   = tl_col + 1
  box_rght  = box_lft + 54

  shft_lft  = box_rght + 1
  shft_rght = shft_lft + 7
```

Initializing the F-Key Values (FKVs)

The F-Key Values, or FKVs, are stored in low-level data files. Actually, low-level is a misnomer, as you will see. These are plain ASCII files that we read and write with low-level access routines.

The setup, in Listing 3–03, consists of reading the file, if there is one, or calling an initialization routine. Once the data is in hand, the values are set into the F keys.

Code Listing 3–03

```
IF FILE( 'fkeys.dat' )
   DO read_fkvs
  ELSE
   DO init_fkvs
ENDIF

DO set_fkvs    && set new values
```

The actual routines that do the work are discussed below.

Final Preparations

The remainder of the preparations are common dBASE setup items, shown in Listing 3–04.

Code Listing 3–04

```
stat = 'norm' && stat is one of 'norm', 'ctrl' or 'shft'
m_act = 0

DO on_keys     && set up F keys

STORE 0 TO dwin_top, dwin_left, dwin_bttm, dwin_rght
STORE 0 TO dwin_hght, dwin_wdth

dwin_smll = .T.
DO dsize WITH dwin_smll

DEFINE WINDOW outdot ;
   FROM dwin_top, dwin_left ;
   TO dwin_bttm, dwin_rght ;
   NONE ;
   COLOR &dw_out_clr
```

```
DEFINE WINDOW dot ;
   FROM dwin_top+1, dwin_left+1 ;
   TO dwin_bttm-1, dwin_rght-1 ;
   NONE ;
   COLOR &dw_con_clr
```

This completes the setup portion of the code.

FKEYS2 Mainline

The mainline code is short, as you see in Listing 3–05. It sets the event traps for keystrokes and mouse actions. Then it calls the display routine.

The guts of the program are in the get_fkvs() routine, which is the main event loop. We will break that one down in considerable detail when we get to it.

Code Listing 3–05

```
* mainline
  ON KEY LABEL Ctrl-O DO ctrl_o
  ON KEY LABEL Ctrl-P DO ctrl_p
  IF ISMOUSE()
     ON MOUSE DO mickey
  ENDIF

  DO dsp_boxes && display the values
  DO get_fkvs  && get new values

  IF LASTKEY() <> 27 .AND. ;
     LASTKEY() <> 17            && Esc and ^Q

     DO set_fkvs  && set new values
     DO writ_fkvs && write the values to FKEYS.DAT

  ENDIF

* exit code
  DO re_set
                                   && end of mainline
```

When we exit from the event loop, we set new values into the F keys and write them out to the file, as long as the exit wasn't done via Esc or ^Q. Finally, a re_set() routine is called to restore all the settings.

Handling the FKVs

If you haven't used dBASE's low-level file routines, you will want to read this code carefully. Many dBASE programmers avoid these routines for the good reason that we are using dBASE, a high-level language. We don't want to code low-level things. C and assembler are more appropriate for low-level coding.

I applaud this thinking. But don't avoid the "low-level" file routines: These routines are misnamed. While they can be used for low-level file access, they handle plain ASCII text files nicely, at a high level.

You'll see that these routines are little ones—a matter of only a few minutes of coding once you know the tricks. To begin at the beginning, we'll start with the initialization routine before we get to the file routines.

Initializing the FKVs

If there is no FKEYS.DAT file, the fkey_vals[] array is initialized to constant length strings holding the dBASE default settings. This is done in init_fkvs(), shown in Listing 3–06.

Code Listing 3–06

```
*****************************************************************
*** init_fkvs — initialize F Key ValueS
*****************************************************************

PROCEDURE init_fkvs
PRIVATE i

* here if there is no FKEYS.DAT file

fkey_vals[1] = str_pad( 'HELP', fkey_len )
fkey_vals[2] = str_pad( 'ASSIST', fkey_len )
fkey_vals[3] = str_pad( 'LIST', fkey_len )
fkey_vals[4] = str_pad( 'DIRECTORY', fkey_len )
fkey_vals[5] = str_pad( 'DISPLAY STRUCTURE', fkey_len )
fkey_vals[6] = str_pad( 'DISPLAY STATUS', fkey_len )
```

```
fkey_vals[7] = str_pad( 'DISPLAY MEMORY', fkey_len )
fkey_vals[8] = str_pad( 'DISPLAY', fkey_len )
fkey_vals[9] = str_pad( 'APPEND', fkey_len )
fkey_vals[10] = str_pad( 'EDIT', fkey_len )

i = 11
DO WHILE i <= 29
  fkey_vals[i] = SPACE( fkey_len )
  i = i + 1
ENDDO

DO set_fkvs && set new values into keys

RETURN                                  && end of init_fkvs
```

Entries 1 through 10 hold the plain F-key values. Entries 11 through 20 hold the Ctrl F-key values and entries 21 through 29 hold the Shift F-key values. (There is no Shift-F10; dBASE uses Shift-F10 for keyboard macros.)

Reading FKVs from Disk

The read_fkvs() function, shown in Listing 3–07, fills the fkey_vals[] array by reading the FKEYS.DAT file. The calling routine already checked to see that FKEYS.DAT existed.

First, it opens the file, returning a "handle"—an integer file identifier used in subsequent file operations. Inside the loop, the FGETS routine returns one line of the file at a time. You call FGETS with the handle; it returns the next line of the ASCII file as a dBASE string. (The *real* low-level work, reading data into a buffer, separating lines by CR/LF markers and so on, is all done by FGETS.)

If you march past the end of the file, FGETS returns null strings. So we can ignore this potential problem. (If the file is less than 29 lines long, we'll want blanks for the extra F-key values, anyway.)

Code Listing 3–07

```
**************************************************************
*** read_fkvs — get F-Key Values from disk
**************************************************************

PROCEDURE read_fkvs
PRIVATE file_hand, i, tmp
```

```
file_hand = FOPEN( 'fkeys.dat' )

i = 1
DO WHILE i <= 29

  fkey_vals[i] = str_pad( FGETS(file_hand), fkey_len )

  i = i + 1
ENDDO

tmp = FCLOSE( file_hand )

RETURN                                    && end of read_fkvs
```

I close the file before leaving this routine. That frees the file handle for further work.

Writing FKVs to Disk

Writing FKVs is no more complex than reading them. Again, the low-level work is done for you by the FPUTS routine. This routine puts one string at a time into an ASCII file. It terminates the strings in the file with DOS CR/LF pairs. (Non-DOS versions of dBASE use the appropriate delimiters, so this code is portable.)

Listing 3–08 shows the writ_fkvs() routine.

Code Listing 3–08

```
*****************************************************************
*** writ_fkvs — write FKEYS.DAT
*****************************************************************

PROCEDURE writ_fkvs
PRIVATE crlf, file_hand, tmp

IF FILE( 'fkeys.dat' )
  ERASE fkeys.dat
ENDIF

file_hand = FCREATE( 'fkeys.dat' )
```

```
i = 1
DO WHILE i <= 29

  tmp = FPUTS( file_hand, RTRIM(fkey_vals[i]) )

  i = i + 1
ENDDO

tmp = FCLOSE( file_hand )

RETURN                                    && end of writ_fkvs
```

Again, the routine closes the file before it terminates.

Setting the F Keys

To set the values into the F keys, we want to use one of these forms:

```
SET FUNCTION F3 TO my_command + CHR(13)
SET FUNCTION Ctrl-F3 TO my_command + CHR(13)
SET FUNCTION Shift-F3 TO my_command + CHR(13)
```

The terminating CHR(13) is the Enter key that executes the command. dBASE also lets you use a terminating semi-colon character for this purpose, but CHR(13) makes more sense to me.

The only real trick here is getting the key name right. That's handled in the DO CASE block in the middle of the routine in Listing 3–09.

Code Listing 3–09

```
*****************************************************************
*** set_fkvs — set the new keystroke commands
*****************************************************************

PROCEDURE set_fkvs
PRIVATE i, j, cmd, key

i = 2
DO WHILE i <= 29

  cmd = '"'+LTRIM( RTRIM(fkey_vals[i]) )+'"' + '+CHR(13)'
```

```
DO CASE
   CASE i <= 10
      key = 'F'
      j = i

   CASE i <= 20
      keyp = 'Ctrl-F'
      j = i-10

   OTHERWISE
      key = 'Shift-F'
      j = i-20

ENDCASE

key = key + LTRIM( STR(j, 2) )

SET FUNCTION &key TO &cmd

i = i + 1
ENDDO

RETURN                                    && end of set_fkvs
```

Do you suppose that "LTRIM(STR(j, 2))" is more efficient than "LTRIM(STR(j))"? I'm not sure, but STR(j, 2) looks right since we're handling numbers from 1 to 29.

The Display Routines

The Display routines are straight dBASE. You may notice that I didn't use a dBASE WINDOW for the main display. Don't read too much into this. I was coding dBASE before there were WINDOWs, so I sometimes don't use one where it might be helpful. Old habits die hard.

Displaying the Boxes

Listing 3–10 shows the dsp_boxes() routine that does much of the display work. It does the F key boxes in five sets of two boxes each, based on the way they are displayed.

There are a lot of lines at the end which make sure that only the correct one of the "Normal," "Shift," or "Control" boxes is highlighted.

Code Listing 3–10

```
***********************************************************
*** dsp_boxes - display the F key boxes
***********************************************************

PROCEDURE dsp_boxes
PRIVATE knum

SET COLOR TO &scrn_clr
@ tl_row, tl_col CLEAR TO tl_row+22, tl_col + 75

row_var = 0

DO WHILE row_var < 5

  col_var = 0
  DO WHILE col_var < 2

    rw = row_var*4 + col_var*2 + tl_row + 1
    cl = col_var*7 + box_lft

    SET COLOR TO &fkey_clr
    @ rw, cl TO rw+2, cl+5
    @ rw+1, cl+1 SAY ' F'
    knum = row_var*2 + col_var + 1
    @ rw+1, cl+3 SAY LEFT( LTRIM(STR( knum ))+' ', 2)

    SET COLOR TO &scrn_clr
    @ rw+1, cl+6 SAY ;
            REPLICATE( '-', 8-7*col_var ) && CHR(196)

    col_var = col_var + 1

  ENDDO

  row_var = row_var + 1
ENDDO

IF stat <> 'norm'
  DO dsp_stat
ENDIF

SET COLOR TO &hilt_clr
@ tl_row, tl_col + 23 SAY "dBASE IV Personal Workbench"
```

```
IF stat = 'ctrl'
   SET COLOR TO &stat_clr
 ELSE
   SET COLOR TO &fkey_clr
ENDIF
do dsp_ctrl

IF stat = 'norm'
   SET COLOR TO &stat_clr
 ELSE
   SET COLOR TO &fkey_clr
ENDIF
do dsp_norm

IF stat = 'shft'
   SET COLOR TO &stat_clr
 ELSE
   SET COLOR TO &fkey_clr
ENDIF
do dsp_shft

SET COLOR TO &fkey_clr
do dsp_esc

SET COLOR TO &wind_clr
do dsp_dot
do dsp_dos

SET COLOR TO &lolt_clr
@ tl_row + 22, box_lft + 24 SAY '(c) 1993, Martin Rinehart'

RETURN                                   && end of dsp_boxes
```

I picked a barely legible "lolt_clr." At least it's barely legible on my machine. You can legally add your name to the copyright notice if you make even the smallest change, of course. Don't be bashful. If you add your name, you might want to make "lolt_clr" something brighter.

Individual Box Displays

Listing 3–11 contains the display routines that show the individual buttons. The only thing to note is that they don't set their own colors. The calling routine sets either a highlight or normal color, and then calls the display routines.

Code Listing 3–11

```
*************************************************************
*** dsp_ctrl — display the CTRL button
*************************************************************

PROCEDURE dsp_ctrl

* color is set by the calling routine

@ tl_row + 1, shft_lft TO tl_row + 5, shft_rght DOUBLE
@ tl_row + 2, shft_lft+1 CLEAR TO tl_row + 4, shft_rght-1
@ tl_row + 3, shft_lft+1 SAY " Ctrl "

RETURN                                  && end of dsp_ctrl


*************************************************************
*** dsp_dos — display DOS prompt box
*************************************************************

PROCEDURE dsp_dos

@ 4, 68 TO 11, 76 DOUBLE
@ 5, 69 CLEAR TO 10, 75
@ 10, 69 SAY 'C:\>'
@ 4, 69 SAY "DOS: ^O"

RETURN                                  && end of dsp_dos


*************************************************************
*** dsp_dot — display dot prompt box
*************************************************************

PROCEDURE dsp_dot

@ 13, 68 TO 20, 76 DOUBLE
@ 14, 69 CLEAR TO 19, 75
@ 18, 69 SAY '. ? x'
@ 19, 74 SAY '2'
@ 13, 69 SAY "dot: ^P"

RETURN                                  && end of dsp_dot
```

```
***************************************************************
*** dsp_esc   - display the ESC button
***************************************************************

PROCEDURE dsp_esc

* color is set by the calling routine

@ tl_row + 19, shft_lft TO tl_row + 21, shft_rght DOUBLE
@ tl_row + 20, shft_lft+1 SAY " Exit "

RETURN                                    && end of dsp_esc


***************************************************************
*** dsp_norm - display the NORMAL button
***************************************************************

PROCEDURE dsp_norm

* color is set by the calling routine

@ tl_row + 7, shft_lft TO tl_row + 11, shft_rght DOUBLE
@ tl_row + 8, shft_lft+1 CLEAR TO tl_row + 10, shft_rght-1
@ tl_row + 9, shft_lft+1 SAY "Normal"

RETURN                                    && end of dsp_norm


***************************************************************
*** dsp_shft - display the SHIFT button
***************************************************************

PROCEDURE dsp_shft

* color is set by the calling routine

@ tl_row + 13, shft_lft TO tl_row + 17, shft_rght DOUBLE
@ tl_row + 14, shft_lft+1 CLEAR TO tl_row + 16, shft_rght-1
@ tl_row + 15, shft_lft+1 SAY " Shft "

RETURN
```

The GET Fields

In an event-driven system such as this one, you constantly need to keep refreshing the GET fields. The only complication in Listing 3–12, the say_gets() routine, is that I am using a little trick to have one routine do each of the normal, shifted, and control F-key screens.

Code Listing 3–12

```
**************************************************************
*** say_gets  — say all the GET fields
**************************************************************

PROCEDURE say_gets

SET COLOR TO &scrn_clr
@ tl_row + 2, box_lft + 14 SAY 'HELP'

SET COLOR TO &fkey_clr

DO CASE
  CASE stat = 'norm'
     start  =  2
     stop   = 10
     offset =  0

  CASE stat = 'ctrl'
     start  = 11
     stop   = 20
     offset = 20

  CASE stat = 'shft'
     start  = 21
     stop   = 29
     offset = 40

ENDCASE

row_var = start

DO WHILE row_var <= stop
  @ tl_row + row_var * 2 - offset, box_lft + 14 ;
          SAY fkey_vals[row_var]
  row_var = row_var + 1
ENDDO

RETURN                                  && end of say_gets
```

As you see, the actual SAY work is done in a loop that runs from "start" to "stop."

The F-Key Status

The last of the display routines, shown in Listing 3–13, is responsible for prefixing the F-key labels with a space, a caret ("^") or an "S." It borrows the loop of five sets of two each from the dsp_boxes() routine.

Code Listing 3–13

```
***************************************************************
*** dsp_stat  - display the F key shift/ctrl status
***************************************************************

PROCEDURE dsp_stat
PRIVATE chr, i, j

DO CASE
  CASE stat = 'norm'
     chr = ' '

  CASE stat = 'ctrl'
     chr = '^'

  OTHERWISE
     chr = 'S'

ENDCASE

SET COLOR TO &fkey_clr

i = 0
DO WHILE i < 5

  j = 0
  DO WHILE j < 2

     rw = i*4 + j*2 + tl_row + 1
     cl = j*7 + box_lft

     @ rw+1, cl+1 SAY chr

     j = j + 1
  ENDDO

  i = i + 1
ENDDO

RETURN                                && end of dsp_stat
```

With those preliminaries out of the way, we are ready to get to the real workhorse: the event loop.

The Event Loop

The event loop is shown in Listing 3–14. I'll describe it here in detail.

First, we set up a string of "exit_keys." This makes our later test for a READ exit simple. Then the main loop starts. I use a perpetual loop: DO WHILE .T.. Software engineering purists object to this. I maintain that this is the cleanest way to write this sort of loop—it runs until the user explicitly exits, which you'll see in code that states this very clearly.

Inside the loop, two variables, "m_act," and "k_act," are initialized to zero on each pass. These variables will be set to either a mouse action (m_act) or a key action (k_act), if required to process one of these events.

Next the routine does some painting setup work. You can see that it paints the word "HELP" next to the F1 key, and the phrase "reserved for keyboard macros" next to the F10 key. It does this without checking to see if they are needed or not. If they aren't needed, they'll be overwritten by the fields, so this is a harmless timesaver.

Next, the routine does GETs for nine or 10 fields, as appropriate for the shift/ctrl status. Then it sets the mouse event trapping to the mickey() routine. The event trapping for ^O and ^P is set by the ON KEY statements in the mainline. The same treatment would have worked for the mouse trapping if there was only one routine that handled the mouse.

But this is not the case. Both the DOS window and the dot prompt window have their own mouse handlers, each of which does its own ON MOUSE handling. So you have to put this ON MOUSE immediately before the READ, as it is here. That way, this ON MOUSE gets reset on each pass through the loop. We don't care if a called routine sets another ON MOUSE handler.

Then we get to the READ statement, which now has a more complicated job than the traditional READ. Let's look at the rest of the code before we discuss READ.

After the READ, we EXIT on any of the exit keystrokes, but only provided that neither "m_act" nor "k_act" has been set. If either of these is set, we continue.

Now let's consider what goes on during the READ. Either the "m_act" or the "k_act" could have been set in the READ. If either is set, the appropriate handling routine, mouse_act() or fkey_act() is called.

dBASE traps ON KEY and ON MOUSE events during a READ (among other commands). The routines you specify (in our case mickey() for the ON MOUSE and fkey() for the ON KEY traps) are called during the READ. So the READ is now a main switching routine, responsible for calling the event setup routines.

I call them setup routines because you usually cannot process the entire event without exiting from the READ. Consider this very reasonable user behavior:

```
(Shift-F8 is blank)
User presses Shift-F8
Screen switches to Shift F keys
Cursor hops to F8
User enters a command in the F8 field
User clicks on the F8 box to execute the command
```

At this point, the user expects the program to execute the command that was just entered into F8. But there is a problem trying to do this during the READ.

Remember that dBASE does not do the assignment of any GET until the READ is finished. (This allows the user to press Esc or ^Q to terminate the READ without saving whatever was entered.) So your program has no idea that the user has typed new data into the Shift-F8 key until the READ is completed.

To accommodate this, the mickey() routine is programmed to fill in the control value in m_act. On the mouse click, the READ command calls mickey(). Mickey() checks the location of the mouse, finding that it is in the F8 box. Mickey sets m_act to 8, and then KEYBOARDs a READ terminating keystroke. In this case it is a ^W.

So the read is completed when it gets the ^W from the keyboard buffer. It will then call mouse_act() with "m_act" set to 8. The mouse_act() routine checks the status, finds it to be "shift"ed mouse_act(), and executes the command in Shift-F8.

Simple? I don't think so. If you don't get this on first read, study Listing 3–14 carefully and then go on. Don't waste time rereading this. It may make sense after you've seen the supporting code. And we will see this technique twice more, in the DOS window and in the dot prompt window.

Code Listing 3–14

```
*************************************************************
*** get_fkvs — get F-Key ValueS
*************************************************************

PROCEDURE get_fkvs
PRIVATE exit_keys, lk, old_stat, start, stop

* Enter, ^Q, ^W and Esc:
exit_keys = CHR(13)+CHR(17)+CHR(23)+CHR(27)

DO WHILE .T.

  STORE 0 TO m_act, k_act

  SET COLOR TO &scrn_clr
  @ tl_row + 2, box_lft+14 CLEAR TO tl_row + 20, box_rght
  @ tl_row + 2, box_lft + 14 SAY 'HELP'
  @ tl_row + 20, box_lft + 14 SAY ;
     'reserved for keyboard macros'

  clrs = fkey_clr + ',' + fkey_clr
  SET COLOR TO &clrs

  DO CASE
    CASE stat = 'norm'
       start  =  2
       stop   = 10
       offset =  0

    CASE stat = 'ctrl'
       start  = 11
       stop   = 20
       offset = 20

    CASE stat = 'shft'
       start  = 21
       stop   = 29
       offset = 40

  ENDCASE
```

```
row_var = start

DO WHILE row_var <= stop
   @ tl_row + row_var * 2 - offset, box_lft+14 ;
             GET fkey_vals[row_var]
   row_var = row_var + 1
ENDDO

IF ISMOUSE()
   ON MOUSE DO mickey
ENDIF

READ

IF m_act = 0 .AND. ;
   k_act = 0 .AND. ;
   CHR( LASTKEY() )$exit_keys

   EXIT

ENDIF

IF m_act <> 0
   DO mouse_act
ENDIF

IF k_act <> 0
   DO fkey_act
ENDIF

ENDDO

RETURN                                 && end of get_fkvs
```

Have you got it? If not, perhaps studying the handling routines will help clear things up.

The Mouse Handlers

By "the mouse handlers" I do not mean the separate handlers for the main loop, the DOS prompt, and the dot prompt boxes. (We'll look at those handlers when we get to the associated window code.) I mean the two separate handlers needed by the main event loop.

The mickey() routine is called during the READ when a mouse event occurs (the user clicks). But mickey() cannot handle the processing, since the READ is not completed. The mouse_act() routine actually performs the action indicated by the mouse. Mickey() and mouse_act() communicate via the "m_act" variable that we are using as a semaphore. If mickey() sets a non-zero value into "m_act," mouse_act() knows that it has work to do. "M_act" is set to a number from 1 to 10 if the user has clicked on one of the F-key boxes, and set values for the other 6 boxes (shift, normal, control, exit, and the two windows) to negative.

Mickey

As you see in Listing 3–15, mickey() is a little routine. It calls its worker, mky_inbx(), which we will get to next. Mky_inbx() returns the code corresponding to the box in which the user clicked, or a zero if the mouse wasn't in a box.

With this value, mickey() checks to eliminate the spurious Shift-F10 key. If it still has a non-zero "m_act," mickey() puts a ^W into the keyboard buffer.

Code Listing 3–15

```
*************************************************************
*** mickey — handle mouse input
*************************************************************

PROCEDURE mickey

m_act = mky_inbx( MROW(), MCOL() )

IF stat = 'shft' .AND. m_act = 10
  m_act = 0
ENDIF

IF m_act <> 0
  KEYBOARD CHR(23)    && ^W
ENDIF

RETURN                                  && end of mickey
```

Note that the very first line of mickey() uses MROW() and MCOL() as arguments to the mky_inbx function. Your ON MOUSE handler should do this, or should set these values into memvars, immediately. MROW() and MCOL() return the current location of the mouse, not its location at the time of the click. You want to grab this location as quickly as possible.

Where Is the Click?

The largest part of mickey()'s job is done in mky_inbx(). The concept is very simple—check each possible meaningful click location. Return the value as soon as you find the right one. The code is shown in Listing 3–16.

The very first CASE in mky_inbx() does a special check. If the user clicks the mouse outside the FKEYS2 area, it is an Exit click. So this CASE checks to see if the mouse is in the top or bottom row, or the two leftmost or rightmost columns. If so, it puts an Esc character in the keyboard buffer and returns a zero semaphore value.

The second CASE is typical of all the rest. Here, it checks to see if the mouse click column is between the left and right "shift" columns. The shift column is the location of the four buttons, shift, normal, control, and exit. If the mouse click was in this range, the row is then checked in the nested DO CASE. The control box runs from rows 1 through 5. If the mouse click was here, −1 is returned. The next three buttons are checked in order, with an appropriate "m_act" code being returned for each. Finally, if all these checks fail (the mouse was between buttons, for instance) it returns a 0. No further checking is required since all other buttons are in different column ranges.

The other CASEs do similar checking. The second one handles the DOS and dot prompt windows, the third one checks for some rows which, if not eliminated in this one, would cause spurious returns in the next two.

The last two CASEs check for clicks in the odd-numbered buttons (left column of F keys) and the even-numbered buttons (right column of F keys). The code is a little tricky in the way it checks for rows, but if you work it through you'll see that it is just checking row ranges, as the second and third CASEs did.

Code Listing 3–16

```
************************************************************
*** mky_inbx — which box is mouse in?
************************************************************


FUNCTION mky_inbx
PARAMETERS mrw, mcl

DO CASE
  CASE mrw = 0 .OR. mrw = 24 .OR. ;
       mcl < 2 .OR. mcl > 77
     KEYBOARD CHR(27) && Esc out
     RETURN 0

  CASE mcl >= shft_lft .AND. mcl <= shft_rght
     DO CASE
        CASE mrw >= tl_row + 1 .AND. mrw <= tl_row + 5
           RETURN -1  && Ctrl

        CASE mrw >= tl_row + 7 .AND. mrw <= tl_row + 11
           RETURN -2  && Normal

        CASE mrw >= tl_row + 13 .AND. mrw <= tl_row + 17
           RETURN -3  && Shift

        CASE mrw >= 20 .AND. mrw <= 22
           RETURN -4  && Exit

        OTHERWISE
           RETURN 0
     ENDCASE

  CASE mcl >= 68 .AND. mcl <= 76
     DO CASE
        CASE mrw >= 4 .AND. mrw <= 11
           RETURN -5  && DOS

        CASE mrw >=13 .AND. mrw <= 20
           RETURN -6  && dot prompt

        OTHERWISE
           RETURN 0
     ENDCASE

  CASE mrw < (tl_row + 1) .OR. mrw > (tl_row + 21)
     RETURN 0

  CASE mcl >= box_lft .AND. mcl <= (box_lft+5)
     * finds F1, F3, ... F9
```

```
   IF MOD( mrw-1, 4 ) = 0
      RETURN 0
    ELSE
      RETURN 2*INT( (mrw-1)/4 ) + 1
   ENDIF

CASE mcl >= (box_lft+7) .AND. mcl <= (box_lft+12)
   * finds F2, F4, ... F10

   IF mrw < 4 .OR. MOD( mrw,4 ) = 3
      RETURN 0
    ELSE
      RETURN 2*INT( mrw/4 )
   ENDIF

ENDCASE

RETURN 0                                    && end of mky_inbx
```

Did you understand that trick in the last two CASEs? Remember that the screen shows each F-key box three rows high, with one row between the boxes. The .T. part of the IF test eliminates those between rows. Then dividing by 4 will get you a number (1 through 5) identifying the F key. You can work out the other adjustments, or ignore them.

Frankly, I'm not sure that this code runs any faster than if I had just written "if row is greater than this and row is less than that" for each of the five cases. I wrote it this way so it would still work in case I changed my mind later and went to bigger or smaller F key boxes. (As it turned out, I never did change from the size you see in the finished product.)

Every screen you do is different in this regard. You may find tricks that shorten the code, and you may be better off if you just check each button or box, one at a time.

Mouse Actions

The other part of the main-event-loop mouse handling is done by mouse_act(), the long routine shown in Listing 3–17. As you can see, this is just a big DO CASE that separates many different activities, each corresponding to the button that the user clicked.

The first three CASEs handle the control, normal, and shift buttons. They display the buttons in the appropriate normal or highlighted colors, set the "stat" flag to the right value, and call the dsp_stat() routine to display the F keys appropriately.

The fourth CASE handles the exit button. It sets the exit button to the highlighted color and the other buttons to the normal color. Then it sets the new F key values into the F keys and rewrites the data file. Hopefully, this takes just long enough so that you can see that it is responding to your exit click, but not so long as to be annoying. Finally, it puts an Esc into the keyboard buffer, to exit from the READ and the main event loop.

The fifth and sixth CASEs are considerably simplified since all the code for their work is done in their own subroutines. We'll get to the DOS window and the dot prompt window later.

Finally, the last CASE handles all positive values. 1 indicates a click on the F1 button, 2 on the F2 button, and so on. F1 help is handled separately. Otherwise, the first job is to decide which is the *real* F key, based on the number and the value of the "stat" flag. (F3 is 3 if "stat" is "norm"; F3 is 13 if "stat" is "ctrl"; and F3 is 23 if "stat" is "shft.")

Given the appropriate F-key number, the processing is the same as if the F key were pressed. It checks to see if there is a command or not. If there is, it executes the command. If not, it stuffs enough Enter keystrokes into the keyboard buffer to move the cursor to the beginning of the appropriate GET field.

The main event loop in get_fkvs() will do GETs for the appropriate set of F key values, so these don't need to be redisplayed here.

Code Listing 3–17

```
****************************************************************
*** mouse_act — process mouse-directed action
****************************************************************

PROCEDURE mouse_act
PRIVATE key_num

DO CASE

  CASE m_act = -1      && Ctrl

     SET COLOR TO &stat_clr
     DO dsp_ctrl
```

```
   SET COLOR TO &fkey_clr
   DO dsp_norm
   DO dsp_shft

   stat = 'ctrl'
   DO dsp_stat

CASE m_act = -2      && Normal

   SET COLOR TO &stat_clr
   DO dsp_norm

   SET COLOR TO &fkey_clr
   DO dsp_ctrl
   DO dsp_shft

   stat = 'norm'
   DO dsp_stat

CASE m_act = -3      && Shift

   SET COLOR TO &stat_clr
   DO dsp_shft

   SET COLOR TO &fkey_clr
   DO dsp_ctrl
   DO dsp_norm

   stat = 'shft'
   DO dsp_stat

CASE m_act = -4      && Exit

   SET COLOR TO &stat_clr
   DO dsp_esc

   SET COLOR TO &fkey_clr
   DO dsp_ctrl
   DO dsp_norm
   DO dsp_shft

   DO set_fkvs
   DO writ_fkvs

   KEYBOARD CHR(27) && Esc

CASE m_act = -5      && DOS
   DO dos
```

```
   CASE m_act = -6        && dot prompt
      DO dot

   CASE m_act > 0

      IF m_act = 1 .AND. stat = 'norm'

         SET COLOR TO
         HELP

      ELSE

         DO CASE
            CASE stat = 'norm'
               key_num = m_act

            CASE stat = 'ctrl'
               key_num = m_act + 10

            CASE stat = 'shft'
               key_num = m_act + 20

         ENDCASE

         cmd = fkey_vals[ key_num ]

         IF LEN( LTRIM(cmd) ) > 0

            DO set_fkvs    && set new values
            DO writ_fkvs   && write to FKEYS.DAT
            DO re_set      && restore everything

            &cmd

            SAVE SCREEN TO scrn_buf
            save_row = ROW()
            save_col = COL()

            DO re_re_set  && resume FKEYS2 settings

         ELSE

            KEYBOARD REPLICATE( CHR(13), ;
                               IIF(key_num<=10, ;
                                   m_act-2, m_act-1) )

         ENDIF && cmd is not empty

      ENDIF && F1 help or other

ENDCASE

RETURN                                   && end of mouse_act
```

Keystroke Events

The keystroke handling is the same concept as the mouse handling. Most keystrokes are handled by the standard dBASE READ. Those set by the ON KEY event traps are the ones we are concerned with here.

Again, half of the handling is done in routines specified by the ON KEY trap. The other half is done in a handler that executes after the READ is finished. The communication between these two is through the "k_act" semaphore.

We have two types of keys set up for event trapping. We have the F keys and the ^O and ^P pair. The F keys present more interesting challenges.

Trapping Keypresses

The routine that actually sets the F-keys is shown in Listing 3–31. It's working part looks like this:

```
ON KEY LABEL F1 DO keys_act WITH 1
ON KEY LABEL F2 DO keys_act WITH 2
ON KEY LABEL F3 DO keys_act WITH 3
```

This continues for all 29 F-key values, each calling keys_act() with a value from 1 through 29. As Listing 3–18 shows, the fkey() routine that handles this is trivial. It just puts the parameter into the "k_act" semaphore and then puts a ^W (to terminate the READ) into the keyboard buffer.

Code Listing 3–18

```
**************************************************************
*** fkey — process F-key presses
**************************************************************

PROCEDURE keys_act
PARAMETER knum

k_act = knum
KEYBOARD CHR(23) && ^W

RETURN                                    && end of keys_act
```

Handling Keypresses

The fkey_act() routine is the one that is called after the READ is completed. As you can see in Listing 3–19, it has a larger job.

First, it checks for F1 and handles this separately. It calls HELP directly, after setting default colors. This lets F1 work without upsetting the control or shift F-key screens.

The next three CASEs are those in which the shift status is not the one shown on the current screen. It has to make the same changes that the mouse event handler did when it handled a click on one of the shift/control status buttons.

Next, it has to either process the command or position the cursor if there is no command in the key. Bear in mind that a READ was just completed that has a possibly new value in the key. So the first action is to set the values into the F keys and then rewrite the data file.

There is a little extra work done here, in case the user's command is a dot prompt command. Everything is returned to the condition it had before FKEYS2 was called, and then the command is run and the original saving/setup process is repeated. This way, if the user is issuing dot prompt commands, the screen will match the user's expectations after exiting from FKEYS2. (The user issues a DIR command from FKEYS2, and then exits FKEYS2. This leaves the DIR listing on the screen.)

Code Listing 3–19

```
*****************************************************************
*** fkey_act  — process F-key-directed action
*****************************************************************

PROCEDURE fkey_act
PRIVATE cmd, enters

DO CASE
  CASE k_act = 1
     SET COLOR TO
     HELP

  CASE k_act < 11 .AND. stat <> 'norm'
     stat = 'norm'
     SET COLOR TO &stat_clr
     DO dsp_norm
```

```
      SET COLOR TO &fkey_clr
      DO dsp_ctrl
      DO dsp_shft

      DO dsp_stat

   CASE k_act < 21 .AND. ;
       k_act > 10 .AND. ;
        stat <> 'ctrl'
      stat = 'ctrl'
      SET COLOR TO &stat_clr
      DO dsp_ctrl

      SET COLOR TO &fkey_clr
      DO dsp_norm
      DO dsp_shft

      DO dsp_stat

   CASE k_act > 20 .AND. stat <> 'shft'
      stat = 'shft'
      SET COLOR TO &stat_clr
      DO dsp_shft

      SET COLOR TO &fkey_clr
      DO dsp_norm
      DO dsp_ctrl

      DO dsp_stat

ENDCASE

IF k_act > 1
   cmd = fkey_vals[ k_act ]

   IF LEN( LTRIM(cmd) ) > 0

      DO set_fkvs    && set new values
      DO writ_fkvs   && write to FKEYS.DAT
      DO re_set      && restore everything

      &cmd

      SAVE SCREEN TO scrn_buf
      save_row = ROW()
      save_col = COL()

      DO re_re_set  && resume FKEYS2 settings

   ELSE
```

```
      DO CASE
        CASE k_act < 11
           enters = k_act - 2

        CASE k_act < 21
           enters = k_act - 11

        OTHERWISE
           enters = k_act - 21

      ENDCASE

      * Enters to position cursor
      KEYBOARD REPLICATE( CHR(13), enters )

    ENDIF && cmd is not empty

  ENDIF && not F1 help

RETURN                                  && end of fkey_act
```

The line that says "KEYBOARD REPLICATE . . ." puts
enough Enter keys into the keyboard buffer to move the cursor
to the beginning of the appropriate field. For instance, it takes two
Enter keypresses to get to Shift-F3 (key 23).

Calling Other Windows

Separate handlers are used to trap ^O and ^P (calls to the DOS window or the dot prompt). They are trivial, as you see in Listing 3–20.

Code Listing 3–20

```
**************************************************************
*** ctrl_o — handle ^O call to DOS
**************************************************************

PROCEDURE ctrl_o

m_act = -5 && simulate mouse click on DOS box
KEYBOARD CHR(23) && ^W to finish READ

RETURN                                  && end of ctrl_o
```

```
*****************************************************************
*** ctrl_p — handle ^P call to dot prompt
*****************************************************************

PROCEDURE ctrl_p

m_act = -6 && simulate mouse click on dot prompt box
KEYBOARD CHR(23) && ^W to finish READ

RETURN                                          && end of ctrl_p
```

The DOS Session

The DOS window is one of those features that I probably would not have coded if I had known in advance how difficult it would be. But it's one of those features that I am glad I coded, since I use it constantly. It turns out to have been worth the effort.

Two separate efforts were required. One, which I anticipated, was putting the DOS window on the FKEYS2 screen and adding the keystroke and mouse handling logic. The other, which I didn't anticipate, was the complication of doing a DOS simulation.

Simulating DOS

You can call any DOS command from dBASE with the RUN or "!" command. So to stimulate DOS, you basically want to get a command, prefix it with a "!" and execute it. In this case, the devil was in the details.

First problem: what to use for a DOS prompt? I assume that you use the common $P $G DOS prompt (drive/directory). You can get this information (almost) from dBASE by asking for the setting of DIRECTORY. Actually, dBASE doesn't read the drive/directory from DOS. It takes the one it had at startup and then monitors SET DIRECTORY commands to track changes. To convince yourself, try this at the dot prompt:

```
? SET('DIRE')
!CD \anywhere\else
? SET('DIRE')
```

The second SET('DIRE') reports the same thing as the first one, even though it is no longer valid. Well, you can't always get what you want. But this seems close enough to still be useful. This is a tool for programmers, after all.

With that understood, let's get to the listing. After doing some setup work, we start another infinite loop and build the prompt from SET('DIRE'). We use this prompt and GET a command that fills the rest of the bottom line. Then we set mouse trapping to dos_mick() and READ.

We process the command in a DO CASE. In this one, the OTHERWISE condition probably handles over 90% of the work. As you see in Listing 3–21, it's simple. Add the "!" and then execute the command as a macro.

All the other CASEs handle little details. First, a null command scrolls the screen. Then the next two CASEs grab "cd" commands and disk drive changes ("X:"). These are changed into dBASE SET DIRECTORY commands to keep our prompt correct. (You can still mess this up by running a batch file or other program that changes directories. You can even get it wrong if you type out "chdir" instead of just "cd," but that still doesn't make this window unimportant. It just makes the prompt suspect.)

The last command turns the DOS "exit" command into a dBASE EXIT command, terminating this loop and returning to FKEYS2.

Code Listing 3–21

```
******************************************************************
*** dos — simulated DOS session
******************************************************************

PROCEDURE dos
PRIVATE prmpt, sav_scr

SAVE SCREEN TO dosbuf
sav_scr = SET( 'SCOREBOARD' )
SET SCOREBOARD OFF

SET COLOR TO W/N, W/N
CLEAR
```

```
DO   WHILE .T.

  prmpt = SET( 'DIRE' )+ '>'
  cmd = SPACE( 79 - LEN(prmpt) )

  DO dos_top  && display top line

  @ 24, 0 SAY prmpt
  @ 24, LEN(prmpt) GET cmd

  IF ISMOUSE()
     ON MOUSE DO dos_mick
  ENDIF
  READ

  IF LASTKEY() = 27 && Esc
     EXIT
  ENDIF

  @ 24, 78 SAY ' '  && reposition cursor

  cmd = LTRIM( RTRIM(cmd) )
  DO CASE
     CASE LEN( cmd ) = 0
        ?

     CASE LOWER( LEFT(cmd, 2) ) = 'cd'
        IF LEN( cmd ) > 2
           cmd = SUBSTR( cmd, 3, LEN(cmd)-2 )
           ON ERROR DO not_a_dir
           SET DIRECTORY TO &cmd
           ON ERROR
           ?
         ELSE
           DO not_a_dir
        ENDIF

     CASE LEN( cmd ) = 2 .AND. SUBSTR( cmd, 2, 1 ) = ':'
        ON ERROR DO not_a_drv
        SET DIRECTORY TO &cmd
        ON ERROR

     CASE UPPER( cmd ) = 'EXIT'
        EXIT

     OTHERWISE
        cmd = '!' + cmd
        &cmd
```

```
   ENDCASE

ENDDO

SET SCOREBOARD &sav_scr
RESTORE SCREEN FROM dosbuf

RETURN                                          && end of dos
```

The rest of the routines that support DOS are all tiny.

Mouse in DOS

The mouse handler checks to see if the mouse is on the top row, where some pseudo-buttons are displayed. If the mouse was clicked in the top row, an Esc character is put into the keyboard buffer to exit from the DOS loop. Listing 3–22 shows this.

Code Listing 3–22

```
************************************************************
*** dos_mick — handle mouse click in DOS window
************************************************************

PROCEDURE dos_mick

IF mrow() = 0
  KEYBOARD CHR(27) && Esc to exit
ENDIF

RETURN                                          && end of dos_mick
```

DOS Top Line

The simple top line code, shown in Listing 3–23, is called after each DOS command. (Each DOS command scrolls at least one line off the screen, so this is forever disappearing.)

Code Listing 3–23

```
***************************************************************
*** dos_top — display top line over DOS screen
***************************************************************

PROCEDURE dos_top

@ 0, 0 SAY REPLICATE( '', 80 )
@ 0, 1 SAY '  '
@ 0, 76 SAY '  '

RETURN                                        && end of dos_top
```

DOS Errors

On an invalid "cd" command, or an incorrect "X:" drive change
command, DOS has trivial error reports. The two routines in Listing
3–24 copy DOS exactly.

Code Listing 3–24

```
***************************************************************
*** not_a_dir — handles invalid directory
***************************************************************

PROCEDURE not_a_dir

? 'Invalid directory'
?

RETURN                                        && end of not_a_dir


***************************************************************
*** not_a_drv — handles invalid drive specification
***************************************************************

PROCEDURE not_a_drv

? 'Invalid drive specification'
?

RETURN                                        && end of not_a_drv
```

These routines complete our simulated DOS session.

Dot Prompt

The dot prompt is my constant companion while I'm coding dBASE. Running FKEYS2 from the dot prompt works well enough, but just doesn't feel right. I was running my editor and other tools under FKEYS2. I was running my .PRGs in dBASE under FKEYS2. So I wanted to run the dot prompt under FKEYS2, as well.

There is only one small problem here. Unlike every other part of dBASE, there is no way to call the dot prompt. You can ask for HELP or ASSIST (or anything else), but not the dot prompt.

Of course, that simply means that you can't really use the dBASE dot prompt. You have to write your own. This is mine.

The Dot-Prompt Mainline

As with FKEYS2, the mainline is simple. The hard work is done in the event loop. Listing 3–25 shows my dot-prompt mainline.

It uses two windows, both borderless. The "dot" window will hold the actual dot prompt session. It fits neatly inside "outdot." Outdot starts one row and column before dot, and it continues for one row and column past dot. As its name suggests, I use it to draw an outline.

dBASE will do scrolling inside a window for you. But if you use a window with a border, dBASE won't let you write special characters on the window border. To get around this, I use a smaller window inside a larger one. Both have no borders. I then draw whatever border I want on the larger one. It's not really a border, just characters in the first and last columns and rows. But it certainly looks like a border. In this case, it is a border with system and resize buttons on the top.

We'll see more of these boxes soon.

Code Listing 3–25

```
*****************************************************************
*** dot — do a simulated dot prompt
*****************************************************************

PROCEDURE dot
ACTIVATE WINDOW outdot
DO dborder
```

```
ACTIVATE WINDOW dot

ON ERROR DO dot_error
SET ESCAPE OFF
DO dot_prmpt
ON ERROR

DEACTIVATE WINDOW dot
DEACTIVATE WINDOW outdot

RETURN                                        && end of dot
```

Dot Prompt Loop

The dot_prmpt() routine is a simulated dBASE dot prompt. Unlike our DOS simulation, which has some rough spots (to say the least), this dot prompt is a pretty good cover for dBASE's dot prompt. The code is in Listing 3–26.

Again, it's a perpetual loop with explicit exit code. It uses a "cmd_line" variable to GET your input. ON MOUSE specifies the dmickey() routine, just before the READ.

Unlike the main FKEYS2 loop, this mouse handler just sets the logical flag "re_size." This is set to .T. if the mouse is clicked on the resize button. Look at the .F. part of the IF test first, as this contains the normal case code.

In the normal case (processing any command except a mouse click on the resize button) we just check for an Esc and EXIT if we find one. Otherwise, after positioning the cursor, we execute the command line as a macro and emit a CR/LF via the "?" command. dBASE handles the job of keeping all scrolling within the active window boundary.

The re_size logic is reasonably straightforward. We first flip the "dwin_smll" logical, then call the dsize() routine to change the global variables "dwin_top" and so on.

Next, the current windows are released and two new windows are defined. You can see that dot is carefully fit within outdot. Finally, we activate outdot and draw our own border. Then we activate dot and are back in business.

Code Listing 3-26

```
****************************************************************
*** dot_prmpt — simulated dot prompt
****************************************************************

PROCEDURE dot_prmpt
PRIVATE clr, cmd_line, i, re_size, scratch, spaces

clr = wind_clr + ',' + wind_clr
spaces = SPACE( dwin_wdth - 2 )

DO WHILE .T.

  SET COLOR TO &clr
  cmd_line = spaces
  re_size = .F.

  IF ISMOUSE()
     ON MOUSE DO dmickey
  ENDIF

  @ dwin_hght-1, 0 SAY '.' GET cmd_line
  READ

  IF re_size && set by mouse

     dwin_smll = .NOT. dwin_smll
     DO dsize WITH dwin_smll
     spaces = SPACE( dwin_wdth - 2 )

     RELEASE WINDOW dot
     RELEASE WINDOW outdot

     DEFINE WINDOW outdot ;
        FROM dwin_top, dwin_left ;
        TO dwin_bttm, dwin_rght ;
        NONE ;
        COLOR &dw_out_clr

     DEFINE WINDOW dot ;
        FROM dwin_top+1, dwin_left+1 ;
        TO dwin_bttm-1, dwin_rght-1 ;
        NONE ;
        COLOR &dw_con_clr

     ACTIVATE WINDOW outdot
     DO dborder

     ACTIVATE WINDOW dot
```

```
    ELSE

    IF LASTKEY() = 27
       EXIT
    ENDIF

    @ dwin_hght-1, 1 SAY ' ' && reposition cursor

    &cmd_line
    ?

  ENDIF

ENDDO

RETURN                                    && end of dot_prompt
```

You can see that this code parallels the main event loop. The mouse event handler sets a flag for code that is called after the READ is completed. In this case, the source code is physically located inside the main loop body, but it has the same effect as calling a subroutine from inside the loop.

Dot Prompt Mouse Handler

The mouse event handler is not quite as simple as the DOS window mouse handler, but is less complex than the main event-loop mouse handlers. Listing 3–27 shows how dmickey() performs chores similar to those in mickey() and mky_inbx().

First, MROW() and MCOL() are stored in variables, so we capture these locations as close as possible to the actual mouse click. Then we figure out where the mouse click happened, and decide how to process it.

If the click was somewhere on the top row of the window, the code checks for a click near the "system" button or near the resize button. In both cases, it accepts a character to the left or right of these as close enough to signal the user's intent.

The system button just keyboards an Esc to exit from the dot prompt. The resize button sets the "re_size" flag to .T. and keyboards an Enter to finish the READ. (There is only one GET in this READ.)

If the click is not on the top row, dmickey() checks for a click outside of the window. If it finds one, it puts an Esc in the keyboard buffer to trigger an exit.

All other locations are ignored.

Code Listing 3–27

```
*****************************************************************
*** dmickey — dot prompt mouse handler
*****************************************************************
PROCEDURE dmickey
PRIVATE mrw, mcl

mrw = MROW()
mcl = MCOL()

IF mrw = dwin_top

  DO CASE
     CASE mcl > dwin_left .AND. mcl < dwin_left+4
        KEYBOARD CHR(27) && Esc out

     CASE mcl < dwin_rght .AND. mcl > dwin_rght - 4
        re_size = .T.
        KEYBOARD CHR(13) && Enter to finish READ

  ENDCASE

ELSE
  IF mrw < dwin_top .OR. ;
     mrw > dwin_bttm .OR. ;
     mcl < dwin_left .OR. ;
     mcl > dwin_rght

     KEYBOARD CHR(27) && Esc out

  ENDIF

ENDIF

RETURN                                      && end of dmickey
```

Dot Prompt Border

The dborder() routine draws a simulated window border on the out-dot window. (Since it uses just single line characters, an @ TO command could have done this more easily. But doing it this way lets you go back and make it fancier later, without too much trouble.)

As you see in Listing 3–28, the two buttons are drawn by the last two @ SAY commands.

Code Listing 3–28

```
**************************************************************
*** dborder — draw dot prompt border
**************************************************************

PROCEDURE dborder
PRIVATE hline, i

@ 0, 0 SAY '' && CHR(218)
@ 0, dwin_wdth+1 SAY '' && CHR(191)
@ dwin_hght+1, 0 SAY '' && CHR(192)
@ dwin_hght+1, dwin_wdth+1 SAY '' && CHR(217)

hline = REPLICATE( '', dwin_wdth )
@ 0, 1 SAY hline
@ dwin_hght+1, 1 SAY hline

i = 1
DO WHILE i <= dwin_hght
  @ i, 0 SAY '|' && CHR(179)
  @ i, dwin_wdth+1 SAY '|'
  i = i + 1
ENDDO

@ 0, 1 SAY ' ' && CHR(240)
@ 0, dwin_wdth-2 SAY ' ' && CHR(25), CHR(18)

RETURN                              && end of dborder
```

Dot Prompt Error Handler

The one thing that we really lose by simulating the dot prompt is dBASE's error handling. The comment in Listing 3–29 correctly identifies the strength of this bit of code.

Code Listing 3–29

```
**************************************************************
*** dot_error — dot prompt error handler
**************************************************************

PROCEDURE dot_error

* world's dumbest error handler
? ' *** Error ***'

RETURN                              && end of dot_error
```

Dot Prompt Size Setting

Listing 3–30 shows the size setting done in dsize(). It sets some global variables that are used to define the outdot and dot windows. The coordinates given are those of the outdot window.

Code Listing 3–30

```
**************************************************************
*** dsize - dot prompt size setting
**************************************************************

PROCEDURE dsize
PARAMETER is_small

IF is_small

  dwin_top  = 15
  dwin_left =  3
  dwin_bttm = 22
  dwin_rght = 60

 ELSE

  dwin_top  =  2
  dwin_left =  3
  dwin_bttm = 22
  dwin_rght = 76

ENDIF

dwin_hght = dwin_bttm - dwin_top  - 1
dwin_wdth = dwin_rght - dwin_left - 1

RETURN                                  && end of dsize
```

The dsizc() routine is the last routine except for some simple support routines.

Miscellaneous Routines

These routines are straightforward. A quick glance should show you how they work.

ON KEY Setup

For a routine like the one in Listing 3–31, it helps to have a nice
macro capability in your text editor. The typing gets boring.

Code Listing 3–31

```
****************************************************************
*** on_keys   — set up F keys
****************************************************************

PROCEDURE on_keys

ON KEY LABEL F1         DO keys_act WITH 1
ON KEY LABEL F2         DO keys_act WITH 2
ON KEY LABEL F3         DO keys_act WITH 3
ON KEY LABEL F4         DO keys_act WITH 4
ON KEY LABEL F5         DO keys_act WITH 5

ON KEY LABEL F6         DO keys_act WITH 6
ON KEY LABEL F7         DO keys_act WITH 7
ON KEY LABEL F8         DO keys_act WITH 8
ON KEY LABEL F9         DO keys_act WITH 9
ON KEY LABEL F10        DO keys_act WITH 10

ON KEY LABEL Ctrl-F1    DO keys_act WITH 11
ON KEY LABEL Ctrl-F2    DO keys_act WITH 12
ON KEY LABEL Ctrl-F3    DO keys_act WITH 13
ON KEY LABEL Ctrl-F4    DO keys_act WITH 14
ON KEY LABEL Ctrl-F5    DO keys_act WITH 15

ON KEY LABEL Ctrl-F6    DO keys_act WITH 16
ON KEY LABEL Ctrl-F7    DO keys_act WITH 17
ON KEY LABEL Ctrl-F8    DO keys_act WITH 18
ON KEY LABEL Ctrl-F9    DO keys_act WITH 19
ON KEY LABEL Ctrl-F10   DO keys_act WITH 20

ON KEY LABEL Shift-F1   DO keys_act WITH 21
ON KEY LABEL Shift-F2   DO keys_act WITH 22
ON KEY LABEL Shift-F3   DO keys_act WITH 23
ON KEY LABEL Shift-F4   DO keys_act WITH 24
ON KEY LABEL Shift-F5   DO keys_act WITH 25

ON KEY LABEL Shift-F6   DO keys_act WITH 26
ON KEY LABEL Shift-F7   DO keys_act WITH 27
ON KEY LABEL Shift-F8   DO keys_act WITH 28
ON KEY LABEL Shift-F9   DO keys_act WITH 29

RETURN                              && end of on_keys
```

Color Set Restoration

The next routine correctly restores 100% of the colors retrieved by dBASE:

```
save_clr = SET('COLOR')

* then to restore:

DO re_color WITH save_clr
```

You can look up SET('COLOR') in Borland's *Language Reference* and figure out what all this does, or just copy Listing 3–32 (L03-32.PRG on your diskette) and let it do the work.

Code Listing 3–32

```
**************************************************************
*** re_color — restores color settings
**************************************************************

PROCEDURE re_color
PARAMETER clrs
PRIVATE clr, cstr, i

SET COLOR TO &clrs

i = AT( '&', clrs )
cstr = RIGHT( clrs, LEN(clrs)-i-2 )

i = AT( ',', cstr )
clr = LEFT( cstr, i-1 )
SET COLOR OF MESSAGES TO &clr

cstr = RIGHT( cstr, LEN(cstr)-i )
i = AT( ',', cstr )
clr = LEFT( cstr, i-1 )
SET COLOR OF TITLES TO &clr

cstr = RIGHT( cstr, LEN(cstr)-i )
i = AT( ',', cstr )
clr = LEFT( cstr, i-1 )
SET COLOR OF BOX TO &clr

cstr = RIGHT( cstr, LEN(cstr)-i )
i = AT( ',', cstr )
clr = LEFT( cstr, i-1 )
SET COLOR OF INFORMATION TO &clr
```

```
cstr = RIGHT( cstr, LEN(cstr)-i )
SET COLOR OF FIELDS TO &cstr

RETURN                                    && end of re_color
```

Setting Restoration

The re_set() code in Listing 3–33, as it says, restores any settings that FKEYS2 might have upset. It attempts to return you to the dot prompt just where you left off when you started FKEYS2.

Code Listing 3–33

```
*****************************************************************
*** re_set    — restores all settings
*****************************************************************

PROCEDURE re_set

RESTORE SCREEN FROM scrn_buf

DO re_color WITH save_colo

SET CURSOR &save_curs
@ save_row, save_col SAY ''

IF ISMOUSE()
   SET MOUSE &save_mous
ENDIF

SET SCOREBOARD &save_scor
SET TALK &save_talk

RETURN                                    && end of re_set
```

FKEYS2 Setting Restoration

The re_re_set() routine in Listing 3–34 is called when you return to FKEYS2 after executing a command. It returns settings to those previously used by FKEYS2.

Code Listing 3–34

```
***********************************************************
*** re_re_set — resumes FKEYS2 settings
***********************************************************

PROCEDURE re_re_set

SET TALK OFF

IF ISMOUSE()
   SET MOUSE ON
ENDIF

SET CURSOR ON

DO dsp_boxes
DO say_gets

RETURN                                    && end of re_re_set
```

String Pad

The str_pad() function shown in Listing 3–35 returns a string padded with blanks to the specified length. It truncates over-long strings to the specified length, too, although it would be more efficient to use the LEFT() built-in function if this were your only purpose.

Code Listing 3–35

```
***********************************************************
*** str_pad — pad string to length
***********************************************************

FUNCTION str_pad
PARAMETERS str, size

* tags "size" blanks onto end of "str" and then
* grabs "size" characters from the left

RETURN LEFT( str + REPLICATE(' ',size), size )
*                                         && end of str_pad
```

Summary

In this chapter we started using FKEYS2, a programmer's work-bench that you can personalize for each of your projects. It puts every file-editing command and all the other operations you commonly need for a project, a single keystroke or mouse click away.

We talked about how FKEYS2 works, including how to use its data files to directly set options. We saw the simulated DOS and dot prompt environments that are part of FKEYS2 and noted their limitations. Then we dived into the code.

FKEYS2 is totally event-driven, allowing you to select operations, including switching data-entry pages, by clicking the mouse or pressing a control key. We looked at each portion of the software, examining the event-driven programming in detail.

The header code begins, as always, with comments documenting the system. It continues setting up variables and arrays that are needed later. Then it calls initialization routines that access low-level data files to set up the F-key assignments.

The mainline code is very short. It calls the GET routine, which does the real work in this event-driven program. For clarity, we proceeded from the mainline to the supporting routines before exploring the event loop.

First, we looked at the F-key handling code. The low-level dBASE file I/O routines are used to read and write the data files. These routines, as we saw, are not, in fact, low level. They provide very convenient access to ASCII text files, which we used here. Other routines handle details such as setting the values we read into an array and into the F-keys themselves.

Next, we looked at the display routines. Each of the main components of the FKEYS2 display screens are handled by their own display subroutine. These are similar to those found in any other program.

After we had explored these supporting routines, we moved on to the event handling code, beginning with the mouse support routines. We saw that the event loop was just a continuous @ GET/READ loop. Mouse handling required provisions for an ON MOUSE subroutine called during the READ process, and an external handler called after the READ. The external handler communicated with the READ subroutine via semaphore variables.

The control-key handling is similar to the mouse event handling in the event loop. During the READ, a control-key subroutine is called via an ON KEY statement. The actual process triggered by the control key is handled in an external routine, called after the READ. It communicates with the ON KEY routine via semaphores.

After looking at the mouse and control-key handlers, we proceeded to the special DOS and dot prompt simulators. The DOS environment is simulated in a window, basically by reading an input line and then running it as a dBASE macro. Routines provide special handling for some DOS commands, as well as a mouse capability. The mouse events in the DOS window are handled in the same manner (under READ and external, communicating via semaphore) as they are in the main loop.

After exploring the DOS window, we went on to the dot prompt window. Again, this was implemented by reading text strings and executing the strings as dBASE macros. Special considerations included error handling and a mouse handler with a window-resizing capability.

Finally, we looked at the miscellaneous supporting routines. Due to the use of FKEYS2, these included particularly thorough routines to save all environment settings, including all color settings, so that your developing systems will run smoothly under FKEYS2.

The techniques in FKEYS2, particularly the event-handling techniques shown in the main event loop, and repeated in the DOS and dot prompt windows, are basic to modern user interface programming. FKEYS2 shows how to handle standard input, mouse input, and control keystroke input simultaneously.

I'm sure you'll want to build this mouse-operable, event-driven capability into your own systems. But before we get on to writing client-server software, we've got to continue to work on our foundation. The next three chapters cover database design.

Are you already an expert? Don't skip over the next section. The more you know about database design, the more the next three chapters will surprise you.

Chapter 4

Keys, Primary and Foreign

To build a sound system, we need a sound database design. As you'll see in Chapter 6, there is a method you can use to generate excellent database designs which focuses on the problem at hand, not on the requirements of relational databases. In this chapter and the next, we'll cover some necessary background material, building the foundation for the ORE&D method discussed in Chapter 6.

In the relational data model, all data is stored in tables. **Relation** is the name given by mathematicians to the structure that you and I think of as a table. Each row in the table, which we commonly call a record, represents one entry or object. Mathematicians call these rows **tuples,** pronounced to rhyme with "couples."

If we look at a table from an object-oriented viewpoint, we can think of the table as defining a class of objects. Each row in the table represents one **object,** or member of the class defined by the table. The fields are the object's characteristics. A PEOPLE table, for example, might have characteristics such as "name," "street," "city," and so on.

Object-oriented theory gives each individual object (or record, to us) a distinct identifier. This identifier is the handle we use to grab a particular object or row in our table.

In relational theory, this identifier is called the **primary key.** A great deal of material has been written that uses the data in the row as a source for this primary key. For instance, in the PEOPLE table, names alone are hardly likely to be unique. But perhaps name plus street address plus postal code would combine to form a unique identifier.

Fortunately, we can discard all the material on primary keys and "candidate keys" if we adopt a simpler solution: the **abstract,** or **factless,** key. An abstract key is a system-generated identifier that is guaranteed to be unique. To a human it looks like a random collection of ones and zeros. But to a computer it has one needed property: no two abstract keys ever have the same value.

If you're ever talking to someone trained in classic relational methodology, a **candidate key** is any set of fields that might uniquely identify a record—a combination of which might be a primary key. For example, a person's name and telephone number might be one candidate key and name plus complete address might be another candidate key. All the fields taken together are always a candidate key.

Classic relational theory devotes a great deal of time to picking a single primary key from multiple candidate keys. We will dispense with all those problems, using abstract keys, as proposed by the noted relational theorist Chris Date.

Implementing Abstract Primary Keys

Implementing abstract keys can be done in several ways. One of the easiest is to simply use numbers. Let's let the first field in the table hold the key value. In a .DBF, I always use a Numeric field, 8 wide, 0 decimal places. The first record added to the table is record "1". The next record is "2" and so on. Within an 8 digit number, this scheme will handle one less than 100 million records. Obviously, if you anticipate needing more records, you can use a larger number.

For a smaller file I could have used fewer than eight digits, but I never have. After considerable testing, I found that locating a single record was just about equally fast with either four or eight digits. I've tested this in dBASE and other major Xbase dialects and always come to the same conclusion: there is either no difference, or the difference is too small to worry about.

Of course, using 8 digits when 4 would be enough wastes space. But two points should be considered. First, the smaller the number of records we have to handle, the less space is taken for keys of any length. Wasting a few bytes per record is not important unless we have a lot of records (millions, for instance). And the more records you have, the more you really need the extra digits.

Additionally, we've passed the point where we can draw simple conclusions about the effect of "wasted" space on actual file sizes. With disk compression (as in Stacker, or DOS 6.x) blank characters get reduced to either no waste, or very little waste. You can now be very generous with blanks in your .DBFs at a very low cost in actual disk space consumption.

All of which leads me to use primary keys of N, 8, 0 for every file. If you're dealing with very large files you might occasionally want a wider field for the primary key. But bear in mind that this field is the record count, not the file size in bytes. If your records are 200 bytes long, N, 8, 0 keys will be adequate up to about 10 gigabytes in a single table.

If you've actually done your own arithmetic, you see that 8-digit keys, times 200 bytes will actually handle 20 gigabytes, not 10. As you'll see, I waste lots of keys—up to 50% of all the available keys. Until your tables push into the gigabyte leagues, this waste is completely free.

My first waste is a little trick I started using long ago. I don't really assign "1" to the first record. I assign "10000000." Why? This makes sure that all your keys are the same length, so trivial programs that dump records line them all up in ncat columns, without any thought to programming them to do so.

How do you generate a unique key when you need one? You need a function you can call that returns the next available key number. This function is responsible for keeping track of the last key it assigned. Warning: You cannot use the record number as a unique key.

Records can be deleted. You must *never* reuse a key. Why? In your archive files, a year or two down the road, you may have lots of deleted customers. What happens if you reassign a customer key to a new customer? Everything works well until you need to reconstruct the records for one of those deleted customers.

The old, deleted customer's key matches the key of a current customer. Your invoices depend on this key to reference the proper customer. But when you recall the old customer, you suddenly have two customers with identical keys. The sole job of the key is to be a *unique* identifier. Reusing a deleted key destroys its uniqueness.

If you write a function that returns the next available key, you can isolate the mechanics in a few lines of code. This means, of course, that you can change methods at a later date by replacing just those few lines of code.

The Last Record Method

The quickest unique key method is to simply look at the key of the last record and add one to it. In pseudo-code, it works like this:

```
FUNCTION get_next_key

go to the last record in the file
read the old key value

RETURN old_key + 1
```

The routine that calls this is the one that appends a new record:

```
* data gathered from user

new_key = get_next_key()
APPEND BLANK
REPLACE key_field    WITH new_key ;
        other_fields WITH other_values
```

Note that you call the get_next_key() routine *before* you append the blank record!

There are some details skipped, of course. The pcode that says "go to the last record in the file" doesn't mention that there are probably two or more indexes in use. These must be turned off to get to the last physical record. Then, they must be turned back on again before appending the new record.

Also, it is a generally bad practice to have a low-level routine such as get_next_key() move the record pointer. Better practice is to store the old RECNO() value, go to the bottom, and finally GO back to the old record before returning. In this case, though, you may be able to skip that step and get away with it. After all, if get_next_key() is only called immediately before an APPEND BLANK, there is no need to store and restore the old record pointer.

I only use this technique in quick and dirty systems. It works for casual use, but when you start to protect it against potential problems, you see that doing a better job in the first place would have been less trouble.

For example, what about deletes? One of your users could have deleted the last record. To get to the bottom, you have to get to the last record, even if it has been deleted. This isn't too much trouble.

But what about the maintenance process that PACKs the .DBF overnight or over the weekend? Here is the old logic for an audit-able table:

```
for all deleted records
  copy the record to a backup table
endfor

PACK
```

Now look at the logic if you are using the last record as a source of key values:

```
for all deleted records
  copy the record to a backup table
endfor

turn off indexes
go to the last record
if it is deleted
  set a flag
  undelete it
endif

PACK

if the flag is set
  delete the last record
endif
```

An auditor might very reasonably spend a great deal of time poring over these details. Why not get it right to begin with?

Using a Key Value File

You can store the highest used key to a .DBF, a memvar file, or a low-level file. Whichever you choose, the algorithm for the get_next_key() function is the same:

```
FUNCTION get_next_key

new_value = read value from file
add one to new_value
write new_value back to file

RETURN new_value
```

I use .DBF files for this purpose, because the record locking is easy to handle. I create a single "MKV" (Maximum Key Value) file for each system. It has one record per .DBF. Each record has two fields: the .DBF name and the last key value.

With locking, the function is:

```
FUNCTION get_next_key

new_value = read value from file
add one to new_value

lock record
write new_value back to file
unlock record

RETURN new_value
```

You can use ON ERROR to trap the occasional failed record lock.

Key Conventions

I always name my abstract keys "<tablename>_K" where <tablename> is the name of the .DBF file in a .DBF-based system, or the table name in an RDBMS-based system. For example, if the PEOPLE table stores names, addresses, and so on, its key is named PEOPLE_K.

I always use the first field in the file for the primary key. This parallels the use of keys in classic relational theory notation. Any other location would work without changing the software, since column positions can be rearranged at will. But using a consistent location helps my mental image of a system's inner workings.

Using Abstract Primary Keys

Using numeric abstract keys makes them readable, but I never show the keys in a user system. I usually produce a "user" system, which is the one you normally think of when building a system, and a "supervisor" system that handles maintenance tasks such as creating files, indexing/reindexing, and so on. The supervisor software may show the abstract keys, but they have no place in my user software.

The user system makes use of the abstract keys as a shorthand notation for naming records. Let's look at a simple billing system.

At the risk of being unrealistic, we'll just have two tables: one for customers and the other for invoices. Let's call them PEOPLE and INVOIC. (My table naming convention needs two suffix characters, so I am limited to six character table names to stay within DOS's eight-character filename limit.)

Each will have an abstract, primary key named, respectively, PEOPLE_K and INVOIC_K. Each record a user adds gets a unique number, starting with 10000001 in each table.

In our system, the user looks at a scroller that can browse through the data, and presses Ins or Del to add or delete records. The data is physically stored in the order it is entered. An index shows it to the user in a sensible order. Data in the PEOPLE table is shown in ascending alphabetic order by last name. Data in the billing table is shown sorted by descending billing date (latest bills first).

Each time the user asks the system to write a new record, a new primary key is assigned. The users are not aware that this happens. They simply see the behavior they expect when they press Ins and add data or Del to delete a record.

Using Abstract Foreign Keys

These keys are critical in handling the tie between the invoices and customers. Each invoice is for a particular customer, of course. The user's view of the invoice shows the customer's name and address at the top, above the other invoice details.

When the user adds an invoice, he or she is shown a point-and-shoot list of customers containing last names and enough other data to correctly identify the person being billed. When the user selects a customer, that person's name and address data is shown on the invoice form.

The person's name and address data is *not* repeated in every invoice record. This would be both inefficient and difficult to maintain. If you change a person's address, for example, you want that change to show up on all invoices for that person. You don't want to have to edit every invoice record—maintaining multiple copies of the same data and keeping them all error-free is nearly impossible.

Foreign keys let us achieve the desired effect: entering the customer's name and address in the PEOPLE table, and having that information shown on invoices as needed. You simply place the PEOPLE_K value into the INVOIC record. This is the only PEOPLE information ever entered into the INVOIC record.

Having a PEOPLE_K value in the invoice lets your system look up the data about that person whenever you need to either show an invoice on-screen or print one. These fragments show the relevant portions of each table.

```
PEOPLE
    Field     Type    Length
    -----     ----    ------
    PEOPLE_K  N          8
    LNAME     C         24
    FULLNAME  C         40
    ADDRESS   C         40
      . . .

INVOIC
    Field     Type    Length
    -----     ----    ------
    INVOIC_K  N          8
    PEOPLE_K  N          8
    AMOUNT    N          6
      . . .
```

With these examples, you begin to see the benefits of a consistent naming convention. By examining the structure of the INVOIC file, you see that it has INVOIC_K. This is the primary key. It also has PEOPLE_K, which, by convention, must be a foreign key into the PEOPLE table. The value of PEOPLE_K in the INVOIC table will match exactly one record in the PEOPLE table.

Here is a portion of the invoice display code:

```
* an INVOIC record has been selected

SELECT PEOPLE    && active INDEX on PEOPLE_K

SEEK invoic->people_k  && find the person
@ r, c SAY people->fullname
@ r+1,c SAY people->address
* etc.
```

This being pcode, no error checking is shown. The SEEK command shown is actually a call to a SEEK subroutine, which handles the case when something has gone wrong and a matching record is not found. In my systems, this condition halts the user program, leaving an error message on the screen. Since this almost never happens in practice, this sort of fatal error handling is acceptable.

Chapter 8 covers relational integrity in depth. For now, let's assume that nothing has gone wrong and when we need a key, we'll find a key.

Primary and Foreign Key Examples

In the following, we'll ignore a lot of irrelevant details that you will have to handle eventually. For example, prices will need some decimal places in many, though not all, currencies. We will focus here on the primary and foreign keys and either ignore all the other details completely or bury them in "(etc.)"—fields your imagination can supply.

The first example is a somewhat more elaborate customer system that assumes that your customers are organizations employing people, not people themselves.

```
PEOPLE
     Field    Type    Length
     -----    ----    ------
     PEOPLE_K  N        8
     LASTNAME  C        24
     (etc.)
     ORGS_K    N        8

ORGS
     Field    Type    Length
     -----    ----    ------
     ORGS_K    N        8
     NAME      C        40
     (etc.)

INVOIC
     Field    Type    Length
     -----    ----    ------
     INVOIC_K  N        8
     INV_DATE  D        8
     ORGS_K    N        8
     (etc.)
```

In the above example, each table has a primary key. The INVOIC table has a foreign key, ORGS_K, which holds the primary key of the organization that purchased your goods or services. The PEOPLE table also has an ORGS_K foreign key. In the PEOPLE table, it identifies the organization that employs the person.

Using this structure, you would store address and phone information for each organization in the ORGS table. The PEOPLE table could have home addresses and personal phone numbers, but would not repeat the data in the ORGS table.

In the next example, we'll show a more realistic invoicing structure where your company sells multiple products, listed in a PRODCT table, and breaks out one line per product sold in the invoice. The line-by-line invoice details are stored in an INVDTL table.

```
PRODCT
     Field    Type    Length
     -----    ----    ------
     PRODCT_K  N        8
     NAME      C        24
     PRICE     N        6
     (etc.)
```

```
INVOIC
    Field    Type    Length
    -----    ----    ------
    INVOIC_K  N        8
    INV_DATE  D        8
    ORGS_K    N        8
    (etc.)

INVDTL
    Field    Type    Length
    -----    ----    ------
    INVDTL_K  N        8
    INVOIC_K  N        8
    PRODCT_K  N        8
    QUANTITY  N        2
```

As always, each table has a primary key that follows our naming convention. Foreign keys attach the invoice to an organization, and in the invoice detail file, they attach each line item to a particular invoice and a particular product.

If you've ever built a billing system, you recognize that the last example has a problem: What happens when you change a price?

This one will generate a current invoice, but it won't correctly price items if you ever need to go back and regenerate an old bill. To do that, you'll need pricing history. The next example shows how a foreign key attaches pricing history information to products.

```
PRODCT
    Field    Type    Length
    -----    ----    ------
    PRODCT_K  N        8
    NAME      C       24
    (etc.)

P_HIST
    Field    Type    Length
    -----    ----    ------
    P_HIST_K  N        8
    PRODCT_K  N        8
    P_DATE    D        8
    PRICE     N        6
```

With all the other uses of foreign keys, your software could simply SEEK for the correct record in the file. With this one, you

SEEK for the product key in the P_HIST file, and then have to look through the file for the most recent pricing date (or another date, for regenerating old invoices). This is a good example of how the complexity of the real world gets mirrored in the complexity of your software.

Summary

A key is an identifier that uniquely specifies a single row in a data table. Mathematicians, who provide the basis for relational database theory, would say that a key identifies a single tuple in a relation. We'll stick to calling them rows in tables.

Multiple combinations of fields, called "candidate keys," could be used as a primary key. Our system is simpler. We use a single, abstract key as the only record identifier.

The abstract key's only required property is uniqueness. The simplest way you can insure uniqueness is to assign the first record the numeric key 1, the second record the key 2, and so on. The only trick is to not inadvertently reassign a key after a record is deleted.

To avoid reassigning key numbers after a deletion, the simplest solution is to keep a small file that holds the highest key assigned in each table. To add a new record, you look up the value in this table, increment it, then assign the new key.

For practical simplicity, I always use 8-digit keys. This wastes only a small amount of space for small tables where a shorter key could work, and keeps all the software the same.

Abstract keys are used as both primary keys and foreign keys. I match key names to the tables. PEOPLE_K is the primary key of the PEOPLE table, for example. Similarly, INVOIC_K is the primary key of the INVOIC table.

To use a primary key as a foreign key, you place the field in a second table. For example, the INVOIC table could also have a field called PEOPLE_K, which would identify the person to whom the invoice was sent. The value of the PEOPLE_K field in the INVOIC table would be the value of one of the PEOPLE_K fields in the PEOPLE table.

Since each PEOPLE_K field is guaranteed to have a unique value in the PEOPLE table, looking up a particular value will find a particular person. A value of PEOPLE_K can appear multiple times in the INVOIC table. Primary keys are unique, but foreign keys may not be. This lets multiple invoices be sent to a single person.

Now that you understand abstract keys, we are ready to go on to relationships. In the next chapter I'll show you that what you thought you knew about relationships (1->M, M->M, and so on) is only the beginning of the story. Then in Chapter 6 we'll get into a brand-new but rigorously sound method of database design, built on these keys and relationship concepts.

Chapter 5

Binary Relationships

Relationships are a key part of database design. Most texts classify relationships as one-to-one, one-to-many, many-to-one, and many-to-many.

This isn't a bad place to start, but it's woefully inadequate as a place to stop. In this chapter, we'll look at that traditional analysis and extend it to an inclusive coverage of binary relationships. We'll also briefly touch on trinary and higher-degree relationships.

Along the way, we'll build a notation that lets us describe binary relationships with precision and economy. We'll use this notation throughout the rest of this book.

Classical Analysis

Let's begin with one-to-many relationships. The common notation is:

```
1->M
```

This is a very common relationship in database design. One customer can have many invoices. One purchase order can specify many individual parts. One shipment can have many cartons.

The many-to-one relationship is the opposite side of the one-to-many. A common notation is:

```
M->1
```

Many invoices can be for one customer. Many individual parts can be part of one purchase order, and so on. In this sense, you can see that a many-to-one relationship is really just a one-to-many relationship, viewed from the opposite side. But do *not* conclude that these relationships are two sides of the same coin.

1->M Is Not M->1

Your software will treat these as two distinct relationships. So far, all our examples have shown the "from" side of the relationship on the left, the "to" side on the right. We have gone from one customer to many invoices (1->M) or from many invoices to one customer (M->1).

To discuss the difference between the two, we will adopt this as a rigorous convention. We always write the "from" side on the left. This means we can substitute a colon for the arrow.

```
1:M — from 1 to Many
M:1 — from Many to 1
```

The "from" here, "to" there distinction is vital in creating quality client-server software. Let's build a system for a local beverage distributor, using 1:M relationships (that's from one to many, of course).

One-to-Many Relationships

Mary, at the Corner Deli, phones in her order to Local Beverages. At Local, the order clerk points to (or clicks on) "Enter Order." Your system presents a picklist of customers. The clerk selects "Corner Deli" and then asks Mary what she needs today.

Mary fills out an order form before her call, and your software shows an on-screen version of Mary's form. The order clerk at Local goes down the form on-screen, filling in quantities as Mary reads them from her order form. Tomorrow morning, Corner Deli's order list (and all Local's other customers' lists) is available in the warehouse in time to load the trucks. Mary's beverages are on their way.

Let's look underneath the screen and see what's going on in the database system. For this discussion, we'll ignore topics such as error recovery that are vital, but will distract us from our main topic.

The clerk at Local Beverages used a point-and-shoot method to pick Corner Deli from a list of customers—more generally, to select the "one" on the from side of a one-to-many relationship. The order entry software created a new, blank order record. Next, this record was assigned a primary key—its Order ID. Then the order software filled in today's date and the Corner Deli's key as a foreign key in the Orders table.

Then this order was used as the from side of another 1 : M relationship, this time between the Orders table and the Order Details table. As Local's order clerk fills in the quantities, your software appends new records to the Order Detail table. Each Order Detail record is assigned its own primary key, and then the Order record's key is entered as a foreign key in the Order Detail record. A product ID and a quantity are filled in to complete each Order Detail record.

When we approach from the one side of the one-to-many relationship, the software passes on a primary key it has already found to a record it is creating. This primary key is entered as a foreign key in the record on the "many" side of the relationship.

The software users' view of the system shows only the records pertinent to a single related record. You might allow the clerk to scroll through the last several days' orders, but only through Corner Deli's orders when Corner Deli has been selected. The orders from all other customers are in the same table, but from the users' point of view, each customer has a logically separate table of orders.

Now let's look at software that supports a M : 1 view.

Many-to-One Relationships

When the clerk at Local Beverages got off the phone with Mary, he suddenly realized that he was speaking to the Mary at North Main Grocery, not the Mary at Corner Deli. Now he had a perfectly good order for the wrong customer. He went in to see his supervisor.

Your system provides supervisors with an M:1 view of the unfilled orders. The supervisor can scroll through the unfilled orders as if they are all entries in a single order table (which, of course, they are). Hopping quickly to the end of the table, the supervisor finds Mary's order.

The supervisor moves the cursor into the Customer Name field, presses Enter to pop up the list of customers, and presses Enter on North Main Grocery. On the order form, the name and address of Corner Deli are replaced with the name and address of North Main Grocery. Problem solved.

Again, let's look under the hood, since the handling was quite different. First, the supervisor located the correct order—the many side of the M:1 relationship. As the supervisor scrolls through the table, the different customers are seen, one for each order. After finding the right order, the supervisor edited the customer field. To the supervisor, it seemed as if the software had entered the customer's name and address as part of the order. Underneath, of course, the software is just scrolling through the customer table and picking an appropriate key.

So you see that the software has important differences. A 1:M view will hide most of the many-side records, showing only those that are relevant to the one-side entry. When the clerk selected Corner Deli, only Corner Deli's orders were visible. An M:1 view allows you to browse the many side across all of the one-side items (or as many as are allowed, subject to security issues). In a 1:M entry, the foreign key (the one-side primary key) is automatically entered into the many-side record.

Many-to-Many Relationships

In our notation, we will use the obvious notation for many-to-many relationships:

```
M:M
```

There is no direct way to represent a M:M relationship in a relational database. M:M relationships are built with separate tables holding multiple foreign keys.

For example, a hospital has many beds and many patients. During a stay a patient might be in one bed when admitted, moved to another after surgery, and then to another for the last days of recovery. Obviously, each bed is used by many patients.

A Who's Where? table could record the data relating beds and patients. Each record in Who's Where? would have a Bed ID, a Patient ID, and start and end dates. This table records the M:M relationship between patients and beds.

In a 1:M (or an M:1) relationship, the one-side record does not record the relationship. The order record had the Customer ID in the example above. The many-side record holds the foreign key. In a M:M relationship, a separate table is required. The relationship between bed and patient is shown in this table as a M:1 relationship between Who's Where? and a patient, along with a M:1 relationship between Who's Where? and a bed.

One-to-One Relationships

One-to-one relationships seldom require anything more than an additional field in a table. For example, the senior officials at your government agency are assigned private parking spaces. You name the parking spaces "P1," "P2," and so on.

When elections trigger a serious change at the top, your personnel system allows the staff to move these names into the new personnel records. Your software does some checking, of course, to see that "P2" is actually allocated just once, but there is only a single table affected.

There is only a single table affected because the object "Parking Space" does not require its own table. Sure, Space 11 is a little farther from the door than Space 12, but it is shaded. That's why it was given number 11—it's better than number 12. You don't need to keep a separate table of parking space characteristics.

On rare occasions, you will need a separate table. This is handled by placing a foreign key in the "to" side (from 1 to 1) of the relationship, just as if it were a 1:M relationship. Your software must then do an additional check of the to-side entry to be sure that the from-side key is not allocated elsewhere. Of course, this is the same as checking that parking space "P2" is only allocated once.

This completes our tour of the classical breakdown of binary relationships. And you should be starting to think about what is missing.

Additional Analysis

So far, we've used two numbers: 1 and "M." How many is M? Frequently it means "zero or more." The "more" part could be one, two, hundreds, or thousands. It isn't specified. The zero could also be a one, as in "one or more."

Let's go back to our beverage distributor. Does your system let a customer be entered before its first order is placed? Many systems will, though you have to decide on a case-by-case basis if this is correct. Local Beverages' system allows zero or more orders per customer.

Now let's look at the Order table. Does your system let an order be entered with zero detail records? This wouldn't be reasonable. If the order clerk doesn't enter at least one item, the order should not go into the table. (You don't want an order for zero of everything, do you?)

So we have zero or more orders per customer, with one or more items per order. To record these facts, I borrow two terms from lexical analysis: **Kleene closure** and **positive closure**, meaning respectively, "zero or more" and "one or more." They are represented by the asterisk and plus sign.

```
M* — zero or more (Kleene closure)
M+ — one or more (positive closure)
```

You will see these symbols in any editor that uses "regular expression" notation for search and search and replace functions. Regarding Local Beverages' system, we could specify:

```
Customer:Order — 1:M*
Order:Order items — 1:M+
```

Of course, this is just a short-hand notation. If we want to cover all the bases, we need to be able to specify an exact range. Local Beverages, for example, stocks 500 items, so its relation-ship is:

```
Order:Order items — 1:1-500
```

And there is no reason to think that zero or more (or one or more) is the full range of minimums. Local Beverages might institute a minimum order policy, where it only delivers orders for 5 or more items. So our relationship could be:

```
Order:Order items — 1:5-500
```

At its most general, our notation for an M:M relationship is:

```
from side:to side

either side can be  1, M+ or M*, or low-high

Examples       5-10:0-100
                  1:M*
                  1:0-1
                  M+:1
```

These next pairs show synonyms:

```
1:M*      or      1:0-M

1:M+      or      1:1-M
```

Now we have a complete range of binary relationships, and an efficient notation to specify them. Why is this important?

Let's look under the hood again.

Implementing 1:M*

This is the easier relationship to implement. For Local Beverages, it means you can enter a customer and write the record to the customer table. Then your software asks the user if there are any orders to enter. If there are, you enter them, and if not, that's fine.

Implementing 1:M+

The positive closure, one or more, requires a bit more work. Let's consider Local Beverages again. You store the order data in RAM until an order-item record is complete. Then you can write the order data into the table. You continue to accept more order-item records, until the user signals that the order is complete.

There is an additional nuisance that must be programmed, too. Your user may enter several line items. You provide a mechanism for editing these entries, of course. These may all get revised to zero amount, thus eliminating the whole order.

(Is this realistic? It's infrequent but not something you can ignore. Mary just started her order, asking for a case of Diet Bubbles, when her boss hollers, "No Diet Bubbles! I just found

3 cases in back." Our clerk zeros out Diet Bubbles. Mary is about to get going again when her boss interrupts. She says, "I'll call you back later." The clerk at Local Beverages now has an order for zero of everything.)

Your software has to be prepared to eliminate the whole order if all the order items are for zero amount. (If you don't trap this condition at order entry time, you'll regret it later. There will be invoices written for zero amount, null packing lists frustrating the crew in the warehouse, etc.)

If the relationship is 1:M+, you have to enforce the "one or more" constraint.

Implementing Minima and Maxima

Similar considerations apply to specified minima and maxima. Obviously, M+ is a specified minimum of one. If Local Beverages institutes a policy of 5 items, minimum order, you have the same sort of programming considerations. You just have to be prepared to back the whole order out if it fails to come up to the minimum specified.

Maxima must be considered on a case-by-case basis. For Local Beverages, the 500 item maximum simply means that they only stock 500 items. Since your system has the clerk scroll through the list entering amounts, there is no chance of going over the maximum. If Mary asks for five cases of whatever, then changes her mind and says, "Better make that seven cases," your clerk just scrolls back to the item and changes a "5" to a "7." There is no provision for the clerk to add another record for two more cases of the same item.

Other systems may require explicit maximum checks, and corrective action based on the application's requirements.

Beyond Binary

So far we have only been discussing binary relationships—relationships between thing one and thing two. There is no limit to the number of participants in a relationship, however. Let's consider a massively complex example, found in almost every home.

You probably have some recorded music. Let's say that you want to catalog the songs in your collection. Let's simplify (we'll need all the help we can get) and only catalog songs—no instrumental numbers.

A 1:1:1 Trinary Relationship

You want to know the lyricist, composer, and singer so that you can pick out all the songs written by David Crosby, for instance. (Or, if you prefer, by Hank Williams or Wolfgang Amadeus Mozart.) Of course, you quickly see that a song, for this purpose, is a trinary relationship: one lyricist to one composer to one singer.

An M:M:M Trinary Relationship

Give the problem some thought and you will see that a song is not really a 1:1:1 relationship. It's a M:M:M relationship, even if we stick to just lyrics, composition, and lead singer. Consider "A Day in the Life" from the Beatles' *Sgt. Pepper's Lonely Hearts Club Band* album. It is two separate songs, tightly interwoven. One is clearly by John Lennon and the other by Paul McCartney, who alternate on lead vocals.

Trinary relationships cannot be correctly represented in a single table. Let's try, using names where a real implementation will use unique keys.

```
Song          Lyrics  Music   Lead vocal
Day in Life   Lennon  Lennon  Lennon
Day in Life   Lennon  Lennon  McC'ny
Day in Life   Lennon  McC'ny  Lennon
Day in Life   Lennon  McC'ny  McC'ny
Day in Life   McC'ny  Lennon  Lennon
Day in Life   McC'ny  Lennon  McC'ny
Day in Life   McC'ny  McC'ny  Lennon
Day in Life   McC'ny  McC'ny  McC'ny
```

Taken together, these eight records are needed to correctly respond to queries such as, "List the songs with lyrics by A, sung by B." If this had been a trio (for example: "words, music, and vocals by Banks, Collins, and Rutherford") we would need 27 records in the table to answer such queries.

Breaking M:M:M into Multiple M:Ms

As before, you must break out the M:M relationships into separate tables. In this example, many lyricists write many songs, many composers compose many songs, and many singers sing many songs. The correct representation is:

```
Song_Lyricist_Table
Day in Life   Lennon
Day in Life   McCartney

Song_Composer_Table
Day in Life   Lennon
Day in Life   McCartney

Song_Singer_Table
Day in Life   Lennon
Day in Life   McCartney
```

In this example, expanding to a trio, each given full credit, would add exactly one more record to each of the three tables.

The real afficionado will want to know about all the musicians on the song, too—not just the lead singer. This quickly expands the trinary song relationship into an *N-ary* relationship. In a rock or country collection, you might want to add the lead guitarist, bass player, and drummer. Of course, you quickly get into trouble there, too.

Leaving M:M:M Alone

Who plays lead guitar on Lennon and McCartney's "Eleanor Rigby"? No one. The instruments are all bowed string instruments. To give credit where credit is due, you want to record the lead violinist, lead cellist, and so on. Obviously, entering a column in the song table for every instrument ever played will quickly get out of control.

Here, you need a table for a trinary relationship:

```
Song            Instrument      Performer
Day in Life     Drums           Starr
Day in Life     Lead Guitar     Harrison
```

If we were using the semantic binary model, instead of the relational model, this choice would be more obvious. This relationship is binary, appearances notwithstanding. Starr on drums can be thought of as a single entity. A song either has Starr on drums, or it doesn't. It either has Harrison's lead guitar or it doesn't. Similarly, it might also have Harrison on sitar, or not. So the relationship is really between the song and the performer/ instrument pair.

Note that this pairing prevents erroneous conclusions. Harrison plays guitar. Harrison plays sitar. Harrison plays on this song. Therefore Harrison plays guitar and sitar on this song. Wrong. (Obviously, Harrison could have played only sitar on one song and only guitar on another.)

Higher-Degree Relationships Summarized

Unfortunately, the relational literature generally gets hopelessly opaque when it expands to trinary relationships. (Look up fifth-normal form in any RDBMS text.) The writing on the semantic model, including the semantic binary model, is all academic so far, so it's not much help either.

The good news is that trinary and higher-degree relationships are rare in practice. Generally speaking, you can break out the M : M relationships into individual tables and achieve a sound design.

In rare cases, such as in the performer/instrument pairing, a pair forms an indivisible entity. If breaking a trinary relationship into multiple binary relationship creates nonsense, you have found one of these cases. When that happens, leave the apparent trinary (or higher-degree) relationship alone.

The same notation that we developed for binary relationships will serve perfectly for the occasional trinary or higher-degree relationship.

Summary

We began our discussion of relationships with the classic relationships. These are one-to-one, one-to-many, many-to-one, and many-to-many. As far as the classical system goes, it works. But it does not consider all the information you need to build systems.

Borrowing terms and notation from "regular expressions," I add the concepts of Kleene closure and positive closure. Kleene closure means "zero or more" and is noted with a "*" as in "1:M*," meaning "one to zero or more."

Positive closure, noted with a "+," means "one or more." The notation "1:M+" means "one to one or more."

In many systems, these are important implementation differences. For example, your system may allow a customer to be entered without any invoices (one customer to zero or more invoices—1:M*). But the same system could prohibit entry of an invoice without at least one detail line showing what was ordered (one invoice to one or more detail lines—1:M+).

We completed our set of binary relations by generalizing to min-max ranges. For instance, a distributor carrying 500 separate items might have an order minimum of five or more items. This would be 1:5–500—one order to from 5 to 500 items.

At its most general, a binary relation is min1–max1:min2–max2. But binary relationships are only a subset of all relationships.

Trinary relationships are those with three related items, of course. An example is a song:composer:performer relationship. We discussed how these can be split into multiple binary relationships to accommodate the relational database requirements. We also discussed when not to split these relationships.

Once you pass binary relationships, database complexity can easily expand exponentially if you are not careful in your analysis. We'll meet trinary and higher-degree relationships in the next chapter, when we look at normal forms higher than fourth-normal form.

In the next chapter, we'll put what we know about keys and relationships to use in a new design methodology that I call "ORE&D." You'll learn how to do your own ORE&D work, and we'll spend enough time comparing ORE&D to classic normalization to convince you that ORE&D is a mathematically sound technique.

Chapter 6

Database Design

I use a semantic, object-oriented approach to database design. By "semantic" I mean that I concentrate on the meaning of the data. By "object-oriented," I mean that I concentrate on the real-world things that are modelled in a database.

In this chapter I'll show you my approach to database design. I'll also discuss the classic "normalization" theory that has been recommended for database design. Critics of relational databases are unanimous in condemning the normalization steps that have been recommended. I agree with the critics, but will give you the normalization steps anyway so you can judge for yourself.

We have agreed to use a relational database since that is the model used by the vast majority of today's available software, including dBASE.

A relational database is one where all data is stored in tables. Whether our back-end is .DBF-based or built around an RDBMS server, our data will be in tables. But how do we organize the data into the right tables? What is the right number of tables? How does a semantic, object-oriented approach yield a relational data-base design?

To answer these questions, let's start with considering our goals.

Design Goals

Other than observing that the number of tables depends on the application, there is no way to make a rule about the right number of tables. But we can identify the characteristics of a good design.

No Redundant Data

First, we do not want redundant data. Every fact we need should have one and only one place in the database. For example, we won't record a customer's name and address on every invoice. That would give us the chance to misspell the name or get the address wrong in many places. It makes it just about impossible to make the needed updates if the customer moves.

We will have a customer table, and store the customer's name and address just once in this table. If we make a mistake, it is then simple enough to correct it. If the customer moves, one change and our whole system is brought up to date.

A warning: There are other design goals that may contradict this one. You can sometimes improve processing speed immensely by storing a small amount of redundant data. Later on, we'll violate this rule, but only very infrequently and very carefully.

No Accidental Deletes

In every active table you will be adding and deleting data. But you don't want this to happen by accident. If your hospital system stores recommended treatments along with the patient's name and bed assignment, you don't want to delete the patient when the recommended treatment is changed.

Every time you store data about two or more independent things in a single record, you risk an unintended deletion. If your hospital billing system stored the insurance company's name and address in the patient record, deleting the last patient insured by a particular insurance company would remove that insurance company from your files.

Update Anomalies

The generic name for problems such as accidental deletes is "update anomalies." At their most subtle, update anomalies can be difficult to predict, and can present serious problems. An inadvertent relational operation could create bogus records (see the "lossless join" in the discussion of higher normal forms later in this chapter).

Update anomalies almost always stem from one design flaw: a single table is used to store data on two or more things. As we get into our design method, we will concentrate on separating our real-world items into individual classes so this will not happen.

Objects and Events

Over the years, I have evolved a design method that I call ORE&D (pronounced ore'n'dee, like R&D). I first starting experimenting with ORE&D when I found that it wasn't possible to teach the classic normalization methodology to my clients in any reasonable length of time.

Why do I need to teach my clients? Only the people closest to the database problem have the knowledge you need to design a database, so it is critical that they understand the database design process. I created ORE&D as a method that could be explained simply to the people who really understood the problems the database system is designed to solve.

In recent years, non-relational database proponents (semantic and object-oriented) have commented extensively on the deficiencies of the normalization process. There is now considerable academic support for abandoning the old approach.

While ORE&D is much simpler than the classic normalization steps, it is not a simplified approach. If this seems like a contradiction, consider two carpenters: one patiently drives nails with a hammer, while the other uses a pneumatic nail gun. In a single "pop" the pneumatic gun drives a nail perfectly.

Obviously, the pneumatic gun achieves the same result as the manual process, but with far less work. Similarly, ORE&D achieves a first-rate, thoroughly normalized design, but with much less work. The last part of this chapter compares ORE&D to classic normalization.

ORE&D depends on a taxonomy of table types. Dividing tables into different classes may seem to contradict one of the most fundamental principles of relational databases: All tables are the same. In fact, there is no contradiction. ORE&D actually classifies real-world entities and places them in tables. The tables are the same from the point of view of the relational model, but are differentiated as to the real-world entities they model.

In the following sections, we'll discuss each table type, starting with the most common, Objects, and ending with Relationships, the least common. (The logical order for this taxonomy is OED&R, but I think you'll agree that ORE&D leads to a better pronunciation.)

Objects

Step one in ORE&D design is listing the real-world Objects that concern your system. Here I am not using "Object" as in "object-oriented." I mean real, tangible, hurt your toe if you kick one, Objects. Buildings, companies, products, customers, people, and employees are Objects for ORE&D work.

If relevant, less-kickable Objects can also be listed. You may list musical compositions or mathematical theorems if they are part of the world your database must model.

Each Object type that you list is a table. Give it a table name and list the facts you need to know about each Object. These Object characteristics, subject to the dicussion below, will become the columns of your table.

Events

After listing the Objects, list the Events that are important to your database. Events are items such as making a sale, admitting a patient, or making a shipment.

If you think of Objects as the nouns in your database, Events are the verbs. Objects are more or less permanent. Events are things that happen at a specific point in time.

Each type of Event that you list is another table. Again, give it a name and list the facts you need to know about the event. There are two things that you will note as you list the characteristics of your Events.

First, you will need a time stamp for each Event. When did it happen? This time stamp must be detailed enough to separate two otherwise identical events. In many cases, recording the date the event occurs will be adequate. In other cases, you will want to know the hour and minute, as well as the day.

A fast-food establishment will want to record the time of each transaction. (How many burgers should we have on the grill at noon? How many at 3:30 P.M.?) A software company that ships products once a month to distributors and dealers will find a date more than adequate for identifying a shipment.

Second, you will notice that Events involve Objects. You ship products to customers, assign patients to beds, purchase components from suppliers. An Event is a transaction among Objects at a point in time.

Some of your Objects may be pieces of paper used to record Events. An invoice, for example, is a paper generated at the time of a sale. You should attempt to classify the real-world Objects and Events and attach data about these pieces of paper to the Events they record. For example, a sale Event may have an invoice number as one of its characteristics. Bear in mind that these pieces of paper are just another model of the real-world Objects and Events you're tracking.

As you list the Objects and Events relevant to your system, you may note that this taxonomy is not exhaustive. Extend it to meet your requirements. You may need to record data about items that are not permanent, like Objects, but that are not happenings at a single point in time, like Events. For example, your employer may build houses.

Biologists call fur-bearing animals that have babies and suckle their young "mammals." Animals that have scales and lay eggs are reptiles. The furry platypus suckles its young, after its eggs hatch. The platypus is neither reptile nor mammal, but this doesn't mean that the distinction between mammals and reptiles is not commonly useful. Similarly, our classification of Objects and Events is also commonly useful, even though it is not exhaustive.

Before you leave Objects and Events, make sure that you have listed an abstract, primary key as one of the characteristics of each Object and Event. Then scrutinize each characteristic carefully. Ask, "Is this really a fact about this Object (or Event)?" Create new tables for any characteristics that are not *completely* part of the subject Object or Event.

Details

Using the relational model, we cannot accommodate data that does not fit in a table. Some of our Objects and Events will require multiple tables to maintain a complete set of data. For instance, an invoice will commonly consist of two tables: one holding items such as the invoice date and the customer, and another listing the products sold, quantity, and price.

Repeating Groups

The invoice is an example of an Event with a repeating group. A sale typically transfers one or more products to a customer. At this point, you should look through your Object and Event characteristics and note all those that involve repeating groups.

Some typical examples are: A patient receives one or more treatments; a shipment is held in one or more cartons; a student enrolls in one or more courses; an employee has one or more dependents. In each case, the repeating group is separated from the parent table into its own Detail table.

The first field in the Detail table is its own primary key. The second field is the foreign key, naming the parent record. For instance, if your SALES table has a related SALDTL (sales detail) table listing the products sold, the SALDTL table would include these fields:

```
SALDTL
    Field     Type     Length
    -------  -------  --------
    SALDTL_K  N          8
    SALES_K   N          8
    (etc.)
```

If you were listing an employee's dependents, your detail table might start like this:

```
DEPENS
    Field     Type     Length
    -------  -------  --------
    DEPENS_K  N          8
    EMPLOY_K  N          8
    (etc.)
```

In the Detail table, you list the characteristics of the repeating item (or move these characteristics out of the Object or Event into the Detail table). The sales detail table would include the product key and quantity. The dependent table would include names, birthdates, and so on.

Occasionally, a Detail table may have repeating characteristics of its own. These are broken out of the Detail table just as other Details were broken out of Objects and Events. Suppose you needed to record the sports in which your dependents participate. (Possibly your medical insurance is more expensive for race-car drivers or cheaper for joggers.) Since each dependent could participate in zero or more sports, another Detail table is required. This is an example:

```
DEPENS
    Field     Type     Length
    -------  -------  --------
    DEPENS_K  N          8
    EMPLOY_K  N          8
    (etc.)
```

```
SPORTS
    Field    Type     Length
    -------  -------  --------
    SPORTS_K  N          8
    DEPENS_K  N          8
    (etc.)
```

Histories

Another type of Detail table is the history table. At this point, go through each characteristic of every Object, Event, and Detail. Ask if historical data will be needed.

Prices are one example of a characteristic for which historical data is normally needed. As with other Details, move the characteristic out of the parent table into its own history table. Here is a price history Detail table, related to a parent product Object table.

```
PRODCT
    Field    Type     Length
    -------  -------  --------
    PRODCT_K  N          8
    NAME      C         24
    (etc.)


P_HIST
    Field    Type     Length
    -------  -------  --------
    P_HIST_K  N          8
    PRODCT_K  N          8
    P_DATE    D          8
    PRICE     N          6
```

Unlike other Detail tables, history tables always require at least one date. More precisely, you must have a start time and an end time for each history item. Frequently, the start date is adequate. (In this case, each start date implies that the previous entry ended the previous day.) However, if your organization changes prices in the middle of a day, for example, you may need a more exact time stamp.

You should be aware that almost every characteristic can change over time. This does not imply that every characteristic should have a history Detail table. For example, people change their names. (Jane marries Bill and adopts Bill's family name.) We can simply edit the record, replacing the old data with new data. Our databases maintain histories via regular backups and audit trails. Before you decide that separate History detail tables are required, ask if the frequency of use of the data justifies the extra effort required to maintain and use history tables.

Relationships

The "R" in ORE&D stands for Relationships. In some cases, fields in your Object, Event, and Detail tables will record relationships. In other cases, additional tables will be required.

1:1

Each student at your university is permitted one major field of study. The major field is simply a characteristic field. If you have a fixed list of major subjects, your software might show the user a picklist and record a two-byte code in the database. This would be structured as follows:

```
STUDNT
    Field    Type    Length
    -------  ------- --------
    STUDNT_K  N         8
    NAME      C        40
    MAJOR     C         2
    (etc.)
```

Alternatively, your university could require that major fields of study correspond to one of the university's academic departments. If academic departments are recorded in an Object table in your database, the STUDNT table could look like this:

```
DEPMNT
    Field    Type    Length
    -------  ------- --------
    DEPMNT_K  N         8
    (etc.)
```

```
STUDNT
    Field    Type    Length
    -------  ------- --------
    STUDNT_K  N         8
    NAME      C        40
    DEPMNT_K  N         8
    (etc.)
```

1:M and M:1

Regardless of the quantity (M, M+, M*, or other) 1:M and M:1 relationships are recorded the same way. In the table of the Many side of the relationship, the key of the one-side is a characteristic.

Here are many invoices, each related to one customer:

```
CUSTMR
    Field    Type    Length
    -------  ------- --------
    CUSTMR_K  N         8
    (etc.)
```

```
INVOIC
    Field    Type    Length
    -------  ------- --------
    INVOIC_K  N         8
    DATE      D         8
    CUSTMR_K  N         8
    (etc.)
```

In the next example, I'll show many cartons as part of a single shipment.

```
SHPMNT
    Field    Type    Length
    -------  ------- --------
    SHPMNT_K  N         8
    (etc.)
```

```
CARTON
    Field    Type    Length
    -------  ------- --------
    CARTON_K  N         8
    SHPMNT_K  N         8
    (etc.)
```

Both types of Detail tables, repeating groups and histories, are examples of M:1 relationships: many details to one parent Object, Event, or Detail.

M:M

Many-to-many relationships almost always require a separate Relationship table, recording the relationship and its characteristics. Here is a table showing which of a chain's stores sell which products.

```
STORE
      Field    Type     Length
      -------  -------  --------
      STORE_K  N           8
      (etc.)

PRODCT
      Field    Type     Length
      -------  -------  --------
      PRODCT_K N           8
      (etc.)

PD_STR
      Field    Type     Length
      -------  -------  --------
      PD_STR_K  N          8
      PRODCT_K  N          8
      STORE_K   N          8
      (etc.)
```

The data "(etc.)" about the PD_STR relationship could include, for example, the number of units on hand if you maintain a chain-wide inventory. If each store maintains its own inventory, the "(etc.)" here might be null. It is not uncommon to have relationship tables that simply record the fact that the relationship exists. If the relationship is temporary, or subject to change, it might include dates (and possibly times) like history tables.

There is one exception: the all-to-all relationship. Suppose that each of the chain's stores sold every product. In that case, a table of all the stores and another table of all the products is adequate. The contents of the relationship table are implied by the fact that each store sells every product.

However, the fact that a relationship is all-to-all does not eliminate the need for the M:M table if other data about the relationship is required. For example, if you maintain a chain-wide inventory where you record the number of each product available at each store, you would still need the M:M table.

ORE&D Summarized

In ORE&D, you first list the Objects and Events relevant for your database system. Each Object and Event is a separate table. You start each table with an abstract, primary key, then add fields for all the other characteristics relevant to your system.

Repeating characteristics are separated into Detail files, as are any characteristics about which you need to record change histories. You repeat this step on the characteristics of the Detail files if they are repeating or require histories.

Relationships are handled by listing a characteristic or foreign key in a 1:1 relationship; including a foreign key on the M side of a 1:M or M:1 relationship, or by including a separate table for a M:M relationship.

Normalization

ORE&D is a simple, teachable method. Your analysis concentrates on the needs of the system, not on abstract database concepts. This is in contrast to the traditional normalization process. In the traditional process, you start with a list of everything you need to know.

First Normal Form

Given a master list, you put your data into tables by removing repeating items. Once all your data is in tables, you have achieved first normal form. Note that at this point you have a master parent table that might include your customers' names, your products' names, and your employees' names.

You then begin to assign concrete keys chosen from the data itself, not abstractly constructed.

Second Normal Form

To achieve second normal form, you separate the data in your tables into individual tables until all the characteristics of each table are "fully functionally dependent" on your keys.

Functional dependence means that a key specifies a value. For example, your personnel file might have an employee number and a social security number. Both are called candidate keys. Both candidate keys have only a single name associated with them, so the name is functionally dependent on both candidate keys.

Candidate keys may be built from multiple fields. For instance, the combination of social security number and name is a candidate key. Each SSNUM–NAME combination specifies a single employee number (EMPNUM), so the EMPNUM is functionally dependent on the SSNUM–NAME key.

Fully functionally dependent means that a characteristic (called "attribute" in normalization) depends on each part of a candidate key. The EMPNUM above is not fully functionally dependent on the SSNUM–NAME candidate key. It is fully functionally dependent on just the SSNUM alone.

If your chain were keeping inventory for all stores, the table that contained STORENUM–PRODUCTNUM–QUANTITY would have STORENUM–PRODUCTNUM as a candidate key. In this table, QUANTITY is fully functionally dependent on this key—you need both parts of the key to select a particular quantity.

Second normal form is achieved when you have a first normal form database with all your attributes fully functionally dependent on each candidate key.

Third Normal Form

Functional dependencies may be transitive: A is functionally dependent on B and B is functionally dependent on C; therefore, A is functionally dependent on C. For example, a shipping company has a shipment table that includes a shipment number, SHIPNUM; an ORIGIN and DESTINATION; and a DISTANCE.

ORIGIN and DESTINATION are functionally dependent on SHIPNUM. (Since SHIPNUM is not a compound key, functional dependence is automatically full-functional dependence.) DISTANCE is also functionally dependent on SHIPNUM, but the relationship is transitive, since DISTANCE is functionally dependent on ORIGIN and DESTINATION.

A database is in third normal form when it is in second normal form and has no transitive functional dependencies. So SHIPNUM–ORIGIN–DESTINATION–DISTANCE is second normal form, but not third normal.

The third normal form would have two relations: SHIPNUM–ORIGIN–DESTINATION and ORIGIN–DESTINATION–DISTANCE. Third normal form avoids update anomalies present in second normal form. For example, under second normal form structure, if you deleted the only shipment from Boston to London, you would lose the distance data between these points.

An equivalent ORE&D design is:

```
ROUTE
      Field    Type     Length
      -------  -------  --------
      ROUTE_K   N           8
      ORIGIN    C          32
      DESTNATN  C          32
      DISTANCE  N           4

SHPMNT
      Field    Type     Length
      -------  -------  --------
      SHPMNT_K  N           8
      ROUTE_K   N           8
```

The complexity of the normalization process stems as much from its opaque jargon as from the concepts themselves. Most opponents of normalization argue that starting with a more meaningful grouping of data items results in a better design.

For example, the ORE&D design above replaces multiple instances of origin/destination pairs with a simple route key.

In much literature, third normal form is considered a "good" database design.

Boyce-Codd Normal Form

Update anomalies are still possible in third normal form. Boyce-Codd normal form solves some of the problems still present in third normal form. Boyce-Codd normal form is of particular interest to us, as it is trivial to prove that any ORE&D design is also in Boyce-Codd normal form.

A database is in Boyce-Codd normal form if it is in first normal form and every functional dependency is an attributes' dependence on a key.

Boyce-Codd normal form does not depend on second or third normal form. It is provable that a relation in Boyce-Codd normal form is also in third normal form, but the reverse is not necessarily true—a relation can be in third normal form but *not* in Boyce-Codd normal form.

This formulation skips some details. First, keys are fully functionally dependent on themselves. This trivial dependence is ignored. The same applies to a part of a key that depends on a compound key. Advanced normalization also introduces the concept of "superkeys" which are combinations of keys and other attributes. A superkey has at least those attributes needed to form a key, and may have additional attributes.

So far I have not discussed certain accidental dependencies that may occur, whatever database design method is used. For example, many addresses include a city and a postal code. In many jurisdictions, the postal code uniquely identifies the city, so city is functionally dependent on postal code.

Most database systems simply ignore these implied dependencies. Of course, a large mail-order concern would have a postal code table, from which the city would be looked up based on the postal code. In designing the database, you should consider any possible consequences of the update anomalies that may result if you ignore the dependency. In many cases, the consequences of entering an impossible combination of city and postal code simply means that the address needs correcting, so this dependency is ignored.

In the U.S., all taxpayers are assigned unique tax identification numbers, whose use as identifiers is legally restricted due to privacy concerns. All employee data is fully functionally dependent on this tax identifier, as well as on whatever employee number system we adopt. But because it is legally restricted, the database design ignores its potential use as a key.

So more correctly, a database is in Boyce-Codd normal form if it is in first normal form and every functional dependency you do not choose to ignore is a dependency of an attribute on a key.

ORE&D designs are obviously in first normal form, since the data is all in tables. Since each table has a unique, abstract key, and since we use no other attributes as keys, every meaningful dependency is a dependency of attributes on a key. So an ORE&D database is, by its definition, in Boyce-Codd normal form.

Fourth Normal Form

Boyce-Codd normal form does not eliminate all update anomalies. Certain bad designs can be in Boyce-Codd normal form, but still have serious update problems. One source of these problems is "multivalued dependencies."

Consider the example we looked at earlier, where we recorded the sports of our employee's dependents.

```
DEPENS
    Field    Type     Length
    -------  -------  --------
    DEPENS_K  N         8
    EMPLOY_K  N         8
    (etc.)

SPORTS
    Field    Type     Length
    -------  -------  --------
    SPORTS_K  N         8
    DEPENS_K  N         8
    (etc.)
```

Now assume that we also need to record any diseases our employees have. Then do not use ORE&D; just place the data in a table that includes DEPENS_K–SPORT–DISEASE. Here is an instance of this table:

```
DEPENS_K           SPORT           DISEASE
----------         ------          ---------------
10000001           Jogging         Asthma
10000001           Skiing          Asthma
10000001           Jogging         Near-sightedness
10000001           Skiing          Near-sightedness
(etc.)
```

A multivalued dependency exists since every value in SPORT implies every value in DISEASE. If our dependent takes up another sport, or develops another disease, we need to add multiple entries to keep this table complete. Similary, dropping a sport or recovering from a disease requires deleting multiple records.

A database is in fourth normal form if it is in first normal form and every multivalued dependency is a dependency of attributes on a superkey. (Note that the single-valued dependencies we have discussed thus far are the minimal case of a multivalued dependency. If A implies B, then A multivalued implies B. So fourth normal form is a higher form of Boyce-Codd normal form.)

In an ORE&D design, the multivalued dependencies are not created. For example, when you see dependents having repeating SPORT and DISEASE attributes, you would create separate detail tables.

```
DEPENS
      Field     Type      Length
      -------   -------   --------
      DEPENS_K  N            8
      EMPLOY_K  N            8
      (etc.)


SPORTS
      Field     Type      Length
      -------   -------   --------
      SPORTS_K  N            8
      DEPENS_K  N            8
      (etc.)


DISEAS
      Field     Type      Length
      -------   -------   --------
      DISEAS_K  N            8
      DEPENS_K  N            8
      (etc.)
```

(Note that the six-character table name limitation is *not* a feature of ORE&D design. It is an unfortunate necessity stemming from DOS filename limitations. Using any design method, you should take advantage of longer table names if they are available.)

Given that each repeating group is separated into its own Detail table, it is also true that an ORE&D design is in fourth normal form.

Higher Normal Forms

If you have followed the discussion of normal forms into fourth normal, you have advanced past the point most normalization achieves. However, additional update anomalies are possible in fourth-normal form designs. These require consideration of the effects of joins on tables.

As if the normalization jargon were not already sufficiently opaque, we will now consider lossless joins. Lossless joins are not at all lossless. On the contrary, some joins can create tables with invalid, extra records. A lossless join is one which does not create these invalid, extra records.

Let's begin by joining a part of a sales detail table with a small product table:

```
SALDTL:
    SALDTL_K, INVOIC_K, PRDUCT_K, QUANTITY
    12345678  22222222  10000001     3
    12345679  22222222  10000015     1
    12345680  22222222  10000023     2

PRDUCT:
    PRDUCT_K, NAME,            COLOR, PRICE
    10000001  Widget           Black  1.95
    . . .
    10000015  Small Widget     Red    4.95
    . . .
    10000023  Gold Widget      Gold   99.95
```

Joining these tables on the product key yields a table that includes these columns:

```
Joined:
    SALDTL_K, QUANTITY, NAME,         PRICE
    12345678     3      Widget        1.95
    12345679     1      Small Widget  4.95
    12345680     2      Gold Widget   99.95
```

(The other columns, not shown here, are INVOIC_K, PRODCT_K, and COLOR.) This is an example of a lossless join, since we did not create any invalid records.

A database is in "projection-join" normal form if the dependencies guarantee that all joins will be lossless joins. An ORE&D design is provably in projection-join normal form. I leave it to you to work out the proof.

Additional normal forms include domain-key normal form and fifth normal form.

In relational theory, the **domain** of an attribute is the set of possible values. The domain of a NAME column might be any combination of alphabetic characters up to the specified length. The domain of a SALARY column might be integer numbers between specified minimum and maximum values. Domain-key normal form uses the concept of domains to eliminate some update anomalies associated with fourth normal form designs.

Fifth normal form considers even more advanced dependencies. Some authors have claimed that fifth normal form is the "final" normal form, although this has not been universally agreed upon.

I have not proved that an ORE&D design is in fifth normal form, though I suspect this to be the case. At any rate, I have never seen an example of an ORE&D design that shows any update anomalies.

Perhaps one of you readers with a mathematical inquisitiveness will answer this question: Are ORE&D designs in fifth normal form?

If you are only interested in designing practical, working systems, be assured that an ORE&D design is guaranteed to be in projection-join normal form, which is substantially better than most practitioners of normalization achieve.

Summary

In this chapter, I proposed a semantic, object-oriented design methodology that yields a relational database design. First, I explained my methodology, and then I compared it with the classic normalization steps.

Our first consideration was the database design goals. We want to have each fact stored in one and only one place in the database. We want to be able to delete a single item, without fear that other data will inadvertently disappear. We considered other "update anomalies" that we want to avoid.

I proposed a way of achieving these goals that is free from the jargon of traditional relational database design methodology. My methodology is called "ORE&D" to help you remember the four basic types of things we will put in tables.

The "O" in ORE&D stands for "Objects." By Object, I mean any durable thing, such as a customer, a product, a machine, building, or hospital bed. You create one table for each separate type of Object that you need to track. The fields in that table are the characteristics of the Object that you need to track: customer's names and addresses, product's weights and prices, and so on.

The "E" in ORE&D stands for "Events." An Event is a transaction among our Objects that occurs at a point in time. A sale is a typical Event, transferring some of our products to a particular customer at the time of the sale. Each class of Event also gets a table, and the fields in those tables are also the characteristics of the Event, such as its time, the Objects involved (specified by foreign keys), and so on.

The "D" in "ORE&D" stands for "Details." We looked at two types of Detail data that you break out of Object and Event tables into separate Detail tables. First, some items are inherently repeating. A sale Event transfers one or more product Objects to a Customer. When there are "one or more" (or "zero or more," or some other number) a Detail table is created. This has a foreign key back to the Object or Event about which it is recording details, and the characteristics of the detailed item, such as the number of products sold.

Another Detail table is created whenever you need to track the history of a characteristic. A price history Detail table might be required to record product prices as they change over time. Each history Detail table records the key of the object about which it records history, the time or time span for which its value applies, and the value.

Relationships are the "R" in "ORE&D" designs. While Event tables show relationships that happened at a single point in time, separate Relationship tables are used for longer-duration relation-ships (excepting 1:1 relationships). If each employee works for a single department, you can simply place a foreign key to the correct department as a field in the employee's record. However, if some employees are on assignments to multiple departments, you create a Relationship table.

Each Relationship table includes foreign keys to the Objects that are related, the time span over which the relationship applies, and any other characteristics of the relationship.

The process of building an ORE&D design is the process of identifying Objects and Events and listing their characteristics. Detail tables are separated out for repeating items and for histories. Relationship tables are created if you need to know about the rela-tionships between or among your other tables. As each table is cre-ated, you reapply the process of separating out Detail tables and creating Relationship tables until you have no additional tables to add. The result is a relational database design.

The ORE&D method appears to be far simpler than the tradi-tional normalization method, so you might reasonably wonder if it results in a design of the same quality. To explore this, I compared it to the classic normalization steps.

Most relational analysts are trained in first, second, and third normal form. First normal form means that all data is in tables, which is true of ORE&D. Second normal form specifies that all data in each table is fully functionally dependent on the primary key, which is also true of ORE&D designs. Third normal form elimi-nates transitive dependencies, which are also eliminated in the ORE&D design process.

There are several higher normal forms, including Boyce-Codd and fourth normal form. Each higher normal form eliminates certain update anomalies, which is one of our design goals. We see that it is trivial to prove than an ORE&D design is in Boyce-Codd normal form and quite simple to extend that proof to show that an ORE&D design is also in fourth normal form.

Higher normal forms come into play when we consider such complexities as trinary and higher-degree relationships. I showed that ORE&D designs are in projection-join normal form. Prov-ing that an ORE&D design is in domain-key normal form or fifth-normal form is left up to you. These advanced normal forms are well past those that most relational analysts consider in practical database design work.

This completes our database design work. Now that you can design solid, projection-join normal form databases (without even needing to know any of the normalization jargon) you are ready to start programming. We'll begin with support software, before we get to the client-side software.

Chapter 7

Server-Support Software

The support software provides the "underware" layer. The support software has two components: client support and server support. The client-support software manages end-user data access. If you choose a .DBF-based system this layer provides the RDBMS services.

As discussed in Chapter 2, using .DBF-based software moves the RDBMS logic from the server to the client. This increases network traffic, but it gives the server a much smaller task, so it can handle many more clients. However, there are some processes that should *never* be run from a client.

Why Server Software?

Server-support software is bundled into a server program that is available to the database administrator for use on the server. A typical server-program job is reindexing the database. During normal use, the indexes are updated as the data is updated, but several conditions may require a complete reindexing.

For example, hardware or software failure could leave the indexes corrupted. In many systems, a portion of the data is received on magnetic media, which is appended to the .DBFs, requiring that the files be reindexed. Other issues, such as B-tree balance, indicate that a complete reindexing may build more efficient indexes than the ones that are generated during normal use. For these and other reasons, experienced administrators regularly reindex their .DBF files.

Reindexing from a client could be disastrous for your network. During the reindexing, the CPU must process every record in every .DBF at least once, and it will read and write every index page at least once (and more likely several times). If you have a large system, running this on a client machine would completely tie up the network. If you run this process on the server, of course, the network will be unaffected.

Redundant data has a similar effect. If you choose to have redundant data for efficiency's sake, the correct way to handle it is to have one and only one set of fields designated as "source" data. The source data is considered correct and all redundant copies are updated from the source. As with indexes, routine operations update the copies, but a special program goes through the entire database updating all redundant information.

This is identical to reindexing in requiring server-based software. (The indexes themselves are, of course, one type of redundant data.) The facility for complete updating needs to be provided for the same reasons (failure recoveries, mass updates, and others) and the process that performs the updating needs to run on the server to avoid massive network overloads.

The server software will also have database recovery capability that is used to rescue the database from human, software, and hardware failures. Additionally, minor chores of interest only to the database administrator are built into the server software.

Presumably, the server software is placed on a server drive with restricted access. The server software locks full files, effectively shutting down client access to the database. These are not functions that you would want to make available to every end user.

Implementing Server Software

The server software is a collection of individual service routines. You could provide these services through separate, stand-alone programs, but it's a bit nicer to bundle them together under a single menu. I use a pull-down as my main menu.

The pull-down main menu is non-standard, so I wouldn't recommend it for your user programs. But for software intended only for the database administrator, it is a fine choice. Unlike a horizontal menu, you can put 20 or so choices on a single pull-down, and you can make the prompts 40 characters wide, or even more, if you like. This requires none of the careful thinking required to organize and economically express concepts under a normal bar menu.

If you haven't yet tried the Application Generator available from the Control Center in dBASE, this would be a good opportunity to do so. As you'll see from my code examples, I use a third-party code generator that supports a data dictionary. If you have a third-party generator, this is a good place to put it to use. If you don't have one, the Control Center's application generator will do a fine job of letting you paint a main menu and hook it to the individual service routines that are discussed in the rest of this chapter.

.DBF File Creation

My server software will begin at the beginning: creating the .DBF files. This is not strictly required, since you could easily use the Control Center for this task. Also, dBASE puts a minor hurdle in our path if you want to include this feature. Why bother?

If there will be exactly one instance of your system, this is a waste of effort. Go to the Control Center, create your files, and you are done. But many systems are not like that. For example, multiple programmers may be working on the system during development. For much of their work, individual, sparsely-populated .DBFs will be most helpful. The ability to create a fresh set of empty .DBFs on demand will prove useful.

More importantly, many client-server systems get installed in multiple branches, departments, or divisions of an enterprise. If you anticipate building your system in office A, then providing copies to offices B, C, and so on, the ability to create fresh, empty .DBFs will be crucial.

Creating Files in dBASE

dBASE falls one step short of providing the ability to create a fresh .DBF under program control, but it does provide enough power to let us work around this limitation.

The dBASE "Structure Extended" file is a .DBF that contains data dictionary information. It contains the information about each field (name, type, length, and so on) that the .DBF header contains. You can also add other fields of your own. Given a Structure Extended .DBF you can create a .DBF with the CREATE FROM command.

Unfortunately, you must have a .DBF to create a Structure Extended .DBF. You can create a Structure Extended .DBF from any available .DBF, including .CATs. You can create any .DBF from a Structure Extended .DBF. But there is no entry into that circle if you don't have an initial .DBF. If you want to distribute compiled dBASE systems, you need to be able to create a .DBF from scratch.

Low-Level .DBF Writing

However, dBASE provides low-level file I/O functions, so we can use these to write an empty .DBF. To do this, I first created a Structure Extended file at the dot prompt, using a handy .DBF. Then I ZAPped the Structure Extended file. From DOS I used the SYMDEB utility to dump the file in hex. Then, courtesy of a print screen and some careful typing, I recreated the hex dump in the program you see in Listing 7–01.

Note that some of the bytes in this file are Reserved. Future versions of dBASE may change some of these. If the code in this listing doesn't work for you, repeat my work: build a Structure Extended file at the dot prompt, ZAP it, then examine a hex dump. Hopefully, you can compare your hex dump to mine and just fix up a byte or two. If you don't know what most of these bytes mean, rest assured that I don't, either.

Code Listing 7–01

```
*************************************************************
*** cre_stru - create STRUCTURE EXTENDED file
*************************************************************

PROCEDURE cre_stru
PRIVATE hand, scratch

* NO ERROR CHECKING!

* This would fail on an "out of disk space" condition or
* on another disk error.  The calling application should
* do any required checking adequate for its needs.

IF FILE( 'creastru.dbf' )
  ERASE ( 'creastru.dbf' )
ENDIF

hand = FCREATE( 'creastru.dbf' )

* Note: this data from a ZAPped, dB4, CREATE STRU EXTENDED

DO hex_writ WITH hand, ;
  ' 03 5D 08 10 00 00 00 00-C1 00 13 00 00 00 00 00'
DO hex_writ WITH hand, ;
  ' 00 00 00 00 00 00 00 00-00 00 00 00 00 1B 39 01'
DO hex_writ WITH hand, ;
  ' 46 49 45 4C 44 5F 4E 41-4D 45 00 43 E1 00 98 0F'
DO hex_writ WITH hand, ;
  ' 0A 00 00 00 01 00 00 00-00 00 00 00 00 00 00 00'
DO hex_writ WITH hand, ;
  ' 46 49 45 4C 44 5F 54 59-50 45 00 43 EB 00 98 0F'
DO hex_writ WITH hand, ;
  ' 01 00 00 00 01 00 00 00-00 00 00 00 00 00 00 00'
DO hex_writ WITH hand, ;
  ' 46 49 45 4C 44 5F 4C 45-4E 00 00 4E EC 00 98 0F'
DO hex_writ WITH hand, ;
  ' 03 00 00 00 01 00 00 00-00 00 00 00 00 00 00 00'
DO hex_writ WITH hand, ;
  ' 46 49 45 4C 44 5F 44 45-43 00 00 4E EF 00 98 0F'
DO hex_writ WITH hand, ;
  ' 03 00 00 00 01 00 00 00-00 00 00 00 00 00 00 00'
DO hex_writ WITH hand, ;
  ' 46 49 45 4C 44 5F 49 44-58 00 00 43 F2 00 98 0F'
DO hex_writ WITH hand, ;
  ' 01 00 00 00 01 00 00 00-00 00 00 00 00 00 00 00'
DO hex_writ WITH hand, ;
  ' 0D 1A'
```

```
scratch = FCLOSE( hand )
USE creastru

RETURN && end of cre_stru
```

Cre_stru() uses the current directory to build CREASTRU.DBF, an empty Structure Extended file. It makes an exact, byte-by-byte copy of one that dBASE created for me.

As you see in Listing 7–01, cre_stru() does no checking. It will crash without grace on an out-of-disk-space error, for example. I wrote this under the presumption that the database administrator was using it on a disk with space for the intended application. If there aren't enough bytes available for this little file, the administrator has clearly made a major mistake. User systems need more careful code than this, of course.

The hard work of the routine is done by the supporting hex_writ() routine. Hex_writ() and its supporter, hval(), are shown in Listing 7–02.

Code Listing 7–02

```
******************************************************************
*** hex_writ — hex words written to low-level file
******************************************************************

PROCEDURE hex_writ
PARAMETERS hand, hex_line
PRIVATE hbyte, scratch, t

* format of hex_line is word, word, word, . . .
*    where word is cxx — c is any character, ignored
*                         xx is two hex digits

* "Hex_line" must be correct — no error checking here.

* "Hand" must be a file handle, open for writing,
* positioned as desired, space available on disk.

t = hex_line

DO WHILE LEN(t) >= 3
 hbyte = SUBSTR( t, 2, 2 )
 scratch = FWRITE( hand, CHR( 16*hval( LEFT(hbyte,1) ) + ;
                              hval( RIGHT(hbyte,1) )) )
 t = RIGHT( t, LEN(t)-3 )
```

```
ENDDO

RETURN
*                                            && end of hex_writ


***************************************************************
*** hval — value of hex digit
***************************************************************

FUNCTION hval
PARAMETERS hchar

* returns numeric value of hex digit

DO CASE
 CASE  hchar >= '0' .AND. hchar <= '9'
   RETURN ASC(hchar) - ASC('0')

 CASE hchar >= 'A' .AND. hchar <= 'F'
   RETURN ASC(hchar) - ASC('A') + 10

 CASE hchar >= 'a' .AND. hchar <= 'f'
   RETURN ASC(hchar) - ASC('a') + 10

 OTHERWISE
   RETURN 256 && error value

ENDCASE                         &&  end of hval()
```

You see that the job these two share is to take a hex-like string (see the comments for the exact format) and emit one byte at a time into an already opened file. It's necessary to go just one byte at a time since you may have CHR(0) bytes. dBASE uses the CHR(0) as a string terminator, so you cannot embed it in a string.

As an exception, to support applications such as this one, the FWRITE() built-in function will correctly handle a single CHR(0). So we write the file just one byte at a time. In practice, although this is very inefficient, it still takes only a few milliseconds to write the entire file.

If you examine hval(), you'll see that it has enough sense to return an error code if it is passed a non-hexdigit character. If you examine hex_writ(), you'll see that it happily ignores the possibility of an error. If the string passed to hex_writ() is not in order, hex_writ() considers that to be somebody else's problem.

Hval() is a generally useful routine that you may want to put into service elsewhere. Hex-writ() is a careless quickie—it works here, but I wouldn't let its bad attitude endanger too much other code.

Given these three routines, you now only need to call cre_stru() and the Structure Extended file CREASTRU.DBF will be created (deleted and then created, if it already existed) in your current directory. It is placed in USE, just before the end of cre_stru(), so you are set to go. You use standard dBASE APPEND BLANKs and REPLACEs to fill in the structure of the .DBF. Here is a sample:

```
APPEND BLANK
DO rep WITH 'PEOPLE_K', "N", 8, 0

APPEND BLANK
DO rep WITH 'REV_NO', "N", 4, 0

APPEND BLANK
DO rep WITH 'LAST_NAME', "C", 20, 0

APPEND BLANK
DO rep WITH 'FULL_NAME', "C", 32, 0

APPEND BLANK
DO rep WITH 'ADDR1', "C", 32, 0

APPEND BLANK
DO rep WITH 'ADDR2', "C", 32, 0

APPEND BLANK
DO rep WITH 'ADDR3', "C", 32, 0

APPEND BLANK
DO rep WITH 'PHONE', "C", 10, 0

APPEND BLANK
DO rep WITH 'ORGS_K', "N", 8, 0
```

This sets up a PEOPLE.DBF structure for a general-purpose PEOPLE file. The rep() routine is a typing saver, as you see in Listing 7–03.

Code Listing 7–03

```
****************************************************************
*** rep — replace in stru extended file
****************************************************************

PROCEDURE rep
PARAMETERS nm, tp, ln, dc

DO CASE
 CASE tp = 'C'
   REPLACE field_name WITH nm, field_type WITH 'C', ;
           field_len  WITH ln, field_dec  WITH 0

 CASE tp = 'N'
   REPLACE field_name WITH nm, field_type WITH 'N', ;
           field_len  WITH ln, field_dec  WITH dc

 CASE tp = 'D'
   REPLACE field_name WITH nm, field_type WITH 'D', ;
           field_len  WITH  8, field_dec  WITH 0

 CASE tp = 'L'
   REPLACE field_name WITH nm, field_type WITH 'L', ;
           field_len  WITH  1, field_dec  WITH 0

 CASE tp = 'M'
   REPLACE field_name WITH nm, field_type WITH tp

 OTHERWISE
   CLEAR
   @ 8,20 SAY 'Fatal error'
   @ 10,20 SAY 'Bad field type: '+tp
   DO my_quit

ENDCASE

RETURN
*                                            && end of rep
```

As you see, rep() is quite careful about its business. Rep() does not use the index field in the Structure Extended file, by the way. I handle indexes separately, as you will see below.

If you want to improve this code, move the APPEND BLANK command into the rep() routine. I have no idea why I didn't do that in the first place.

With the "cre_stru" routine as the bottom layer, you will need a top layer controller and one middle-level file creator. The complete file creation sub-system looks like this:

```
PROC file_create_controller

FOR each .DBF in system

    IF .NOT. .DBF already built
        DO build_a_new_one WITH which_one
    ENDIF

ENDFOR

PROC build_a_new_one
PARAMETER which_one

SELECT area_you_choose
DO cre_stru

DO CASE
    CASE which_one = first_one
        * APPEND BLANKs and REPLACEs

    CASE which_one = second_one
        * APPEND BLANKs and REPLACEs

    CASE (etc.)

ENDCASE

CREATE <dbf_name> FROM creastru
ERASE creastru.dbf
USE    && to clear this work area

RETURN && end of build_a_new_one
```

Once this is built, you need only edit the CASEs in the build_a_new_one() code as your database design is perfected. Warning: In a multi-programmer project, you must be certain that all programmers use identical copies of this routine.

MKV File Creation and Updating

As discussed in Chapter 3, I use a file to hold the Maximum Key Value (the highest key number assigned to each .DBF). This is a .DBF that holds one record for each system .DBF. Here is an instance of the MKV .DBF:

```
<sys>_K.DBF:
     DBF_NAME   CURRENT   MKV
     --------   -------   ---
     PEOPLE       .T.     10000456
     ORGS         .T.     10000123
     INVOIC       .T.     10002345
     INVDTL       .T.     10008901
```

This MKV .DBF is handling a simple, four-.DBF system: PEOPLE, ORGS, INVOIC, and INVDTL. The MKV field shows the highest number assigned so far as an abstract, primary key for each file. The CURRENT field is a logical field that may flag certain exceptional error conditions (such as a hardware failure during an update of the MKV file).

Listing 7–04 is code that creates an MKV file, if it does not already exist. Note that it contains certain pseudo-variables, enclosed in angle brackets ("<>") that must be replaced by constants or variables suitable for your needs. (The supporting routines, such as say_win(), are included at the end of this chapter.)

Code Listing 7–04

```
**************************************************************
*** MKV_GEN — Maximum Key Value file generator
**************************************************************

PROCEDURE MKV_GEN
PRIVATE text_var

DO clear_win
DO say_win WITH "Generating maximum key values"
in_scratch = INKEY( 1.1 )
DO say_win WITH ""

SELECT 1
* must have full drive:\path\spec in <mkv_path>
name = <your_name>
```

```
IF FILE("<mkv_path>"+name+'.DBF')

 USE ("<mkv_path>"+name)

 SET INDEX TO ("<mkv_path>"+name)
 REPLACE ALL current WITH .F.

ELSE

 DO cre_stru

 APPEND BLANK
 REPLACE field_name WITH 'dbfname', ;
         field_type WITH 'C', ;
         field_len  WITH 8

 APPEND BLANK
 REPLACE field_name WITH 'current', ;
         field_type WITH 'L'

 APPEND BLANK
 REPLACE field_name WITH 'mkv', ;
         field_type WITH 'N', ;
         field_len  WITH 8, ;
         field_dec  WITH 0

 CREATE ("<mkv_path>"+name) FROM creastru

 USE ("<mkv_path>"+name)
 ERASE creastru.dbf
 INDEX ON dbfname TO ("<mkv_path>"+name)

ENDIF

* (routine continues)
```

Mkv_gen() uses the cre_stru() routine (discussed previously) if the MKV file does not exist. It fills in the CREASTRU.DBF values in the Structure Extended file and uses CREATE FROM to build the MKV file. Finally, it indexes the new file and deletes the CREASTRU file. If the MKV file already existed, it sets all the "current" flags to .F., as it is in the middle of an update.

After building, or USEing the MKV file, this routine continues to construct or maintain the MKV file data, one .DBF at a time. For each database .DBF, it first checks for an existing record in the MKV file, and, if needed, adds the record.

Then it uses the database .DBF, turns indexes off, and goes to the bottom of the file. It examines the key value found there, and either reports that the MKV file is OK, or does the needed update and reports that fact.

There are delays of 1.1 seconds between each report, so the database administrator can watch this process. (I pick 1.1 so I can easily change all the "1.1" to "0.1" for debugging.) Presumably, reports other than "xxx OK" are a cause for concern, except when building a new database.

Listing 7–05 shows the code for a single .DBF. You must repeat this code once for each system .DBF. Note that I have the MKV opened in area 1, and the .DBFs open in SELECT areas 3, 4, and so on. You may adopt this convention or pick another, modifying this code appropriately.

Code Listing 7–05

```
SELECT 1
SEEK "<dbf_name>"

IF .NOT. FOUND()
 DO say_win WITH "Creating record for <dbf_name>"
 APPEND BLANK
 REPLACE dbfname WITH "<dbf_name>"
ENDIF

SELECT 3
 * in USE: <dbf_name>

SET INDEX TO
GO BOTTOM
M->mkv = <dbf_name>_k
SELECT 1
IF M->mkv <> sample_k->mkv
 text_var = "<dbf_name>: replacing "
 text_var = text_var + LTRIM( RTRIM(str( sample_k->mkv )) )
 text_var = text_var + " with "
 text_var = text_var + LTRIM( RTRIM(str( M->mkv )) )
 DO say_win WITH text_var
 REPLACE sample_k->mkv WITH M->mkv
ELSE
 DO say_win WITH "<dbf_name>: OK"
```

```
in_scratch = INKEY( 1.1 )
ENDIF
REPLACE current WITH .T.

* (code continues)
```

Repeating this code for each system .DBF completes the MKV
handling routine. You may want to make an actual subroutine out of
the last group, calling it as needed. This would be an improvement,
but it wouldn't make sense to spend too much time on this rarely
used code.

Index Creation and Updating

dBASE's production indexes make index creation and maintenance
very simple. If you use the INDEX ON TAG command, a production index is created automatically (if needed), and the tag is added
or updated as required.

The only trick is deleting the tag, when it exists, prior to updating to avoid onscreen messages asking if you really want to update
the index. (If you just DELETE TAG, you get messages when the
tag doesn't exist.)

Fortunately, the TAGNO() function is just right for this purpose. It reports the number of a tag in the index order set. This
would be its number in the production index if you had not used
a command such as SET ORDER to modify the value. If the tag
does not exist, TAGNO() returns 0. Fortunately, if the .MDX does
not exist, TAGNO() still returns 0.

So the code you want just marches through the files doing
SELECTs and index updates via:

```
IF TAGNO( '<tag_name>' ) > 0
   DELETE TAG <tag_name>
ENDIF
INDEX ON <expression> TAG <tag_name>
```

Listing 7–06 shows part of a reindexing routine from one of
my systems. Yours will, of course, reflect your file and tag names,
and your SELECT area scheme.

Code Listing 7–06

```
DO say_win WITH "Working on CUSTS"
in_scratch = INKEY( 1.1 )
SELECT 3
custs_sel = 3

SET INDEX TO
PACK
DO say_win WITH '               index CUSTS_K'
in_scratch = INKEY( 1.1 )
IF TAGNO( 'CUSTS_K' ) > 0
  DELETE TAG CUSTS_K
ENDIF
INDEX ON custs_k TAG custs_k

DO say_win WITH '               index CUSTS_S'
in_scratch = INKEY( 1.1 )
IF TAGNO( 'CUSTS_S' ) > 0
  DELETE TAG CUSTS_S
ENDIF
INDEX ON lname TAG custs_s

DO say_win WITH ''

DO say_win WITH "Working on ITEMS"
in_scratch = INKEY( 1.1 )
SELECT 4
items_sel = 4

SET INDEX TO
PACK
DO say_win WITH '             index ITEMS_K'
in_scratch = INKEY( 1.1 )
IF TAGNO( 'ITEMS_K' ) > 0
  DELETE TAG ITEMS_K
ENDIF
INDEX ON items_k TAG items_k

DO say_win WITH '             index ITEMS_S'
in_scratch = INKEY( 1.1 )
IF TAGNO( 'ITEMS_S' ) > 0
  DELETE TAG ITEMS_S
ENDIF
INDEX ON price TAG items_s
```

Do not forget the MKV file when you do this reindexing.

The PACK command here is convenient for some systems, wrong for others. PACKing prior to reindexing makes the indexes slightly faster, recovers wasted space, and is otherwise beneficial.

On the other hand, if you have large files (over 100MB is large as I write this—next year or the year after it won't be more than moderate) you may wish to make the PACKing a separate server menu option. Your maintenance program might dictate reindexing nightly, but PACKing after the full back-up on the weekend, for example.

Bear in mind that the audit trails maintain a complete record of the deletions, so audit concerns are satisfied however you do this.

Some of you recycle deleted records, using the old space in lieu of APPENDing new records, whenever possible. This is generally not an acceptable practice for auditable systems. Leave your deleted records alone until the .DBFs, deleted records included, are properly backed up, then PACK the waste space out of existence.

Other

Your system will have its own server-software requirements. Low-activity systems may simply accumulate data until it's time to buy a larger server. On the other hand, a high-activity system will require regular copying of Event records to secondary storage, with reasonable totals (see Chapter 12) left online.

(Copying to secondary storage is probably the same as copying to your backup medium—anything from floppies to high-speed tapes. Secondary storage is best if you can use removable disks, of course. I call it secondary storage to indicate that this process is done *in addition to* your regular backup procedures.)

Similarly, audit trail data may need regular copying to secondary storage. You may wish to keep only the latest month, or even the latest week of audit trail data online. These are simple maintenance routines that should be accommodated in the server software.

It is highly likely that a very few of your .DBFs will consume the vast majority of your total disk storage, so you will want to treat these files specially.

Three other classes of server functions will be covered at the appropriate places later in this book.

Damage Repair

As you will see, audit trails can also be used for damage repair. They can be used to roll the current data files backwards, eliminating transactions entered by, for instance, a user without adequate training.

The same files can be used to recover damage from hardware or software failures. If a hardware failure damages your .DBFs, for instance, you can reconstruct the .DBF by rolling forward from the most recent backup copy, having the server software automatically re-enter all the transactions.

The rollback and rollforward processes are covered under the appropriate chapters later in this book.

Posting

Also covered later in this book is the posting process. Many currency amounts are captured on a transaction-by-transaction basis, but regularly analyzed only in aggregated form. Sales data is typically collected with every transaction, but is primarily interesting when aggregated by product, location, or otherwise, over some time period (days, weeks, and months or whatever is appropriate).

Automatic posting updates total records as individual transactions are entered. The totals are redundant data, based on the individual transactions. Posting allows users to query the totals directly without going through each transaction, so this is a case where redundancy may be a serious efficiency device.

If posting is done, your server system should have custom software that will recalculate all the posted totals. This is the equivalent of reindexing in its demands on the server and the network.

Other Redundancy

Posting is a large class of redundancy, but there are many other areas where you may wish to have redundant data. For instance, your financial statements files could include redundant customer name and address information to simplify access by your telemarketers.

Again, whenever data is redundant, you must create software that does mass updates, to insure that the redundant data remains synchronized with the source data.

Support Routines

The above routines all keep the database administrator informed of database activity through messages written within these support routines. These routines give the server software the appearance of polished code, without requiring a great deal of thought or trouble to program.

The basic routine is say_win(). This writes a line to a window, teletype style. It wraps the line to fit, if needed, and forces the window to scroll when you reach the bottom. Onscreen, you get the scrolling window display overlaid on the fixed window displays. It's reasonably pleasing considering the minimal effort needed to program it.

As you'll see in Listing 7–07, the wrapping algorithm is as simple as possible: chop off the part that doesn't fit and pickup again at the start of the next line. Some simple capability to look for a word break might be nice, but I seldom pass say_win() an over-length line. This is really just a safety net, not a regular operation.

Code Listing 7–07

```
****************************************************************
*** say_win — write a line in the window
****************************************************************

PROCEDURE say_win
PARAMETERS text_var
PRIVATE line

DO WHILE .T.

 IF LEN(text_var) > window_width
   line = SUBSTR(text_var,1,window_width)
   text_var = RIGHT(text_var,LEN(text_var)-window_width)
 ELSE
   line = text_var
   text_var = ""
 ENDIF

 DO say_win_line WITH line
 IF LEN(text_var) = 0
   EXIT
 ENDIF
```

```
ENDDO

RETURN
*                                              && end of say_win
```

Your code must have set up the window, and related global variables, including "window_width," prior to calling say_win(). Once this setup is done, you just say_win() with the text to be displayed: say_win ("show this").

Say_win() itself relies on say_win_line() to do the serious work of deciding where to put the line in the window, and when to scroll the window. This is shown in Listing 7–08.

Code Listing 7–08

```
*****************************************************************
*** say_win_line — write a single line in window
*****************************************************************

PROCEDURE say_win_line
PARAMETERS s
PRIVATE i

SET COLOR TO &boxcon_clr

IF window_line > window_height && scroll!
 @ 1, 1 CLEAR TO window_height, window_width
 i = 1
 DO WHILE i < window_height
   win_lines[i] = win_lines[i+1]
   @ i, 1 SAY win_lines[i]
   i = i + 1
 ENDDO
 win_lines[ window_height ] = s
 @ window_height, 1 SAY s
ELSE
 win_lines[ window_line ] = s
 @ window_line, 1 SAY s
 window_line = window_line + 1
ENDIF

RETURN
*                                              && end of say_win_line
```

As you see from this code, the actual windowing software was ported from another dialect of Xbase that did not directly support

screen windows. It is written in generic Xbase, and will run under
all the major Xbase dialects. You could certainly save some CPU
cycles by replacing the array of lines used to scroll with a
SCROLL() function, but that would make this code non-portable to
dBASE IV 1.5.

Since dBASE IV 2.0 is a major improvement over 1.5, why
would you want this backward compatibility? Certainly, you won't
be building systems that will run on servers with less than the 2MB
RAM that dBASE IV 2.0 requires, will you? Probably not. But
before you rush to make the switch, ask yourself what happens
when you want to demonstrate this system on a small notebook
computer. You may decide that dBASE IV 1.5 compatibility is a
good idea.

As you see, this code requires additional global variables. The
full requirements are set out below, so I won't repeat them here.

Listing 7–09 shows two support routines that create a new,
cleared window, and clear the existing window, respectively.

Code Listing 7–09

```
*****************************************************************
*** clear_win — pops up a new, cleared window
*****************************************************************

PROCEDURE clear_win

SET COLOR TO &border_clr
@ 0, 0 TO window_height+1, window_width+1 DOUBLE
SET COLOR TO &boxcon_clr
@  1, 1 CLEAR TO window_height, window_width
SET COLOR TO &shadow_clr
@ window_height+2, 2 CLEAR TO window_height+2,window_width+1
@  1, window_width+2 CLEAR TO window_height+2,window_width+2
window_line = 1

RETURN
*                                        && end of clear_win


*****************************************************************
*** erase_win — disappearing act for window
*****************************************************************

PROCEDURE erase_win
```

```
SET COLOR TO &screen_clr
@  0, 0 CLEAR TO window_height+2, window_width+2

RETURN
*                                              && end of erase_win
```

While you could set up multiple windows for multiple processes, my server code just uses one window. It is set up in the mainline by initializing these variables:

```
window_line = 1
window_height = 20
window_width = 40
DECLARE win_lines[ window_height ]

screen_clr = 'N/W'
border_clr = '+GR/BG'
boxcon_clr = '+W/B'
shadow_clr = 'N/N'
```

You can see that the window defaults to appearing in the upper-left corner of the screen. This lets you use just "window_height" and "window_width" to specify the coordinates.

The colors are:

```
screen_clr = background screen
border_clr = window border
boxcon_clr = window contents
shadow_clr = shadow (lower and right sides) of window
```

There is enough wrong with this code to have made me hesitate to let it be seen in public. The fixed location of the window and the use of unnecessary globals are not up to my highest code standards.

But this is a good example of real code from a real, working programmer. As you might guess from looking at it, this code was done quickly to have something that met the need at hand. It was needed as a little piece of a large system. So I threw together something that worked and went on. At the time, I intended to write something better the first time I got the chance.

That was five years ago. This code is still in lots of systems, and it still runs and causes no trouble. I leave it up to you if you want to make improvements. For me, fixin' what ain't broke doesn't bubble up to the top of the priority stack.

Summary

In client-server systems, some operations should be performed on the server. This speeds up the operation itself and eliminates potentially extensive network traffic.

As an example, RDBMSs provide routines to rebuild their indexes. If we are using a .DBF-based system, we must write this routine ourselves. Running this software on a client would cause our entire database to cross the network at least once—and probably several times—which could bring a network to its knees.

To create your server software, start with a simple menu of the server actions. The first action we considered was creating the data tables.

dBASE makes it easy to create .DBFs with its built-in tools. But there are good reasons to build this process into a program. You may need to recreate these data tables several times during development of the system. You may need to repeat this process at many sites if you deploy the system at multiple locations. In any case, I show you ready-to-use software that does .DBF creation and can be built into your system.

The next menu item we considered was the creation and maintenance of the small but critical control file that holds the highest keys used as primary keys in each table. I gave you routines that create and, if needed, rebuild this file.

Following this, we looked at the routines that create and update the indexes. In .DBF-based systems, there is no theoretical need to ever rebuild your index files. There are, however, several practical reasons to do this, even if your hardware and software never malfunction. I showed you some sample routines that handle these chores.

Then we considered other possible server chores that you may want to program, depending on your particular needs. These included routines that post individual transactions into appropriate sub-totals and totals, and routines that maintain deliberate redundant data that is introduced for efficiency. They also included routines that provide data recovery after errors. We'll discuss both these topics in greater detail in Chapter 11 and Chapter 12.

Finally, I showed you several supporting subroutines that simplify your job in programming this server-support software.

With this background, we are ready to go on to record reading and locking. If you remember, at the end of Chapter 2 I told all of you database-design experts to pay close attention because the information in the next three chapters was original. Well, here the exact opposite is true. If you've been correctly handling record reading and locking with memory variables or arrays and a semaphore-based locking system, skim the next chapter quickly. You already know this information.

On the other hand, lots of you have come from building single-user systems that didn't need locking, or building "glass house" systems where the operating system or DBMS software did it all for you. For you, Chapter 8 shows a simple, foolproof way of handling record locking.

Chapter 8

Record Reading and Locking

Most dBASE programmers have adopted some system for reading user data into memvars or arrays. Some, especially self-taught dBASE programmers, GET into the fields themselves, which is dangerous. The first section in this chapter will explain the tradeoff between reading into memvars and reading into arrays. Then we'll get into record locking.

If you are using a software server back-end, you will never meet record locking. The server does it for you. If you are arriving from a mainframe or mini-computer environment, the system may have always taken care of this detail for you.

If you are using a .DBF-based system, you have to handle record locking yourself. Lots of things can go wrong if you don't handle record locking properly. Fortunately, the whole locking concern is a solved problem. There is a practical, simple method for doing it right that will produce 100% error-free results.

Record Reading

In personal systems, you can just @ GET a field directly. If you enter bad data, you can always use the Control Center or dot prompt to fix the problem. This is a habit you cannot carry over into client-server programming, and certainly not into mission-critical, auditable systems.

You should do all your GETs into temporary locations. You cannot tell until the user is finished what he or she will decide to do with the data. One case is that the user will want the data placed in the database, of course.

But there are lots of other possibilities. Another case is that the user needs some clarification and calls someone. That person is out, so the user leaves a message. Then the user presses Esc to exit from the data-entry screen and files the source document, waiting for that return phone call.

Another possibility is that the user will make a mistake. Then, another mistake will happen while trying to fix the first mistake. From there on it runs downhill until, again, the user presses ^Q or Esc to exit.

In general, your user doesn't make a final decision to commit the data to the database until he or she completes the data-entry screen or presses an action key such as ^W. You cannot place the data into the database until you get a positive signal that all is well.

This means that the data must be held in memory while the user is entering it. There are two good choices to handle this: memvars and arrays.

Memvar-Based READs

One tradition for editing data is to read it from the database into memvars. Then all editing is done on the memvars. If the user signals successful completion, the memvar data is used to REPLACE the fields in the database. A common naming convention was to use an "M" in front of the field name for the memvar name. So the "name" field was read into the "Mname" memvar, the "address" field was read into "Maddress," and so on.

With that convention, typical code looked like this:

```
* to read the record:
SKIP && or whatever gets to the record
Mname = dbf->name
Maddr1 = dbf->addr1
Maddr2 = dbf->addr2
Mcity = dbf->city
* etc.

* to edit the record:
@ r1, c1 GET Mname
@ r2, c2 GET Maddr1
@ r3, c3 GET Maddr2
@ r4, c4 GET Mcity
* etc.
READ

* update the fields if OK'd by user
IF LASTKEY () <> 27 .AND. ;
   LASTKEY() <> 17          && Not Esc nor ^Q

   REPLACE dbf->name  WITH Mname
   REPLACE dbf->addr1 WITH Maddr1
   REPLACE dbf->addr2 WITH Maddr2
   REPLACE dbf->city  WITH Mcity
ENDIF
```

(This code ignores key ingredients, such as data validation, to illustrate the main point.)

Many people still use this system, either exclusively or occasionally. I am in the latter camp. The alternative is to use arrays.

Array-Based READs

Arrays are a structure of memory data, but the name "memvar" is commonly used to indicate a single variable, reserving the term "array" for groups of memory variables. I use that convention here.

The memvar-based READ has a major problem. The field names may not be unique across the whole system. How many Objects, for example, have a "name" characteristic. Certainly customers have names, products have names, suppliers have names, employees have names, and patients have names. No matter what your enterprise does, you are likely to have several different tables with a "name" field.

If you use the "M" in front of the field name convention (or any other consistent convention, for that matter) you will have "Mname" applying to your sales contacts, your parts suppliers, your hotel guests, or whatever. If your system uses point-and-shoot look-ups, with one scroller calling another as suggested here, there is no telling which "Mname" is active at any given point. A rigorous system of PRIVATE variables might still make "Mname" unique at any moment, but it is an invitation to trouble.

A simple solution is to create an array with one element for each field in the table. Let's build "people_a[]" and duplicate the example code above.

```
* somewhere near the start of the system,
* assuming PEOPLE.DBF has 20 fields:
  DECLARE people_a[20]

* to read the record:
SKIP && or whatever gets to the record
people_a[1] = dbf->name
people_a[2] = dbf->addr1
people_a[3] = dbf->addr2
people_a[4] = dbf->city
* etc.

* to edit the record:
@ r1, c1 GET people_a[1]
@ r2, c2 GET people_a[2]
@ r3, c3 GET people_a[3]
@ r4, c4 GET people_a[4]
*etc.
READ

* update the fields if OK'd by user
IF LASTKEY() <> 27 .AND. ;
   LASTKEY() <> 17          && Not Esc nor ^Q

   REPLACE dbf->name  WITH people_a[1]
   REPLACE dbf->addr1 WITH people_a[2]
   REPLACE dbf->addr2 WITH people_a[3]
   REPLACE dbf->city  WITH people_a[4]

ENDIF
```

This could give us a doctor's name in md_a[3], a patient's name in ptient_a[5], and a supplier's name in supplr_a[4]. They will never get confused, no matter how many scrollers pop up other scrollers in the data-entry process.

Why not always use the array solution? Well, sometimes the cure is worse than the disease. The trouble with the array-based solution is that you can never be sure that you are dealing with the right array element unless you keep your documentation close at hand.

If I saw a variable called "addr2" in your code, I would guess that it was the second line of an address. If I saw "Maddr2" I would know that it was the memvar copy of a field called "addr2." But what should I assume about "people_a[3]"? Clearly, it's the memvar equivalent of the third field in the "people" table. But what in the world is it?

Worse, suppose we refine our design and decide to add another field. Suppose we decide to add the field near the front of our table. If you do that, you cause havoc. You give the new field the next sequential number (so your record goes something like people_a[1], people_a[2], people_a[21], people_a[3], and so on) and your code looks silly, at best. Or you remember the fields' array equivalents, which requires a very careful edit of a lot of .PRGs. (I predict a lot of bugs eventually if you don't renumber, and a lot of bugs immediately if you do renumber.)

My recommendation is to dig into your pockets or purse for a coin and flip it. Neither memvars nor arrays are a totally satisfactory solution. Luckily, record locking presents no such problems.

Locking Errors

I am tempted to just tell you how to do locking right and skip the next section. But I'm not very good myself about just following orders when I don't understand the reasons, and a lot of you are probably the same. So we'll start by considering some of the things that can go wrong if you don't do record locking correctly.

Files or portions of files can be "locked" by programs under DOS and almost every other operating system. The locked file, or file area, cannot be written by any other program until the lock is released. In .DBF work, dBASE locks a single record, or, if requested, an entire file.

No Locking

What are the consequences of not using locking? The most damaging errors will occur when users A and B both attempt to update the same data at roughly the same time. User A makes one set of changes and user B makes other changes. Both write to the file. Whichever user writes *last* makes the changes that stick. Neither user knows that there was a problem.

File Locking

I didn't name this chapter "File and Record Locking" because file locking is almost always a mistake. The user data-entry systems work on one record at a time—either adding, deleting, or changing one. So it only needs to lock the record it is updating.

File locking effectively turns a multi-user system into a single-user system, blocking out all but the user who asserts the lock. I allow file locking only in the supervisory software that runs on the server. Operations such as loading bulk data from tape, complete reindexing, or other mass-update operations may require that the system temporarily lock out all other users.

In dBASE, commands that update multiple records automatically lock the entire file. For example, the PACK command locks the entire file. This is a good example of a command that should only be part of the supervisory software run on the server.

In general, file locking should never be part of a multi-user system. Use it only when you want to turn your system into a single-user one.

Long-Term Record Locking

Your system should lock individual records, and then only when it is ready to write the data to the file. A common error is to lock a record when the user selects the record for editing, and unlock the record when the user completes the edit.

This invariably leads to a user locking a record at the beginning of an edit, then discovering that some additional data is needed. After a couple of phone calls, the user decides that the person with the data won't be back for half an hour, so this makes a good time to break for lunch.

In the meantime, anyone else who needs to update the locked record can't get access to it.

The correct technique is to let the user read the data, not locking the record. The user edits the data, goes to lunch or whatever, and no one else is slowed down. Eventually, if the user completes the edit and tells the system to write the record, the system then locks the record, writes the new data, and unlocks the record— holding the lock for only the miniscule fraction of a second needed for this process. Semaphores, discussed in the next section, handle the problem of another user also updating the record.

Done correctly, there should never be any user input allowed between asserting the lock and unlocking the record.

Uncoordinated Edits

Just as in a system without locking, users A and B can both edit the same record. If they attempt to write the updated data roughly simultaneously, the first one to complete the edit locks the record for writing, writes the new data, and unlocks the record.

In the meantime, the second one waits a few milliseconds while the first one's edits are written. Note that the delay is imperceptible to the human user. When the first lock is released, the second one's edit locks the record, writes new data, and then unlocks the record. The effect is to destroy the first one's work, entirely.

What is needed is a coordinating system that will catch those occasions when two or more users edit the same record at the same time.

Deadly Embrace

Another problem can occur if two or more records must be locked to complete a transaction. User A's entry gets a lock on record i and then attempts to lock record j. Meanwhile, user B's work has locked record j and is attempting to lock record i.

Both users' software assumes that a record lock only lasts a few milliseconds, so each calmly repeats the lock request, waiting for the needed record to be unlocked by the other user. This is total gridlock. The transactions have halted each other.

Fortunately, none of these problems need trouble us if we use a simple semaphore-based locking scheme.

Locking with Semaphores

Developed before radio, semaphore flags were waved at sea so that ships could communicate with each other, well beyond shouting distance. Railroads use mechanical signals that are also called semaphores to signal to oncoming trains. Software has borrowed the term semaphore to refer to any small piece of data that one process uses to communicate with another. In the case of record locks, we use a revision-number semaphore.

Always Lock Records

Before we get to semaphores, let's consider some of the problems mentioned above. First, we'll use locking, but we will not use file locking under normal circumstances. We'll only lock records.

Lock for Minimum Time

Our software will only lock a record after the user has signalled "write this data." We'll use a simple sequence:

```
* at user's "write it" command
lock the record
write the record
unlock the record
```

That way, we'll not need to worry about a user going to lunch in the middle of an edit. No lock should last more than a few milliseconds.

Use a Revision-Number Semaphore

To coordinate edits, we'll use a revision-number semaphore. In each record, include a numeric field to hold the record's revision number. This is set to one when the record is first written. Each process that rewrites the record increments the revision number field.

In dBASE, if you CONVERT your .DBFs, a semaphore field called "_dbaselock" is added to your structure. Its default width is 16 bytes. I use my own semaphore field, 4 bytes wide. If you use the CONVERT and _dbaselock method, you will save a small amount of trouble by using the dBASE's built-in CHANGE() function. More importantly, you can use the built-in LKSYS() function to find the name of the user who has locked the record, when there is a record lock. I prefer to use my own semaphores since I don't need this capability and I gain the advantage of code that is portable to other Xbase dialects.

When a record is read, its revision counter is stored. Prior to a record write, the revision counter is re-read after the lock is asserted. If it does not match the stored value, the new record is not written. This is the algorithm:

```
start
   read the record
   store the revision number semaphore

   * user edits the data, then,
   * at user's "write it" command

   lock the effected record

   reread the revision number
   if same # as the one we stored
     write record
     unlock record
   else
     unlock record
     display error message for user
     go back to start
   endif
```

Now when users A and B attempt to write the same record at roughly the same time, the first one done still gets the data rewritten. The second one sees an error message and is then shown the new data. At that point, the second user needs to decide what to do.

Eliminate Deadly Embrace

Finally, there is the matter of deadly embrace. This has always been a pernicious problem, but it has never been a necessary problem. In cases where two or more records must be locked to complete a transaction, on any locking failure your system should unlock all the records it has and start over. It should never keep a lock. This is the correct algorithm:

```
start
for each record that you need to update

    attempt to lock the record
    if lock fails
        unlock any locked record(s)
        go back to start
    endif

endfor

update each record
unlock each record
```

Naming Convention

I always use a four-digit, no-decimal, numeric field for the sema-phore. I always use the name REV_NO, which reminds me that this stores revision numbers. I always make this field the second field in each table, immediately following the primary key.

You can adopt these conventions, or invent others of your own. You will find that consistently following a convention simplifies your programming.

Summary

We looked at record reading and record locking in this chapter. Record reading presents three choices: read into the fields, read into memvars, or read into array elements. Reading directly into fields is not really satisfactory, except for simple personal systems.

Reading into memvars is the classic solution, though some programmers prefer to read into arrays. Given any naming convention, reading into memvars may lead to non-unique names, which an array-based solution avoids. On the other hand, the array-based solution leads to less-readable code, and has serious problems if you need to add fields to your databases. You must pick whichever system promises the least amount of trouble.

Record locking, fortunately, has a simple prescription. Before getting to the prescription, I showed you some of the problems that incorrect locking poses.

Without locking, two users can update a single record, each oblivious to the work of the other. With file locking, you avoid this problem, but a single user can halt the work of many others. Long-term locking (say, while entering a screen of data) inevitably leads to a user leaving a screen in process and going to lunch, locking many others out of the system.

Uncoordinated edits lead one user to replace the work of another as easily as non-locking would permit. In the worst case, a "deadly embrace" lets two users effectively lock each other out of the system, hanging both offending processes, and possibly many others.

The solution is a semaphore-based record locking system. With this system, records are locked after the user presses ^W, or otherwise signals that it is time to write the data to the database, and are kept locked only during the actual record-writing process. This is a matter of a few milliseconds, at most.

With a semaphore system, the software ensures that the record has not been updated since the user read the data into memory. If the record has been updated by another user in the interim, you tell the user that there is new data, and give him or her another chance at the editing.

Deadly embrace is eliminated by simply releasing all locks as soon as a lock request fails. The algorithm presented completely eliminates this problem.

By using the recommended locking method, with either memvar or array-based record reading, your systems will never experience a record locking management problem.

Record locking is very simple, once you see how it should be done. Now that you can do this correctly, we'll move on to a subject that is much less simple. We'll be writing our own dBASE-like routines that will let us use indexes as filters, for high-performance file access.

Chapter 9

Indexes and Filters

Our data tables will be indexed on at least two or three fields or expressions. We'll also frequently be filtering out most records. The most efficient filter is one that uses the index. In this chapter I'll show you the .DBF access routines that make this filtering as efficient as possible. This is key to minimizing disk accesses and network traffic.

If performance isn't one of your highest priorities, you can skip this whole chapter. In fact, I would recommend that, in many cases, the smart thing to do is to forget this whole subject until your system is running and performance becomes an issue. You'll find the techniques suggested here are very easy to retrofit to a running client-server system.

On the other hand, many of you will want your system to start out with top performance. If that's you, this chapter shows you a cover for dBASE's lowest-level routines that will make high-performance your trademark.

Indexes

We need at least two indexes for every table, before the additional requirements of your application are considered. We will have one index on the primary key and another on whatever will keep your data in the best order for your users. Foreign keys will also be indexed.

Primary Key

The index on the primary key allows you to SEEK the associated record whenever your key is used as a foreign key. For example, the invoice application will SEEK for the associated customer record to get the name and address. The invoice detail records will hold keys into the product table. A SEEK on the product's key will be done to get the product names, part numbers, and prices.

Scroll Order

We will also be showing the user the table's data in a scroller. This requires an index that puts the data in an order that makes sense to a user. Customers and products can be indexed alphabetically by name, for instance. Invoices might be stored by customer, and in reverse date order for each customer.

Foreign Keys

Each foreign key also requires an index. You must be able to quickly find, for example, all the invoices for a particular customer, or all the invoice detail lines for a particular part. With an index you can SEEK for the first one, and then SKIP forward, processing the records until the foreign key changes.

Filters

dBASE has become very smart about using indexed data for efficient file access. Still, there is no way that general-purpose access routines can compete with software that you supply, tailored exactly to your application.

SET FILTER

The SET FILTER command allows you to create a logical database that only includes records that are relevant to the task you have in mind. Here are some examples:

```
SET FILTER TO customer->region = "North"

SET FILTER TO product->color = "red"

SET FILTER TO invoice->cust_k = cust->cust_k
```

The last example is the one we will focus on. It is an example of matching a foreign key in one table to a primary key in another table.

The problem with a SET FILTER command is that dBASE may not be able to take advantage of the fact that the data is already indexed on the filter. Even though it tries, several situations defeat its best intentions.

If your software is not processing data a set at a time, you cannot depend on dBASE to handle the indexed accesses properly for you. For example, you may be processing all the invoices for the month, using the same customer key to look up and print a single customer's name and address repeatedly.

If you have multiple filter conditions, you may also defeat dBASE's efforts to use indexes. For example, you may want to know how many invoices included orders for red products sold to customers in the North region. You can do this with a complex SET FILTER expression, or you can do it by taking advantage of your indexes.

Index-Based Filters

Since you have indexes on primary and foreign keys, finding all the invoices for one customer is simple. This is the technique in pcode:

```
SELECT cust
* user picks a particular customer
SELECT invoices
SET ORDER TO cust_k index in invoices
SEEK cust->cust_k

DO WHILE invoices->cust_k = cust->cust_k
   * do whatever with the invoice
   SKIP
ENDDO
```

What we are doing is using the index on customer keys to SEEK the first invoice for a particular customer. Then we SKIP through the invoices, processing until the customer key in the invoice table changes.

I've found this very simple to implement using cover routines that simulate dBASE commands and functions. I let these routines hide the details of index-based filtering. For example, my higher-level code uses them so that it can function as if the invoice file only contains invoices for a single customer.

In the following routines, the variable "sele_area" holds the numeric value of the work area currently SELECTed. The first .DBF is opened in area 5. (I use the first four for non-data items, such as help screens and password/permission data.) So "sele_area − 4" returns the character position of the filter status in the filter string.

I keep four data structures. Two strings record the EOF() and BOF() status of each table. Each string has one "T" or "F" for each .DBF. "T" indicates that the condition is true, and "F" indicates that the condition is false.

Two arrays, filt_str[], and filt_val[], contain the name of the key and its value, respectively. For example, assume that the invoice table is the third .DBF. Setting the invoice table to just the value of the current customer key would be done as follows:

```
filt_str[3] = 'cust->cust_k'
filt_val[3] = cust->cust_k
* we SEEK and find the first invoice
```

```
my_bof = STUFF( my_bof, 3, 1, "F" )
my_eof = STUFF( my_eof, 3, 1, "F"
```

As you'll see in the code, there are enough details to handle, so functions are used to hide each of the data structures.

Let's look at these routines, beginning with the simplest. Listing 9–01 shows the is_bof() and is_eof() routines, which I call in lieu of the BOF() and EOF() built-in functions.

Code Listing 9–01

```
****************************************************************
*** is_bof — are we at the beginning of the file
****************************************************************

FUNCTION is_bof

RETURN SUBSTR(my_bof,sele_area-4,1) = "T"    && end of is_bof


****************************************************************
*** is_eof — are we past the end of the file
****************************************************************

FUNCTION is_eof

RETURN SUBSTR(my_eof,sele_area-4,1) = "T"    && end of is_eof
```

As you can see, these just check that the appropriate character in the string is "T."

These values are set True by set_bof() and set_eof(). They are set False by reset_bof() and reset_eof() functions. Burying the data in these functions means that I can change the data structure just by changing these six functions, of course.

Listing 9–02 shows these set and reset functions.

Code Listing 9–02

```
****************************************************************
*** reset_bof — turn bof flag off
****************************************************************

PROCEDURE reset_bof

my_bof = STUFF(my_bof,sele_area-4,1,"F")

RETURN                                    && end of reset_bof
```

```
**************************************************************
*** reset_eof — turn eof flag off
**************************************************************

PROCEDURE reset_eof

my_eof = STUFF(my_eof,sele_area-4,1,"F")

RETURN                                      && end of reset_eof


**************************************************************
*** set_bof — turn bof flag on
**************************************************************

PROCEDURE set_bof

my_bof = STUFF(my_bof,sele_area-4,1,"T")

RETURN                                      && end of set_bof


**************************************************************
*** set_eof — turn eof flag on
**************************************************************

PROCEDURE set_eof

my_eof = STUFF(my_eof,sele_area-4,1,"T")

RETURN                                      && end of set_eof
```

The filtered() function, shown here in Listing 9–03, checks for a non-blank string in the appropriate filt_str[] array element.

Code Listing 9–03

```
**************************************************************
*** filtered — is a filter set?
**************************************************************

FUNCTION filtered

RETURN .NOT. str_mt( filt_str[sele_area-4] )
                                      && end of filtered
```

Listing 9–04 shows the supporting str_mt() routine. (Pronounce it "string empty" to make sense of the name.)

Code Listing 9–04

```
***************************************************************
*** str_mt — are there non-white chars in string
***************************************************************

FUNCTION str_mt
PARAMETERS str

RETURN LEN( LTRIM(str) ) = 0                    && end of str_mt
```

Str_mt() is also called by set_filter(), which is shown in Listing 9–05. As you see, this is a non-trivial function.

Code Listing 9–05

```
***************************************************************
*** set_filter — sets index-based filter
***************************************************************

PROCEDURE set_filter
PARAMETERS fname, value

filt_str[sele_area-4] = fname
IF PCOUNT() > 1
  filt_val[sele_area-4] = value
ENDIF

IF str_mt(fname)                && removing previous filter

  IF .NOT. BOF()
    DO reset_bof
  ENDIF

  IF .NOT. EOF()
    DO reset_eof
  ENDIF

ELSE                                      && adding new filter

  SEEK value
  DO reset_bof
```

```
IF .NOT. FOUND()
  GO BOTTOM
  SKIP
  DO set_eof
 ELSE
  DO reset_eof
ENDIF

ENDIF

RETURN                                  && end of set_filter
```

With the ability to set a filter, we can now create routines that go to the logical bottom and logical top of the file. Listing 9–06 shows these routines.

Code Listing 9–06

```
**************************************************************
*** go_bottom — to end of file
**************************************************************

PROCEDURE go_bottom

DO reset_bof

IF .NOT. filtered()

 GO BOTTOM
 IF EOF()
   DO set_eof
  ELSE
   DO reset_eof
 ENDIF

ELSE

 SEEK plus(filt_val[sele_area-4],1)
 SKIP -1

 IF in_filter()
   DO reset_eof
  ELSE
   DO set_eof
 ENDIF

ENDIF
```

```
RETURN                                         && end of go_bottom


****************************************************************
*** go_top - go to (logical) beginning of file
****************************************************************

PROCEDURE go_top

IF .NOT. filtered()

 GO TOP
 IF BOF()
   DO set_bof
 ENDIF
 IF .NOT. EOF()
   DO reset_eof
 ENDIF

ELSE

 SEEK ( filt_val[sele_area-4] )
 DO reset_bof

 IF FOUND()
   DO reset_eof
 ELSE
   DO set_eof
 ENDIF

ENDIF

RETURN                                         && end of go_top
```

The logical top of the file is the first record that matches the filter value, so a simple SEEK works. The only complication is that we have to keep the bof and eof flags set correctly.

The plus() function called in go_bottom() is not needed if you are only going to use the numeric keys suggested here. I used character string primary keys at one time. Plus() will add two numbers or it will add a number to a character string. (You do this by replacing the last character with CHR(ASC(last_char)+1).

However you do it, the goal is to SEEK with NEAR ON, the first value after the key you want. Then SKIP −1 will back you up to the last entry (the one you want). The other code reflects the fact that the file may be logically empty (there are no invoices for a customer, for example).

In Listing 9–07, you see the routine that checks whether you are currently in the filter range.

Code Listing 9–07

```
****************************************************************
*** in_filter — is the current record within filter scope?
****************************************************************

FUNCTION in_filter
PRIVATE val, macro

IF EOF() .OR. BOF()
 RETURN .F.
ENDIF

IF filtered()
 macro = filt_str[sele_area-4]
 val = &macro
 RETURN val=filt_val[sele_area-4]
ENDIF

RETURN .T.                              && end of in_filter
```

This is used by the SKIP replacement, my_skip(). Like the dBASE SKIP command, my_skip() has to check that the record it skips to is within the filter condition, then correctly set the BOF and EOF flags. Listing 9–08 shows this routine.

Code Listing 9–08

```
****************************************************************
*** my_skip — skips, respecting index-based filters
****************************************************************

PROCEDURE my_skip
PARAMETERS n

IF pcount() < 1
 n = 1
ENDIF

IF n > 0 .AND. is_eof()
 RETURN
ENDIF
```

```
IF n < 0 .AND. is_bof()
 RETURN
ENDIF

DO reset_bof
DO reset_eof

DO CASE
 CASE n = 1
   SKIP
   IF .NOT. in_filter()
     DO set_eof
   ENDIF

 CASE n = -1
   SKIP -1
   IF BOF()
     DO set_bof
    ELSE
     IF .NOT. in_filter()
       DO set_bof
       SKIP
     ENDIF
   ENDIF

 CASE n = 0

 CASE n > 1
   j = 0
   DO WHILE j < n
     SKIP
     IF .NOT. in_filter()
       DO set_eof
       EXIT
     ENDIF
     j = j + 1
   ENDDO

 CASE n < -1
   j = 0
   DO WHILE j > n
     SKIP -1
     IF BOF()
       DO set_bof
       EXIT
      ELSE
       IF .NOT. in_filter()
         SKIP
         DO set_bof
```

```
      EXIT
    ENDIF
    j = j - j - 1
  ENDIF
 ENDDO

ENDCASE

RETURN                                    && end of my_skip
```

The next pair of routines are ones that I wish had matching dBASE built-in functions. Is_bot() and is_top() return .T. when you are at the first or last record, respectively. After a GO TOP, is_top() returns True. You don't need to attempt a SKIP backward. Similarly, is_bot() returns True when you are at the last record, not when you have SKIPped past the end to the ghost EOF record.

Listing 9–09 shows these handy routines.

Code Listing 9–09

```
****************************************************************
*** is_bot — are we at the bottom of the file
****************************************************************

FUNCTION is_bot
PRIVATE at_bot

DO my_skip WITH 1
at_bot = is_eof()
DO my_skip WITH -1

RETURN at_bot                             && end of is_bot



****************************************************************
*** is_top — are we at the top of the file?
****************************************************************

FUNCTION is_top
PRIVATE at_top

IF is_bof()
 RETURN .T.
ENDIF
```

```
DO my_skip WITH -1
at_top = is_bof()
IF .NOT. at_top
 DO my_skip WITH 1
ENDIF

RETURN at_top                                && end of is_top
```

As you see, these two routines do their job by calling the other routines in this set. They are no more complex than equivalent routines calling dBASE built-ins.

The last function is not really part of the set, but it is very handy when, for example, you want to find a customer name and address if you are in the invoice table. As you see in Listing 9–10, seek_ctl() is nice for doing a SEEK in a secondary table without upsetting your current settings.

Code Listing 9–10

```
*****************************************************************
*** seek_ctl — general purpose SEEK routine
*****************************************************************

PROCEDURE seek_ctl
PARAMETERS area, key_value

SELECT (area)

SET ORDER TO 1
SEEK key_value

IF .NOT. FOUND()
 DO seek_err
ENDIF

SELECT (sele_area)

RETURN                                       && end of seek_ctl
```

Note that this routine assumes that the index on the primary key is always the first index. You can make an appropriate adjustment if this is not your convention. It *is* important, however, that you adopt and follow a consistent convention.

Summary

In this chapter we looked at the need for indexes and discussed using index-based filters. The techniques discussed here minimize disk accesses and network traffic. That means you get the ultimate in performance.

You need indexes for the primary key, for the natural order (the way your data will be presented to your users), and for each foreign key. The primary key index lets foreign keys quickly locate the referenced entry in the related table. The natural order index is used by your scrollers to let your users examine the data. The foreign key indexes let you quickly locate all the records that are "children" of a parent record.

You will use additional indexes, as always, to support whatever special requirements your application imposes, such as the need for fast queries and reports.

The SET FILTER command can be used to select children of a parent record, but under many conditions it is slow. A better method is to use indexes directly.

If you SEEK the first child record, using the table's appropriate foreign key index, you can then just SKIP through the records until the foreign key changes. This is a very efficient way to process all the children of a parent record.

The way I suggest to achieve this is to program routines that let you call functions that emulate the basic dBASE file access routines. Code that does this is provided here. For example, the "is_bof()" function is equivalent to dBASE's built-in BOF() function.

I build these dBASE-equivalent functions on data structures that mimic dBASE's internal structures. As with the dBASE built-in commands and functions, these data structures are used only by the dBASE-equivalent functions.

For example, the my_skip() routine provides the same service as the dBASE SKIP command. It examines a flag that is set if the record pointer is already at a logical eof condition. On the actual SKIP, it uses the data structures to see if there is an index-based filter set, and, if so, it checks to see if the filter condition is met. The my_skip() code sets a flag in the appropriate structure if it SKIPs past the logical end of file. This does a lot of work in the client CPU, eliminating a lot of disk accesses and network traffic.

The routines shown here let your higher-level code issue dBASE-equivalent commands, while using index-based filters. The result is very fast access to precisely the data you want.

With these high-performance routines in place, we can go on to consider topics that may be new to many of you: auditors and audit trails. Don't skip this next chapter, even if you don't have an immediate need for auditable systems. When we get on to rollback and rollforward recovery you'll see that we use audit trails for more than just audits.

Chapter 10

Auditors and Audit Trails

Most dBASE systems do not maintain audit trails, which is unfortunate. Audit trails are vital for auditable, mission-critical systems. As you will see, they are also incredibly handy even in simple departmental systems.

An audit trail records every change to the database. Each record that is added is also added to the audit trail. Every deletion and edit is also recorded in the audit trail. Along with the actual data change, the audit trail records the time and date of the change and the name of the user making the change.

One reason for having an audit trail is to let an auditor answer such questions as: "Who gave the programmer a $100,000 raise?" By tracing the data in the audit trail, the auditor will discover that it was the programmer himself at midnight after the Christmas party. As any auditor will point out, just having the ability to track these changes is an excellent deterrent.

As we will discuss in Chapter 11, audit trails provide all the data needed to do rollback/rollforward recovery. If every add, delete, and edit to the database is recorded in an audit trail, it is obviously possible to use this data to either back changes out of the database (rollback) or to recover a more recent database version given a backup and the audit trail data (rollforward). We'll see that this is not just theoretically possible; it's extraordinarily simple to code if your audit trails anticipate this use.

The best news about audit trails is that they are simple to implement and impose very little overhead on the system. At first glance, it appears that the audit trail means that your system must write every record twice, adding 100% overhead. It's true that you write every record twice, but the overhead is actually less than 10%.

I like to begin by explaining how low the overhead actually is, so you'll be eager to get to the implementation details to build audit trails into your own systems. Unfortunately, if you do not know how they are built, you cannot calculate the overhead they impose. So I ask you to accept my statement that the overhead is under 10% for the moment. We'll get into this in enough detail that you can estimate your own figure for your own systems before the end of this chapter.

First, let's discuss your relationship with the auditor.

Working with the Auditor

Different enterprises have different auditors. Government agencies are audited by government auditors. Public companies are audited by independent accounting firms. Enterprises such as banks, public utilities, and insurance companies are often audited by an accounting firm and several government agencies. Additionally, most large enterprises have an independent internal audit staff.

If your system is mission-critical chances are good that you will meet your enterprise's auditors. This meeting can be a mutually rewarding experience, or a cause for panic. I have reviewed my audit trail design with four of the "Big Six" accounting firms, and it has passed muster. But just implementing this design is not a sure prescription for an auditable system.

Auditors have a broad range of concerns, many of which are outside the scope of this book. All auditors will review your computer system's physical security, for instance. Are there locks on the doors? Do you have a disaster-recovery plan? Software is one important part of the overall system, but it is only one of the auditor's concerns. Within the software, the audit trail system is, again, an important part, but only one of the things the auditor will be examining.

Fortunately, there is a simple technique for building systems in which you can have complete confidence when the auditor comes around.

The Auditor Is a Partner

Remember that the auditor is on your side. All the auditor's goals are legitimate concerns of the enterprise. You want to avoid theft. You want to track your enterprise's assets and liabilities. You want to avoid casual mistakes and deliberate fraud. Start from the premise that the auditor's goals are your goals, too.

With that in mind, there are two times when you can have an auditor take a first look at your system: when it is running or while you are still designing it. Remarkably, most auditors are excluded from the design process.

This is foolish, of course. If the auditor detects a problem in your design, it is cheap to fix it at design time—and expensive to fix it after the system is built. This is no different from any other design change. Any problem you fix in the design stage is trivial when compared to making the same fix in a completed system.

This means that the correct relationship with your auditor is proactive, beginning with the system design. Early in the process, ask to meet with your auditor. Show him or her your plans and ask for a critique. Work with your auditor on the design.

I have always been astounded that this is almost never done. Auditors are often pleasantly surprised to be brought in at the design stage. They enjoy the work.

If we are calling in auditors from an independent accounting firm, they will, of course, bill your enterprise for their time. When justifying this expense, bear in mind that the same auditors will bill your enterprise for their time if they are brought in to audit the completed system—bills that will typically be much larger than bills incurred at design time.

If the auditor sees weaknesses in your completed system, fixes will be required to bring the system up to standard. Paying for a day or two of time at the design stage is orders of magnitude cheaper than retrofitting fixes in a running system.

This is especially true for client-server systems. Unlike "glass house" systems, client-server systems require more work to make them secure. Additionally, there are no firm standards for audit requirements—this is still a developing technology. You want your auditors' insights at design time. You also want to be able to say, "We built it this way because you told us to build it this way." (Bear in mind that the auditor who reviews the completed system may be a different person than the one who participated in its design. In fact, you'll probably see a different person every time an audit is done.)

There is one problem with this policy, if you are an independent consultant.

The Auditor Is a Competitor

Most of the accounting firms have large systems-consulting practices. Accountants, including auditors, are paid by their companies for bringing in business. If you have an auditor look at a client-server system, he or she is trained to see a potential consulting job for the systems side of the accounting firm.

For the independent consultant, this means that inviting the auditor in may also be inviting a competitor in. One personal anecdote: I asked a major client's auditors to review a design. By the time they finished bringing in their systems consultants, they had taken a $50,000 job away from me.

Remember, while you're in the trenches building a system, the systems partner from the accounting firm is probably at the club playing squash with your client's CFO. The partner will say that you seem to be doing a fine job, but then suggest that it would be wise to invite his staff to look the project over. After all, the breadth of experience of his staff could check that there were no loose ends—the last thing you want.

The way to handle this problem is to head it off before it starts. When you are ready to invite the auditors in at the design stage, explain the situation fully to your client. Explain the reasons for inviting the auditors in (to save your client money!) and explain that some accountants will take this as an opportunity to invite the other side of their firm to compete with you.

Tell your client in advance that you don't consider this ethical and that you expect them to "Just say no" as long as you are keeping their project on track. Ask for a five-minute meeting with the most senior officer you can possibly see, to lay out the situation. The simple truth is that you are putting your client's best interests ahead of your own in this situation, so don't be bashful about saying so.

Make sure that you are directly involved in calling in the auditors. If someone says "system" the accounting firm will transfer the inquiry straight to the systems consulting side. Repeat the word "auditor" as often as necessary to get a meeting with real auditors, not systems consultants.

When you first meet with the auditors, welcome them and set out the situation frankly. Tell them that you value their input, but that you would consider it completely unethical of them to take this as an opportunity to invite in the other side of their firm.

At the first meeting, the auditors will be thinking about their own billable hours; the potential for the other side of their firm is not at the top of their list at this point. After your comment they'll think twice before calling in the systems people.

With that said, let me contradict the heading of this section. The auditor is not your competitor, but other people at the auditor's firm could be. Address the problem in advance and you will be serving your client well.

Implementing Audit Trails

There are only three transactions that can change records in your database: adds, edits, and deletes. We need to design and build a system that records each of these three transactions, along with the name of the user and a time-stamp. Additionally, we want to synchronize the recording of data in the audit trail and in the .DBFs.

None of this is difficult.

Designing the Audit Trail Files

First, since we are using dBASE we might as well use .DBF-format files to record the audit trail data. All the tools in the Control Center (queries and reports, for instance) will be available for use on our audit trails. Now let's consider the data we need to record.

With each transaction, we want one field for the user's name, another for the date of the transaction, and a third for the time. I'm going to add one more field, a logical value called "complete." We'll use this one when it is time to actually write the data.

```
Audit trail overhead fields
---------------------------
USERNAME   C      16
ADATE      D       8
ATIME      C       8
COMPLETE   L       1
```

(Time could be stored in an N,5,0 field, as the number of seconds since midnight, for example. The above field holds the standard HH:MM:SS form without conversion. But check the actual storage used—after compression—before you commit to this added complication to save these bytes.)

Now let's consider the data we need to record for each of the three transaction types. For an add we need to record the contents of every field in the added record. (If some fields were left blank, we want to know that, too. With today's disk compression techniques, storing blank fields takes minimal disk space.)

For an edit, your first thought is that we need the before and after contents of the record. But in reality, the after contents are enough. We already have the before contents in the audit trail. The record contents are there for the original record add. Another audit trail record holds the contents after every other change, so we can find the before contents simply by looking backward for the correct previous audit trail record. Recording just the after image of the changed record gives us all the data we need to reconstruct our database at any point in time.

So for either adds or edits our format is the four overhead fields we first mentioned, plus the fields in the .DBF we are tracking. We will use one audit trail .DBF to track changes to each .DBF in the system. This is the form of our audit trail:

```
Audit trail design
---------------------------
USERNAME   C      16
ADATE      D       8
ATIME      C       8
```

```
COMPLETE   L       1
field_1, primary key, from the related .DBF
. . .
field_n from the related .DBF
```

This form handles both adds and edits. The only transaction left to consider is the delete.

For a delete, we need to record the overhead data (who and when) and the key of the record deleted. For simplicity, I use the same record as for adds and edits. There is an extra byte in every .DBF record containing the deleted status. A DELETE command sets the flag in this byte. For deletes in the audit trail, we can just copy the deleted record and then do a DELETE on the audit trail record.

Are you concerned that we haven't distinguished between a record add and an edit? If we SEEK backward in the audit trail looking for another record with the same primary key, we will find out which it is. If another record with the same key exists, this is an edit; otherwise, it is an add. Finding out this way seems like a lot more trouble than adding another field for transaction type. But, as you will see, in practice this problem disappears.

Opening the Files

For each .DBF in the system we will also have an audit trail .DBF. I open the .DBFs in low work areas, starting at some base number. My first .DBF might be open in area 5, the next in 6, and so on. (I use the first few numbers for miscellaneous files, such as password/permission and help.)

I add an offset, such as 20, for each audit trail file. The .DBF in area 5 has an audit trail in area 25; the .DBF in area 6 has an audit trail in area 26, and so on. Obviously, your scheme should reflect your system's number of .DBFs and other requirements.

My systems have an active index on each .DBF's primary key and almost always another one for natural order (UPPER(last_name), for example). Then they have additional indexes as needed. I average about 3 indexes per .DBF. A key to the efficiency of the system is the fact that the audit trails do not have any indexes.

Coding the Audit Trail Add

Presumably, your user-system code has the user enter all the data for the new record into an array or into memory variables. You only do an add after the user confirms this data, such as by pressing ^W.

After the data is available, an add is a two-step process in dBASE. First you APPEND a BLANK record, and then you REPLACE the fields with the values in memory. This means that you can break your add into an APPEND BLANK routine and then call your general-purpose REPLACE routine, as if you were doing an edit. This is the control algorithm:

```
* the .DBF workarea is already SELECTed
DO add_blnk
DO the_replace && same as an edit
```

This is the algorithm for the add routine. Note that it handles every .DBF/audit trail pair in the system.

```
PROCEDURE add_blnk

* assume that the .DBF workarea is SELECTed
APPEND BLANK

SELECT current_workarea_number + audit_offset
APPEND BLANK
SELECT current_workarea_number - audit_offset

RETURN
```

We now are positioned on blank records in the .DBF and in the audit trail.

Coding the Audit Trail REPLACE

Now let's get to the actual code for a REPLACE. Here is where we use the COMPLETE field to make sure that our data is written correctly. The algorithm is:

```
SELECT audit trail
REPLACE complete WITH .F.
REPLACE data in audit trail

SELECT the .DBF
REPLACE data in the .DBF
```

```
SELECT the audit trail
REPLACE complete WITH .T.
```

Note that this process gives you a partial entry, with COMPLETE set to .F., if your system crashes in the middle of the REPLACE. You may never see this in practice, but you should be prepared to deal with it. It is simple to write a little utility program that opens each audit trail, goes to the bottom record and looks at the COMPLETE field.

If you ever find a COMPLETE set to .F., manual intervention is needed. There is no way of telling at what point in the process the system failed. You may have no data in the audit trail, or data in the audit trail but not in the .DBF, or good data in both (if the crash happened after the .DBF REPLACE but just before the COMPLETE field was re-written).

Note that using BEGIN TRANSACTION/END TRANSACTION in conjunction with ON ERROR ROLLBACK is not a substitute for using COMPLETE. There is no guarantee that the crash did not occur during the transaction, or during the ROLLBACK. In fact, Murphy's Law virtually guarantees that the crash will be in the worst possible place.

In any case, if your equipment is reasonably reliable, you will find that manual recovery is an extremely uncommon experience. The COMPLETE field lets you know when you have a problem, and helps you pinpoint the problem.

The only two points that we have not covered are the actual REPLACE commands:

```
REPLACE data in audit trail
. . .
REPLACE data in the .DBF
```

If you use the same field names in the .DBF and audit trail, this is simple.

```
* in the audit trail:
REPLACE username WITH the_users_name ;
        adate    WITH DATE() ;
        atime    WITH TIME() ;
REPLACE field1   WITH memory_value_1 ;
        field2   WITH memory_value_2 ;
        . . .
        fieldn   WITH memory_value_n
```

```
* in the .DBF
REPLACE field1    WITH memory_value_1 ;
        field2    WITH memory_value_2 ;
        . . .
        fieldn    WITH memory_value_n
```

Note that the code following the overhead items in the audit trail is identical to the code in the .DBF. You decide if this should be done with a single REPLACE procedure or by just copying the code.

Coding the Audit Trail Edit

The REPLACE routine just discussed handles both record adds and record edits. The only other concern with edits is a bit of preparation. You must lock the .DBF record and APPEND a BLANK record to the audit trail prior to doing the REPLACE.

Prior to this, the user had come to the relevant record in the .DBF. At the user's EDIT command, the data was read into memory variables or an array. The user then edited the data and gave a confirm command, such as ^W. (With a non-confirm command, such as ^Q or Esc, you will not execute this update code. You proceed as if the user simply looked at the data. If you use any of the dBASE @ GET-based techniques, LASTKEY() reports the user's exit keystroke.)

The following algorithm presumes that the proper work-area has been SELECTed and that the record pointer has not been moved since the record's data was read into memory variables or arrays.

```
PROCEDURE on_edit_get_ready_to_replace

lock_flag = .F.

ON ERROR ask_user_if_you_should_retry

DO WHILE .T.
   IF RLOCK()
      lock_flag = .T.
      EXIT
    ELSE

      IF user_says_keep_trying
         LOOP
```

```
        ELSE
           EXIT
        ENDIF

     ENDIF
ENDDO

IF lock_flag
   DO the_replace
   ELSE
   any_lock_failure_recovery_goes_here
ENDIF

RETURN
```

You do not need to code a separate version of this procedure for every .DBF. You can use just one procedure, and pass it the name of the REPLACE routine. Or you can put the REPLACE code for each .DBF into a single routine.

The universal REPLACE routine is very long, but is simple in concept:

```
PROCEDURE all_replaces

dbfnum = figure_out_which_dbf_this_is

DO CASE
   CASE dbf_num = 1
      REPLACE dbf1_k    WITH memory_1_1 ;
              dbf1_fld2 WITH memory_1_2 ;
                . . .
              dbf1_fldn WITH memory_1_n

   CASE dbf_num = 2
      REPLACE dbf2_k    WITH memory_2_1 ;
              dbf2_fld2 WITH memory_2_2 ;
                . . .
              dbf2_fldn WITH memory_2_n

   CASE etc.
ENDCASE
```

If you recall that these REPLACEs work for both the audit trail file and the .DBF, you see the point of the "figure_out_which_ dbf_this_is" item. If your scheme has the first .DBF in work-area 5 and its audit trail in 25, as suggested above, that code would be like this:

```
dbf_num = SELECT( ALIAS() ) - 4
IF dbf_num > 20
   dbf_num = dbf_num - 20
ENDIF
```

This code sets "dbf_num" to 1 for either the first .DBF or its associated audit trail. That lets you use the same REPLACE code for both the .DBF and the audit trail. You will, of course, substitute code for your own work-area convention if you have a different scheme.

Coding the Audit Trail Delete

This brings us to the subject of deletes. These are the simplest to implement. I presume that your user has given a delete command with the correct work-area selected and the record pointer at the record to be deleted. The record data has been read into memory.

```
lock the current record
append a blank record to the audit trail

* set the COMPLETE field to .F.

replace the audit trail data with the memory data
delete the audit trial record
delete the .DBF record

set the COMPLETE field to .T.
```

Again, you can write this as a general routine, so that you only have the code once, not once for each .DBF. When you APPEND BLANK, logical fields are initialized to .F., so you do not need to actually set the COMPLETE field. I suggest that you include a comment about this if you do not actually do a REPLACE, since you don't want the next person who reads the code to miss this key point.

Audit Trail Overhead

By now it should be clear that we are flipping back and forth between the .DBF and the audit trail file with every database update. At first glance it looks like our database update overhead exceeds 100%. This is totally incorrect.

First, let's consider the overhead factors. There is a small overhead for processes in RAM (choosing the correct work-area) and a large overhead for actually reading and writing disk records. In practice, most RAM-based processes are completed while the user is typing and/or looking at the data. The overwhelming majority of available CPU cycles are spent waiting for the user. Therefore, we can safely ignore the CPU overhead, and concentrate on the disk overhead.

Disk Accesses

Now let's think about indexes. Borland and its competitors are constantly working on their indexing schemes, so it is impossible to be too definitive here. But the general techniques are fairly constant. You can do your own measurements using the actual dBASE version you have in combination with your server's operating system. (Disk blocking and compression/decompression algorithms are vital—timings on my machine suggest little and prove nothing about timings on your machine.)

With these caveats, indexes all have the same job. They provide rapid access to the data in the same way that a library's card file lets you find a particular book without searching through all the stacks.

If you haven't been introduced to B-tree indexes, this is how they work. A very high-level index divides the index into parts. Purely for illustration we'll assume this is 10 parts. If the index is on character data, it might put A through C in part 1, D through F in part 2 and so on.

At the next level, each part is divided again into 10 more parts. Aa through Ah might be in part 1, Ai through At in part 2, and so on. This division continues until we get down to the actual record level. Each division into parts is called an index page. This corresponds to the unit of data actually read from disk.

Actually, the index page doesn't really match what is read from disk. Real disk reads go through decompression algorithms, so you couldn't judge the actual size even if all DOS/disk combinations used the same blocking factors, which they don't.

What you can count on is that the engineers at Borland compete fiercely with their peers at Microsoft and the other Xbase vendors to build the most efficient possible indexes. A small page size, such as 10, means that the system has to read 1 page for 10 records, 2 pages for 100 records and so on. A larger page size, such as 100, means only one index read for 100 records, 2 reads for 10,000 records and so on. On the other hand, the larger the page size, the slower the process of finding a particular item in the page. Fortunately, we don't have to be concerned with these tradeoffs. Borland's people do this with awesome skill.

A reasonable estimate is that a medium file might require 3 to 5 index page reads to get to the correct data page. Let's use the smaller of these figures and assume that only 3 reads are required. To update the data, 3 writes will then be required. If your .DBF has 3 indexes, 10 writes will be required: 3 writes per index times 3 indexes, plus one write for the actual data record. If you add an audit trail, this expands to 11 writes. (The audit trail has no indexes.)

But we have not yet looked at the process in much detail. Let's suppose that a clerk is changing an existing order. Of four items on the order, the clerk will change "3 widgets" to "4 widgets."

First, the clerk looks up the customer in the customer table. Working with hyper-efficiency, the clerk might find the right customer with 3 index page reads and 1 data read (again assuming 3 page reads per index). A less-efficient clerk could easily do several times this number.

Next, the clerk selects the appropriate invoice for that customer. Again, with hyper-efficiency, this might require 4 reads. The software automatically seeks the correct entry in the invoice Detail table—another 4 reads. The clerk corrects the order detail line and it is written to disk. We now have 12 reads and 1 write. The audit trail adds a second disk write.

But we have consistently assumed an unrealistic hyper-efficient clerk/software combination. Recount the number of disk reads if the customer is named "Smith" and the clerk enters the first three letters, "SMI" while scrolling through the customer table. At the "S" the software seeks the first "S" in the name index and reads 20 or so records, updating the display on the clerk's screen. That's 4 reads, minimum—maybe 5 or 6 if getting 20 records requires more than one read.

The same process is repeated for the "M" and the "I." We could easily have 20 disk reads in finding the correct Smith. Assuming that each read is buffered and that the software is very smart about looking in RAM for buffered data (which it is) this might happen in as few as 10 reads.

The same 10 to 20 reads would also be required to locate the correct invoice for the customer. The invoice details would probably take fewer reads to accommodate the clerk, but might have more index pages to handle because the table is larger.

And we have ignored the fact that the invoice detail records contain keys into a product table. At least two or three reads will be required to use the product table keys to find each product name. If there are only five invoice line items, this is 10 to 15 more reads.

So, instead of the 12 reads we first estimated, we are now looking at 35 to 50 reads in a more realistic scenario. As you can see, adding one disk write to support the audit trail is a negligible overhead.

Disk Space

Of course, the audit trails also take up disk space. If there were no edits or deletes, the audit trail files would have as many records as their associated .DBFs, with each audit record slightly larger than its counterpart .DBF record due to the four overhead fields.

Edits and deletes have no impact on the size of the .DBF, but add records to the audit trail. The audit trails can easily grow to several times the size of their associated .DBFs.

On the other hand, there is no need to maintain the audit trails in online storage. Audit trail data can be written out to tapes or other removable media as often as the .DBFs are backed up. The actual frequency will be determined by the amount of activity in your system, which determines the amount of data accumulated in the audit trails; your available disk space; and the tradeoff between the cost of moving the audit trail data offline and the cost of maintaining it online.

Your system could move a month's audit trail data to offline storage, perhaps 90 days in arrears. At the end of May, for example, you would move February's audit trail data to tape. At the end of June you would place March's audit trails offline. This way you always have three to four month's audit trail data online, where it is convenient for rollback/rollforward recovery and other uses. The rest of the data is available as needed, though less conveniently than its online counterpart.

Of course, you can use a more frequent schedule if you need, or a less frequent schedule if your disk space permits. Bear in mind that a typist working at 60 words per minute, continuously for 8 hours a day, 5 days a week will enter fewer than 200K characters per week.

As a rule of thumb, allowing for generous margins, figure 1MB per month for every 5 full-time data-entry clerks. Of course, that's for clerks working from well-designed forms, with no need to check on the data. If the clerks are checking data as they work, that figure could drop by an order of magnitude.

As I write this, a gigabyte of hard disk costs about $2,000. That gigabyte will store 5,000 clerk/months' data entry.

In building your systems, you might want to leave the audit trails' offlining sub-system as a task to begin after the system is fully operational. You will then be in a better position to judge its storage needs and frequency. And, many of you will find that the cost of online storage drops fast enough to make it uneconomic to ever implement this procedure.

Summary

In this chapter we discussed working with an auditor and building audit trails. The audit trails are only one of the many concerns that an auditor will have. Doing them properly, however, has substantial benefits that come at very little cost.

The first principle in working with an auditor is that the auditor's concerns should also be your concerns. The auditor will be looking for systems that are secure from careless errors, as much as from deliberate misuse. These are your goals, also.

If you bring the auditor into the system at the design phase, any changes will be relatively inexpensive. You will also complete the design with confidence in its ability to be audited after it is running.

The audit trail files are .DBFs similar to the source .DBFs. They have all of the same fields, plus four more for the date and time of the change, the user name, and a flag used for insuring the integrity of the transaction.

We looked at code that implements audit trails and saw that it is simple to implement. The file opening can be done by opening each audit trail .DBF in a work-area that is a selected increment above the source .DBF. For example, the .DBF in work-area 5 might have an associated audit trail in work-area 25.

We also examined code that does record adds, edits, and deletes, and we looked at code for general-purpose replace routines. Programming with audit trails is not complex; the one non-obvious technique is to make the audit trail change first, setting the integrity flag to False. Then the source .DBF is updated and finally the integrity flag is reset to True. With the help of a trivial routine that examines each audit trail for a False integrity flag, this lets you instantly find any compromised tables after a system crash.

While the techniques for creating and maintaining audit trails are simple enough, it first appears that audit trails may add a 100% or greater overhead to the system. We examined the overhead in detail.

On closer inspection, audit trails are not likely to add even as much as 10% overhead to disk accesses and the related network traffic. Additions to the source files require multiple accesses to update indexes, search for related records, and more. In contrast, the audit trail is not indexed and is updated with a single disk access.

The audit trails do require disk space, but this requirement can be controlled by regularly transferring older audit trail data to removable media.

As we will see in the next chapter, the audit trails also serve as the base for a data rollback and rollforward recovery system, allowing you to gracefully recover from system and human failures.

Chapter 11

Rollback/Rollforward Recovery

The audit trails we discussed in Chapter 10 provide complete logs of every change to your database. They are ideal sources for database recovery.

Of course, if hardware, software, people, and data were perfect, there would be no need for recovery. dBASE's built-in TRANSACTION/ENDTRANSACTION mechanism will automatically recover from some types of failures. But there are still lots of things that can go wrong.

First, computers have power cords that can be pulled, power switches that can be flicked to "off," and reset buttons. While each of these serves a vital purpose, each is also a source of database crashes that cannot be helped by TRANSACTION-type recovery.

Software can fail too. Operating systems, dBASE itself, and your code are all potential points of failure. Combine these sources of failure with potential hardware failures, and add the inherent complexities of a network (everything depends on multiple computers, simultaneously) and the wonder is really that most of it works, most of the time.

While these are all serious problems, the worst problems are human- and data-related. One untrained operator can enter more errors in an hour than you will get from every hardware failure you experience in your lifetime. And even the best-trained, most intelligent, and conscientious operators will not be able to eliminate bad data.

For a simple personal system, or a system that is not mission-critical, you can ignore recovery, trusting to a good backup system. For mission-critical, auditable systems, however, recovery capability is vital. Using the system defined here, you will be pleasantly surprised to find that recovery is simple.

Rollforward

It was only 9:15 on Monday morning. A panicked voice summoned you to the server, double-quick. There was smoke coming from the disk array. You grabbed the fire extinguisher and hit the circuit breaker.

That was an hour ago. Your quick action saved the day. The power supply failed, but you were ahead of this one. You had a spare power supply on hand. It's installed and your hardware is back up and running. Now, what about the database? Exactly what was happening when you hit the switch?

Backups

The first line of database security is regular backups on a device that is matched to the size of your databases. Designing your backup system is outside the scope of this book. One common system would have regular nightly backups and weekend backups that were duplicated, with one copy be stored off-site.

Regular backups are a necessary measure. Our recovery system depends on the availability of a backup at some point reasonably close to the time of failure. The words "reasonably close" may mean within 24 hours for an active system, or within a month for a low-activity system.

After you devise your recovery system, you can calculate the time required for full recovery based on the amount of data in your system. Then you can estimate the length of time required to recover based on a backup that is a day old, a week old, and so on. Finally, you can ask if the time required to recover is consistent with your system's use. Is an hour of downtime acceptable? (Downtime costs money, of course. Arranging for rapid recovery also costs money, too.)

Hardware Redundancy

Modern RAID (Redundant Array of Inexpensive Disks) disk servers allow you to pull a failed drive out of a running server, and replace it with a fresh drive. You can do this while the server is running, and without losing a single byte of data.

Of course, if your failure stemmed from bad data given to an inexperienced operator, this only insures continuous availablity of a seriously compromised database. It is no substitute for the recovery procedures discussed here.

One source of hardware redundancy is required: availability of either the source .DBFs or of the audit trails. Our recovery depends on the audit trails surviving any damage that might occur to the source .DBFs.

If you have a large RAID server with mirroring and hot-replacement capability, hardware redundancy is not a problem. For the rest of us, the best solution is to keep the audit trails on one server and the .DBFs on another server. If two servers are not available, keeping the audit trails and source .DBFs on different physical disks is almost as good.

Modern disk drives generally have MTBFs (Mean Time Before Failure) of 8,000 hours or more. 8,000 hours is about 11 months of continuous operation, or about 4 years of 8 hours per day, 5 days a week. The probability of two drives' random failures occurring at the same time is so close to zero that you can safely ignore it.

But the key point there is "random failures." If a single power supply lets a large surge pass into your server, it could easily blow two drives together. These single-source failures in both the .DBFs and the audit trails are the ones to avoid.

Using the Audit Trails

Now that you have good backups and you have made sure that your audit trails will survive a failure in the source .DBFs, how does recovery work? It is simple. As we'll see, a short program handles the recovery. You can even do the job working from the dot prompt.

Step one is to delete the damaged .DBF(s) and their associated index and memo files. Replace them with the backup .DBFs and associated files. You can restore the indexes from the backup media, or you can choose to restore just the .DBFs and reindex them after they are restored. It's a cost tradeoff between backing up more data (.DBFs and indexes) versus slowing down the recovery process somewhat by doing a complete reindex.

Step two is to find the first record in the audit trail whose time/date is later than your backup time/date. The audit trails have a record of every change entered. So, you now want to re-enter the audit trail data from the time of the backup to the time of the failure.

Step three is to process each record in the audit trail, adding, deleting, or changing data in the .DBFs. This is the algorithm:

```
FOR each audit trail record

    key = <dbfname>_K in the audit trail record
    SEEK key in the .DBF

    DO CASE
       CASE the .DBF record is not FOUND()
          APPEND the audit trail data to the .DBF

       CASE the audit trail record is DELETED()
          DELETE the .DBF record

       OTHERWISE && the .DBF record is FOUND()
          REPLACE the .DBF data with the audit trail data

    ENDCASE

ENDFOR
```

You can automate this whole process with special-purpose recovery software. Alternatively, you can do this work manually after a failure. If you (or another suitably adept person) are guaranteed to be available at the time of a failure, you might want to skip writing the recovery software.

If you want a well-trained operator to do the recovery, then you want to provide the software. But think through the possibility of your well-trained operator not being available at the time of the failure. What happens when an untrained person mounts the backup for one date, and then runs the recovery software for a different date? (Check the algorithm: it works correctly if audit trail records preceding the date of the backup are processed. It fails if audit trail records subsequent to the backup are missed.)

The rest of this section will show sample software for steps two and three. First, the audit trails are not indexed, so you cannot just SEEK the right record. They are built, however, in date/time order, so you can do a binary search, either manually or via software. Start with a record in the middle. If it is too late, backup a quarter of the way. If it is too early, skip forward to three quarters of the way through the audit trail.

Checking the record you find after the skip, you hop forward or backward by an eighth. Repeat this process until you come to the right record. Listing 11–01 shows a pair of routines that do this. You first open the audit trail .DBF in the current workarea, then call fixd_search() with the date and time of the backup.

Code Listing 11–01

```
***************************************************************
*** fixd_search — binary search for starting audit record
***************************************************************

PROCEDURE fixd_search
PARAMETERS dt, tm
PRIVATE delt

GO BOTTOM
delt = INT(RECNO()/2)

DO WHILE delt > 0
```

```
 IF toolate()
   SKIP -delt
  ELSE
   SKIP delt
  ENDIF

 delt = INT(delt/2)
ENDDO

DO WHILE toolate()
 SKIP -1
 IF BOF()
   EXIT
 ENDIF
ENDDO

DO WHILE .NOT. toolate()
 SKIP
 IF EOF()
   EXIT
 ENDIF
ENDDO

RETURN
*                                     && end of fixd_search


*****************************************************************
*** toolate — audit date is later than selected date
*****************************************************************

FUNCTION toolate

IF when_d > dt
 RETURN .T.
ELSE
 IF when_d < dt
   RETURN .f.
  ELSE
   RETURN when_t > tm
 ENDIF
ENDIF

RETURN .F.
*                                     && end of toolate
```

The first DO WHILE loop in fixd_search() does the binary searching. It will quickly get to within a single record of the one you want. (About 20 reads will find one record in a million. 30 reads will find one record in a billion.) It may be off a bit because it is constantly dividing unequal parts (odd numbers divided by two).

The next two DO WHILE loops in fixd_search() compensate for any slight misses due to rounding up or down, or to the date/time being past one of the ends of the audit trail file.

Listing 11–02 shows a routine that actually does the data correction. You can see that Listing 11–01 showed general-purpose code that you can plug right into your own system. Listing 11–02 is system-specific code that you can use as a model, but you'll need to modify it for your own system.

This sample is from a simple, two-table system. As the number of tables grows, the DO CASE switches expand, but the rest of the code stays the same.

Code Listing 11–02

```
****************************************************************
*** fixd_update — update dbf from adt in Fix dbfs
****************************************************************

PROCEDURE fixd_update
PARAMETERS fil
PRIVATE key, del

dt = end_date
                              && globals for toolate()
tm = end_time

DO WHILE .NOT. ( EOF() .OR. toolate() )

  DO CASE
    CASE fil = 1
      val = PEOPLE_adt->PEOPLE_k

    CASE fil = 2
      val = ORGS_adt->ORGS_k

  ENDCASE

  del = DELETED()
  SELECT (fil+2)
  SEEK val

  IF del

    text_var = "deletion"
```

```
  IF FOUND()
     DELETE
  ENDIF

ELSE

  * either edit or append
  IF FOUND()

    text_var = "edit"

  ELSE

    text_var = "append"
    APPEND BLANK

  ENDIF

  DO fixd_rep WITH fil

ENDIF

SELECT ( fil + 12 )
IF .NOT. EOF()
  SKIP
ENDIF

ENDDO

RETURN
*                              && end of fixd_update
```

The algorithm and code shown here assume that you did *not* have a failure in the middle of a .DBF update. This is the final concern we need to address, before we have a complete rollforward recovery system.

Mid-Transaction Failures

I have simulated failures that left the COMPLETE field set to .F. in the audit trails, but I have never seen this happen in actual use. As we discussed in Chapter 10, the ratio of disk reads to disk writes may be about 30 to 1. This means that for a server whose disk utilization is 100%, your chance of a failure occurring during a write is about 3%. If your disk utilization is 50%, that figure drops to 1.5%.

At 1.5%, with today's hardware you may *never* see a mid-transaction failure. It takes about 46 failures to yield even a 50% chance of a mid-transaction failure, at 1.5% possibility per failure. That should be far more hardware failures than you see in a typical system's life.

On the other hand, Murphy's Law virtually guarantees that you will see a mid-transaction failure at the worst possible time, if you are not prepared to deal with it!

First, have a utility program that searches the audit trails for a record where the COMPLETE field is .F. Run this routine prior to every backup. You should never find this condition, but if you do, you should take it very seriously.

Of course, you will run this program after any failure, *before* you use the audit trail for recovery. Chances are excellent that your audit trails are OK. The procedure that follows lets you handle the rare problem you might encounter.

First, remember the order of audit-trail-based updates:

```
APPEND BLANK record to audit trail
* COMPLETE field is now .F.

REPLACE audit trail data (possibly DELETE)

REPLACE .DBF data (or APPEND or DELETE)

set COMPLETE field .T.
```

Working at the dot prompt, check the audit trail record. If it is blank, your failure occurred just after the APPEND BLANK to the audit trail. Just delete the audit trail record—the .DBF was not affected by the failure.

If the audit trail data is filled in, SEEK the appropriate primary key in the .DBF. If it is not found, there was a failure between updating the audit trail and updating the .DBF. Look for a blank record in the .DBF. If you find one, fill it in with the audit trail data. If you don't find one, add one and fill it in with the audit trail data.

If the .DBF record is found, check that its data matches the data in the audit trail record. This indicates a failure after a successful update of the .DBF, just prior to resetting the audit trail COMPLETE flag. Again, either your .DBF is OK, or you need to fill in part of the record from the audit trail data.

After you finish, manually set the COMPLETE field to .T. if you did not delete the audit trail record. You have now manually completed the interrupted update.

Rollback

Rollback is also possible from our audit trails, but it is a good deal more complex. If you think there may be some reason that will require you to do true rollbacks, you may want to revisit the audit trail structure. You might want to store both the before and after images, although this data is not really required.

Fortunately, there is a simple solution.

Rollforward as Rollback

The simple way is to rollforward, not backward. Assume that today is Friday. You know that your database was OK on Wednesday. But, beginning Thursday morning, you were visited by a swarm of bad data. What you want to do is rollback all the work done yesterday and earlier today, and start over from Wednesday evening.

Simply rebuild the database, starting with last weekend's backup and entering all the audit trail transactions for Monday through Wednesday. You may have noticed that the software in Listing 11–02 checked for .NOT. toolate(). This routine enters a specified date/time range.

You can see that rolling forward from a good backup to a cutoff time results in exactly the same database as rolling backward from the present to that same cutoff time. Either way, you get to the "good" database as of, for example, Wednesday evening.

Rollback for Human Error

Rollback is most frequently used in the case of severe or extensive human error. Let's be a bit more realistic about the example above. You weren't really visited by a swarm of bad data affecting everyone equally. Actually, your best data person came down with the flu and you had a temporary worker in as a replacement. Eager to keep productivity up, your data supervisor let this temp get started without adequate training.

What you have is five operators entering good data and one temp making a mess of your system. You really want to rollback just this one user's entries. This is surprisingly simple.

Again, you "rollback" everything to Wednesday by rolling forward from the previous weekend's backup. Then you roll forward from Thursday through today, but you plug a little IF into the logic. You only enter the transactions IF the username field in the audit trail is not that of your ill-trained temp. You end with a database that's missing the entries of one person during Thursday and Friday. You have rolled back just that user's entries.

This may not be entirely possible, however. I'll discuss referential integrity in detail in Chapter 15, but we have to consider it to some extent at this point. If the ill-trained temp entered a new customer, and then your other people entered invoices for that customer, you have a problem.

What do you do? For now, your procedures should be designed to avoid this problem, if possible. If not possible, then you need to modify the roll forward to pause to show each record entered by the ill-trained temp to a competent data person who will correct the errors as the update progresses.

All of the other rollback and rollforward procedures we have discussed, by the way, maintain complete domain and referential integrity.

Summary

In this chapter we discussed the use of your audit trail files as the source of data rollback and rollforward recovery. This capability allows you to recover from rare hardware failures, or less-rare human errors.

The first requirement for rollback or rollforward recovery is a good backup system. You must have a data backup system that copies your .DBFs to removeable media whose size and speed is appropriate to the size of your database. Your data backup frequency must be matched to the amount of data being entered on your system.

Hardware redundancy is an important way to avoid single-source errors that can damage both your .DBFs and your audit trails. Our recovery depends on at least one of these surviving. Modern RAID servers provide the ultimate in hardware redundancy. More modest solutions include storing the audit trails on one server and the .DBFs on another, or using separate hard disks within a single server.

To rollforward from a backup point, you copy the audit trail information into the .DBF from the point of the backup forward. Software was shown that does a binary search to efficiently locate the correct audit trail record. Algorithms were presented to perform the update. With the possible exception of the search algorithm, the actual recovery programs are simple to code.

Although mid-transaction failures are exceedingly rare, a due respect for the power of Murphy's Law requires that we be ready to handle them. A mid-transaction failure is shown by the COMPLETE flag in the audit trail record being set to False. Manual procedures were discussed to recover the damaged record.

Rollback, based on our after-image audit trail data, is a more complex job. However, it can be effectively simulated by rolling forward. To rollback the dastabase from Friday to Wednesday evening, for example, you can restore from the last weekend's backup and rollforward to Wednesday evening. The resulting database is identical to one that would be constructed through true rollback.

Rollback is particularly important as a way to recover from human errors. For example, to eliminate a single, ill-trained operator's entries for the last two days, you again use the rollforward from a backup to restore the database as of two days ago. Then you continue to rollforward, but this time insert an IF test into the rollforward program that excludes the work of the ill-trained operator.

Doing this successfully requires that you not create referential integrity problems. These could occur if your ill-trained operator entered new customer names, and other operators subsequently entered billing data for those customers, for example. Data entry procedures should be designed to minimize this problem.

Chapter 12

Posting and Data Redundancy

By "posting" I mean the process of updating sub-totals and totals at the same time the source data is entered. When you sell a widget, you could decrement the "widgets-on-hand" total; increment the "widgets sold" total; increment "gross sales, month-to-date," and so on.

Posting fields are part of the parent record. For example, the product table could have one field for month-to-month sales, in dollars, and another field for quantity-on-hand. As you add each invoice detail record, the dollar amount adds to sales, and the units sold decrement the quantity-on-hand.

Posting slows down the data update process, but may dramatically speed up database queries. However, posted totals are redundant data. Therefore, posted totals, like other forms of redundant data, require special handling.

The first rule about redundant data is: "Don't do it!" Let's take a typical example. You decide to copy the product name and price from the product table into the invoice line-item detail record. Repeating this data saves an indexed lookup (maybe three or four disk reads) for every line item in every invoice. That could reduce server overhead and cut out a lot of network traffic.

Well, I strongly recommend that you don't do it. At least not yet. Before you add a deliberate redundancy, wait to see if it addresses a real problem. On those invoices, I'll bet that 90% of the time, the data-entry person just builds an invoice on screen and then moves on to the next invoice. Duplicate data only hurts the first time you build an invoice.

Deliberate redundancy doesn't avoid the initial reads from the product table when the data is looked up. In fact, you will ultimately be writing *more* data, so redundancy may actually add a disk write or two when you build the record. Are your data people or tele-marketers really going to be looking at old invoices regularly?

Next, when you discover a redundancy that could solve a *real* problem, (one you're experiencing, not one you just think might happen), look for another solution. Let's say that out in the ware-house your people really do run the invoice program to generate a fresh invoice to enclose with each package. This operation is slow-ing your server and network and you think that repeating the prod-uct information in the invoice detail records will save as much as 70% of the resources going into these invoices.

As you'll see in this chapter, writing the code to handle data redundancy in a robust way is non-trivial. Before you undertake a major programming job, look for a simple solution. Maybe you can run the invoices overnight and have them waiting in the warehouse in the morning?

Well, you've got so much already being done overnight that you are still having a problem with network response when you run the invoices. If network load is the problem, move the invoices off the network! Plug a printer directly into your server and run the invoice print job directly on the server. That offloads 100% of the network load. Chances are pretty good that an extra printer is a lot cheaper than the time you'd spend writing a good redundancy fea-ture into your software.

However, there is one type of redundancy that frequently pays off: posting. People seldom need another invoice, but frequently want to know the invoice totals. How many widgets have you sold? How much does a customer owe you? These questions can be answered without any access to the invoice line-detail file, if the totals are posted.

As you'll see, it takes a lot of work to support posting. The same work is needed for other sorts of data redundancy. Posting can, however, turn a slow system into a slick system.

The same might be true of some other data redundancies, but I'd guess that 90% of all data redundancies I've seen are bad choices made by inexperienced designers. Remember rule one: "Don't do it!" The rest of this chapter applies to those few cases where you decide to violate rule one.

Server-Based Posting Software

The problem with redundant data is, of course, that it can get out of sync. The name of the product in one record might not match the name in another record. Worse, the price of the product in one record might not match the price in another record. The flight might have available seats on one screen, after the last seat was sold elsewhere.

To avoid this condition, you have to design carefully (it may be acceptable for one invoice to call it a "purple widget" and another to use the new "mauve widget" name). Then you need to regularly run an updating, or "sync," process on the server.

First, decide which records are going to be the official "source" data. The fundamental ORE&D design (see Chapter 6) should provide an obvious source table. Then write a server program that will update every record that stores a redundant copy of the source data.

Posting is a complex form of redundant data. Your invoice detail records may be the source data for your invoice sub-total. Shipping cost will come from the invoice record. Sales taxes are calculated from the invoice detail record and stored in the invoice record. All of this is put together to form an invoice total.

Typical posting processes may push sub-totals upward into progressively higher realms. The invoice total is posted to the customer total. The customer total is posted to the regional total, and so on. As a designer, you have to decide how far to automatically carry this process, when you build the client-based posting software.

On the server side, each posting or other redundancy has to be able to be recreated in a mass update that guarantees a single, consistent set of data. A typical time to run this server software is immediately before each nightly backup.

Will an auditor find your posting or other redundancy acceptable? Answers may differ, so to get a hard answer, you have to consult your particular auditor about your particular system. One general case where you should expect a "yes" answer is when the posting provides temporary summary data for decision makers, but not for actual accounting.

If the actual invoices are generated overnight from the source data, the fact that you also store invoice totals for quick lookups will not generally be a problem. If the data used to total accounts receivable and sales also come from the invoice process that builds from source data, your auditor will probably not care that the sales department uses possibly erroneous summary data during the day.

Now let's look at the actual software. We want to do two things. First, we want to do the posting work, in the correct order. Second, we want to show the operator a display that reports the progress we are making.

Server-Based Posting Display

Do you need to program this display? I'd say "yes." It only takes an hour or so, and you will need it. First, you'll want it when you are testing the server-based postings. After that, your backup operator will want to check the display to see how much time is left until the backup starts.

Of course, once the operator knows that the job runs 17 minutes each night, he or she will probably forget your display and use that time to start brewing a fresh pot of coffee. But you will still have interested parties.

Your auditor will probably be keenly interested in your treatment of redundant software. Even if an auditor finds your treatment provisions theoretically sound, he or she may still want to look at the actual operation. Starting a program that just spins the drives for

17 minutes is not a good match for a program that neatly reports what it is working on, and how far along it is.

For this, you want two windows. One large window should display the posting operations as they are being done. The key point to review is that your postings are done from the bottom up. (Get an invoice total; update the customer total from the invoice totals; update the regional total when the customer totals are done, and so on.)

A second display can show the status of each posting. A typical progress indicator says "0%" at one end and "100%" at the other. As the posting routines progress through a table, use a graphics character to fill in the appropriate amount of the indicator.

The progress indicator is usually horizontal, since you can fit more characters. The key point is to show regular motion—delays of several seconds make you wonder if the job is hung or still working. One nice trick to use when you have a slow job is to use CHR(219) (a solid block of color) for the progress indicator. Then use CHR(221) (a solid block on the left) to show completion of a half increment. Listing 12–01 shows the basic idea.

Code Listing 12–01

```
clear
i = 0
do while i <= 20

   @ 1, 10 SAY replicate( CHR(219), i )
   k = inkey(.5)   && simulated work

   @ 1, 10+i SAY CHR(221)
   k = inkey(.5)   && simulated work

   i = i + 1
enddo
```

(The all-lowercase style in Listing 12–01 is one that I use for throwaway code that I only use to test or check something.)

Server-Based Posting

With displays in hand, the next process is to carefully examine the posting process to list all of the required steps from the bottom up. In many of your systems, this can take a lot more thought than our simple examples. Obviously, you have to post to the customer totals before you can use these totals to post to regional totals.

Then you can build a control routine, which looks like this:

```
clear screen
SET cursor, etc. OFF

initialize variables and DECLARE arrays

open all required .DBFs for EXCLUSIVE use

DEFINE and ACTIVATE windows

DO lowest_level_posting
DO next_lowest_level_posting
. . .
DO final_posting

RELEASE windows
```

For testing, write a little "zoop" driver that doesn't really do any work, but neatly fills up your progress indicator. Take the code in Listing 12–01, for instance, and cut the delays down so that it only takes a second or two for the whole thing.

If you use Listing 12–01 as a base for your zoop() code, bear in mind that INKEY() is working off the PC's clock-tick update code. This gives an update 18.2 times per second, so delays of less than $1/18.2$ (about 0.055) seconds are not really delays. INKEY(0.06) works fine, but INKEY(0.05) doesn't delay at all. This delay is independent of your PC's CPU speed.

Given a zoop() that pretends it's doing work, you can test the whole program with stub routines, such as these:

```
PROCEDURE lowest_level_posting
DO update_big_window WITH 'Posting lowest level'
DO zoop
RETURN

PROCEDURE next_lowest_level_posting
DO update_big_window WITH 'Posting next level'
DO zoop
RETURN
```

Finally, you can write the actual posting code. For some items, such as calculating an invoice total, you can just cycle through

all the records in a table, calling a routine that is common to both
server and client code. I try hard to have both the server and client
routines use common posting code, but this seldom works out in
practice.

Your client-side code will be worrying about record locking
(see the later discussion of this) and other details that are irrelevant
to the server process. Equally, your added sale on the client side
adds an increment to the customer total. The increase in the customer total is added to the regional total, and so on.

On the server side, the customer total starts at zero, and then
adds up each of the invoice totals. The regional tables are updated
by starting the sub-totals at zero, then adding in each customer total.
The processes are very different.

On the other hand, for simple postings, such as just maintaining totals, this is only a minor concern. It is the more complex operations, such as invoice totals, where you probably can continue to
use common code in both the server and client routines.

These are typical examples of posting operations:

```
PROCEDURE inv_totals

SELECT invoices
GO TOP

DO WHILE .NOT. EOF()
   REPLACE invoic->total WITH calc_invt()
   SKIP
ENDDO

* calc_invt() is a routine called here and by
* the client-based code
```

That example, and the following, omit the display update calls
in the interest of clearly showing the basic work.

```
PROCEDURE cust_tot

SELECT cstmers
GO TOP

tot = 0.0
DO WHILE .NOT. EOF()

   SELECT invoices
```

```
* set filter: invoic->cust_k = cust->cust_k
DO go_top
DO WHILE .NOT. ie_eof()
   tot = tot + invoic->total
   DO my_skip
ENDDO

SELECT cstmers
REPLACE cust->inv_tot WITH tot

  SKIP
ENDDO
```

Note that the invoice processing uses the index-based filtering code we discussed in Chapter 9.

These examples have brought us to the bottom-level code in the server-based posting software. Add the display update code to them and you're in business. For that, you go to the bottom of the table before starting. Divide the total number of records by the number of increments in your display routine. Then, update the display each time MOD(RECNO(), # per increment) equals zero.

If you have other types of redundant data, handle them the same way.

Client-Based Posting Software

There are two areas to consider before you build posting into your client programs. First, there is the locking issue. In our other updates, we locked the record we were updating. In posting, we may want to update several records, so we need to lock them all before proceeding to post.

Second, the dBASE language is designed to work on only one .DBF at a time, via the SELECT mechanism. In posting, we frequently need to hop from one .DBF to another. Worse, within each .DBF we may want to do considerable work with related .DBFs, so we cannot be sure that things will be just as we left them when we return to another SELECTed workarea.

A .DBF stack lets us conveniently push the status of one .DBF just before we leave it, and then pop the status when we return.

Transaction-Style Locking

In Chapter 8, we looked at locking the record we wanted to update. There is a more general case to consider, and we meet it here. A single transaction may require updates to several records. (In the most general case, a distributed database, a transaction may require updating multiple records in multiple databases, which uses these principals.)

The basics of this type of locking are the same as in single-record locking. You must lock before you update. You must have all relevant information in memory, so that you can lock, update, and immediately unlock. Finally, you can use semaphores to check that no updates took place between the time you read a record and the time when you are ready to update the record.

Most posting transactions work their way up one or more data trees. For example, you might post a sale up to a customer total, then up to a regional total, and so on. Simultaneously, you might post the sale up to a product, then a product class, then a division, and so on. When you design the postings, consider the locking consequences carefully.

If you post every sale all the way up to the "year-to-date sales" entry in the general ledger, chances are pretty good that your system will never have time to get any real work done. If you try to post all the way up to total sales, every person attempting to enter a single line item in an invoice will need to lock the record that holds total sales.

When every transaction in every sub-system needs write access to a single record, work grinds to a halt.

When you design, remember that a standard query can total conveniently from one level to another. It is no problem to use the dBASE Control Center to ask for a regional sales total, for example. RDBMS-based systems all have convenient SQL-based query mechanisms.

While these queries are not quite as simple as just looking at a single record, they are fairly easy to use and do not require exclusive access to a record. Everyone in the enterprise can be busy querying the system without the kind of stoppage that occurs when several people try to lock the same record at the same time for updating.

The system should be designed to stop the posting process at a level that avoids frequent multiple-access problems. But your update code also has to be built on the assumption that you do have multiple-update problems.

To do a posting, you first need to calculate the delta in the amount being posted. If you have added an invoice, the delta is the new invoice amount. If you have edited an invoice, the delta is the new invoice total minus the old invoice total. In an add, the invoice total is zero immediately after the APPEND BLANK, so actually you can just use the latter rule. The delta to post is the new amount minus the old amount.

With the delta in hand, you are ready to post the affected totals. You replace each total with:

```
REPLACE thisdbf->total WITH thisdbf->total + delta
```

(Actually, that "+" might be a "–" in some cases. You could be deducting amount sold from amount in stock.) As you work up the tree, you post the same delta at each stage. You ignore the intervening totals, as this illustrates:

```
REPLACE cust->total WITH cust->total + delta
REPLACE region->total WITH region->total + delta
```

This implies that each record has been located, and then locked. Locate all your records first, then lock them all, as the following shows:

```
* SEEK cust record done during invoice update
SELECT region
SET ORDER TO region_k && index on primary key
SEEK cust->region_k   && find the right region

DO WHILE .T.
   SELECT cust
   IF RLOCK()
      SELECT region
      IF RLOCK()
         EXIT
      ENDIF
   ENDIF
   * do something about lock failure
ENDDO
```

```
REPLACE region->total WITH region->total + delta
UNLOCK

SELECT cust
REPLACE cust->total WITH cust->total + delta
UNLOCK
```

Note that relational integrity is maintained by the system, so your SEEK commands will work as you move up the system. You do not need to check FOUND() after each SEEK. Or do you? Set that aside for the moment.

What you need right now is some code to handle the problem of the failure to RLOCK() one of the records you want. I display a message to the user asking if another try is desired. Normally, the user just says "yes" and the message/response process provides enough delay to get the record available. In exceptional conditions, repeated requests to try again will not work. (Some programmer or database administrator may have grabbed a table for exclusive access.)

If this is the case, you set an error flag and exit from the loop. The following code that does the REPLACE/UNLOCK process has to check this flag.

Now about that SEEK. The good news is that your system will maintain bullet-proof relational integrity so you can SEEK with confidence. The bad news is that programmers such as yourself and database administrators can still get manual access to the files and make human mistakes, so you can never be sure.

I use a general-purpose SEEK that triggers a fatal error on a relational integrity fault. It looks like this:

```
PROCEDURE gnrl_seek
PARAMETER seek_value

SEEK seek_value

IF .NOT. FOUND()
    * write as much data as you can
    * to an on-screen error message

    * close all open files

    * tell the user to fetch the database
    * administrator
```

```
* leave the message on the screen
IF the DBA provides special go ahead
   QUIT
 ELSE
   * the system must be rebooted
 ENDIF
ENDIF

RETURN
```

The error condition shown here should seldom, if ever, be encountered. You want the DBA (or programmer, or whomever) to be involved if it does, because the relational integrity violation must be tracked down and corrected. Chances are that it was caused by someone doing manual data updates, ignoring the protections provided by the system.

At this juncture, you don't really mind if the user is getting angry at the powers that caused this interruption in his or her work. (You don't mind, that is, unless you were the person that messed up the data. If it was you, you'll hear from the database administrator. Next time, use your own system!)

Stack-Based .DBF Status

One other technique makes the posting process much easier to code reliably. That is using a .DBF status stack. Here is what we want to do:

```
push current status onto stack

* we go elsewhere, updating who
* knows what

pop current status from stack

* and the former status is restored, regardless
* of what the intervening steps were
```

Remember that the intervening process between a push and a pop could, itself, have triggered multiple pushes and pops. It might have had reason to access the work area that was current before the push.

There are hardware stacks for system programmers, but there are no stacks in dBASE. Even if dBASE could access the hardware stacks directly, they wouldn't be much help, since we want a push() to record many individual facts, and a pop() to do a lot of database work.

But it is simple enough to use an array and a pointer to create our own stack. Assume that you have five status items to store and that you want to be able to push up to 10 status sets. This declaration will work:

```
DECLARE stat_stk[50]
stat_s_ptr = 0
```

Now you can create push and pop routines. They look like these:

```
PROCEDURE push_dbf

IF stat_s_ptr = 50
   * Fatal error!  out of room
   * close files
   * display message
   QUIT
ENDIF

stat_stk[stat_s_ptr + 1] = first item
stat_stk[stat_s_ptr + 2] = second item
stat_stk[stat_s_ptr + 3] = third item
stat_stk[stat_s_ptr + 4] = fourth item
stat_stk[stat_s_ptr + 5] = fifth item

stat_s_ptr = stat_s_ptr + 5

RETURN


PROCEDURE pop_dbf

IF stat_s_ptr = 0
   * Fatal error!  out of room
   * close files
   * display message
   QUIT
ENDIF
```

```
stat_s_ptr = stat_s_ptr - 5

restore first item
restore second item
restore third item
restore fourth item
restore fifth item

RETURN
```

Typical data-saving code could include:

```
stat_stk[stat_s_ptr + 1] = sele_area
stat_stk[stat_s_ptr + 2] = RECNO()
stat_stk[stat_s_ptr + 3] = is_eof()
```

Typical restoration code could include:

```
SELECT( stat_stk[stat_s_ptr+1] )
GO stat_stk[stat_s_ptr+2]

IF stat_stk[stat_s_ptr+3]
   DO set_eof
 ELSE
   DO reset_eof
ENDIF
```

In my push and pop routines, I generally track the current select area, the current record number, the current index tag, and the status of my eof and bof indicators. Your system will probably need these items, as well as other, system-dependent data.

As in any stack-based work, you must push and pop in pairs. I suggest that you always type (or write an editor macro that always types):

```
DO push_dbf
DO pop_dbf
```

You can put whatever you like between these two calls, but make sure that you never fail to use them in pairs. This push/pop process makes lots of otherwise complex posting operations relatively simple.

Other redundant data is handled the same way as posting on the client-side.

Summary

Posting is the process of accepting a source entry and then updating a sub-total or total. For example, an invoice detail entry might increase total sales in the customer's record and in a product record and might decrease the inventory total for the product.

Posted totals are one form of redundant data. Rule one about redundant data is to eliminate it. There are times, however, when you want to violate this rule to increase system efficiency. This chapter suggests procedures to help you do this as safely as possible.

To keep redundancy acceptable to auditors, decide which data is the source data, and build all auditable reports directly from the source data. Create batch update programs that rebuild all totals or other redundant data directly from the source data, and run these programs regularly—normally prior to each backup.

These batch update jobs are run directly on the server. Various pieces of server software are shown that effectively display the batch posting. You can expect auditors to examine these processes. The importance of the audit examinations, as well as the inherent dangers in data redundancy, suggest that you spend more time with these programs than is devoted to other server-side utility routines.

On the client side of your system, posting and other redundant data transactions require particular care with record locking. The source data may be posted using the locking techniques already discussed. Then all affected redundant data records should be locked before updating any of them. The same procedures that were discussed in Chapter 8 continue to apply.

Since you will, in the posting process, be using tables that may have been involved in other ways in your system, the posting process should not disturb your database by moving record pointers, changing index order, or otherwise failing to leave things undisturbed.

I showed you software for a stack-based .DBF-manipulation system that allows you to "push" current status information onto a stack. After updating whatever records, the status is simply "popped" from the .DBF stack to restore the original conditions. This greatly simplifies the rest of the posting or other redundant-data updating processes.

This chapter completes our consideration of the systems "underware" layer. Now we have the basics in place and are ready to get on to the software that our users will see. We'll start with building our own menuing engine to get the security capabilities that client-server systems demand.

The menu code in Chapter 13 shows techniques that you'll expand on in Chapter 14, when we look at scrolling. Even if you don't need this security just yet, at least spend enough time here to understand how the code works. Menu and scroll engines are some of the most rewarding things you'll ever program.

Chapter 13

Client-Server Menus

dBASE has built-in menuing commands that provide both horizontal and vertical menus. Additionally, the Control Center provides menu painting and code-generation tools, so you never have to code a menu. Well, you never have to code a menu unless you want to go beyond the capabilities of the built-in tools.

One reason that client-server programs generally don't use the built-ins is security. In many applications, not all users should have access to all of the options on the menu. Your code can do a check after each option selection, of course. But this requires that your system sometimes give the user a "Sorry, you're not allowed in there" message.

One of the things wrong with this approach should be fairly obvious. The way to discourage unauthorized access to salary data is *not* to post a sign over a file cabinet that reads: "Salary data locked up in here!" For physical security, you don't want people to know where private data is stored, and you don't want to remind unauthorized people that the data even exists. The same applies to computer systems.

A user should never see a menu option that provides access to data that the user is not allowed to access. If there is no menu option that says "Salary data," users will assume that the salary data is in some other system. Or perhaps just not even think about salary data, which is your first line of defense against unauthorized access.

In this chapter, I'll show you how to build a menu engine. Those of you who have done this before will want to skim forward until we get to the section on Adding Security to the Menu Engine. Those of you who have not done your own menuing are in for a pleasant surprise. This coding is very rewarding.

Writing a Menu

We'll start with a simple pulldown menu. In dBASE IV, you build a pulldown menu with POPUP and BAR commands: DEFINE POPUP, DEFINE BAR, ACTIVATE POPUP, and so on. As you'll see, dBASE has a built-in menu engine and these commands are your vehicle for providing data to the internal engine. We'll build our own engine and pass data to it through standard coding practices.

But before we build an engine (a general-purpose version), we'll write one menu the long way, so you can see clearly how this works. The techniques used here will carry forward to Chapter 14 when we cover scrolling.

Menu Structure

All menus share common code components. These are setup code, a highlight/lowlight system, a keystroke (or event) handler, and action-processing code.

The setup code handles initialization activities, as setup code does in any sub-system. In our first menu, this will be very brief. It is critically important, though, when we get to the secure menus that eliminate options for which the user is not authorized.

The highlight/lowlight system is the one that displays menu options as either selected or unselected. In DOS systems, this is usually done by showing a selected color (or inverse video, in monochrome). When you get to graphics systems, you can use a variety of different techniques, such as showing buttons up or pushed down. These all work in the same structure.

Menu Setup Code

For this menu, setup is simple. We define and activate a window for the menu, then establish some control variables. This is shown in Listing 13–01.

Code Listing 13–01

```
PRIVATE i
SET TALK OFF
SET CURSOR OFF

DEFINE   WINDOW menwin ;
         FROM 5, 10 ;
         TO   15, 34 ;
         DOUBLE ;
         COLOR +W/B

ACTIVATE WINDOW menwin

STORE 1 TO hi_opt, i
num_opts = 4
```

In most menus, you will not need the SET commands, as these settings will be taken care of in the system startup code. Here, "hi_opt" is the number of the option that is highlighted; "i" is a loop-control variable that we use to initialize the display, and "num_opts" is the number of options.

Next, we need to display the first option highlighted and the other options lowlighted.

Menu Highlight/Lowlight System

The key to giving the appearance of a moving highlight bar is the highlight/lowlight routine. It is called with a menu option number, and a logical flag that is set to True to show the option in the highlighted color.

Listing 13–02 shows a typical example.

Code Listing 13–02

```
*****************************************************************
*** men1_hilo — hilite/lolite for menu 1
*****************************************************************

PROCEDURE men1_hilo
PARAMETER opt_num, is_hi

IF  is_hi
  SET COLOR TO +W/BG
ELSE
  SET COLOR TO W/B
ENDIF

DO CASE
  CASE opt_num = 1
     @  1, 1 SAY " Everyone's option    "

  CASE opt_num = 2
     @  3, 1 SAY " Universal option     "

  CASE opt_num = 3
     @  5, 1 SAY " Private option       "

  CASE opt_num = 4
     @  7, 1 SAY " Very private option "
ENDCASE

RETURN                                    && end of men1_hilo
```

As you see, this routine selects a color depending on the "is_hi" parameter, and then displays the selected menu option. Note that all the text strings in the @ SAY commands are the same length.

We put this to use at the end of the menu setup code to initialize the menu option display, as shown in Listing 13–03.

Code Listing 13–03

```
DO WHILE i <= num_opts
  DO men1_hilo WITH i, i=hi_opt
  i = i + 1
ENDDO
```

Menu Keystroke Handling

When I build a menu from scratch, I always do this much, then write a stub keystroke handler that looks like this:

```
DO WHILE .T.
   last_key = INKEY(0)
   DO CASE
      CASE last_key = 27 && Esc
         EXIT
   ENDCASE
ENDDO
```

This loop does nothing but wait for an Escape key. It's just enough to test the menu code you've seen so far. Once this works (usually only a matter of wiggling the display coordinates until it looks good) I add an Up and Down arrow CASE. They look like this:

```
CASE last_key = 5 && Up arrow or ^E
   DO men1_hilo WITH hi_opt, .F.
   hi_opt = IIF( hi_opt = 1, num_opts, hi_opt-1 )
   DO men1_hilo WITH hi_opt, .T.

CASE last_key = 24 && Down arrow or ^X
   DO men1_hilo WITH hi_opt, .F.
   hi_opt = IIF( hi_opt = num_opts, 1, hi_opt+1 )
   DO men1_hilo WITH hi_opt, .T.
```

This code lowlights the current menu option, increments or decrements the "hi_opt" pointer, and highlights the next option. I use an IIF() function to wrap from top to bottom and vice-versa. You may not want menu wrapping if your users are beginners.

This lets you see the menu come to life, bouncing the light bar in response to the arrow keys. Once this works, you can fill in the keystroke loop. Listing 13–04 shows a full example.

Code Listing 13–04

```
* keystroke loop
DO WHILE .T.
  last_key = INKEY(0)

  DO CASE
```

```
      CASE last_key = 17 .OR. ;
           last_key = 27 && ^Q or Esc
         EXIT

      CASE last_key = 13 .OR. ;
           last_key = 23 && Enter or ^W
         DO men1_action WITH hi_opt

      CASE last_key = 5 && Up arrow or ^E
         DO men1_hilo WITH hi_opt, .F.
         hi_opt = IIF( hi_opt = 1, num_opts, hi_opt-1 )
         DO men1_hilo WITH hi_opt, .T.

      CASE last_key = 24 && Down arrow or ^X
         DO men1_hilo WITH hi_opt, .F.
         hi_opt = IIF( hi_opt = num_opts, 1, hi_opt+1 )
         DO men1_hilo WITH hi_opt, .T.

      OTHERWISE
         * do nothing or ?? CHR(7) (beep) if you want

   ENDCASE
ENDDO
```

This calls men1_action() on an Enter or ^W keypress. To test it, you need to provide a stub routine.

Menu Action Code

The full menu action routine is generally very simple. It is typically a DO CASE switch that selects from one or more subroutines (which are often calls to major sub-systems).

Listing 13–05 shows a sample action routine that is handy for testing this menu. (Real action routines are frequently even simpler than this one.)

Code Listing 13–05

```
**************************************************************
*** men1_action — action code for menu 1
**************************************************************

PROCEDURE men1_action
PARAMETER opt_num
PRIVATE k
```

```
DEFINE  WINDOW fake_win ;
       FROM  8, 40 ;
       TO   12, 66 ;
       PANEL ;
       COLOR W/R

ACTIVATE WINDOW fake_win

DO CASE
  CASE opt_num = 1
    @ 1, 1 SAY "This is fake action # 1"
  CASE opt_num = 2
    @ 1, 1 SAY "This is fake action # 2"
  CASE opt_num = 3
    @ 1, 1 SAY "This is fake action # 3"
  CASE opt_num = 4
    @ 1, 1 SAY "This is fake action # 4"
ENDCASE

k = INKEY(0)
RELEASE WINDOW fake_win

RETURN                              && end of men1_action
```

As you can see, there is nothing particularly complex about a menu routine. Of course, this omits some small details, like cleaning up the window after you exit from the menu. Listing 13–06 shows the complete code, with nothing left out.

Code Listing 13–06

```
* MENU1.PRG - menu sample 1
* copyright 1993, Martin L. Rinehart

PRIVATE i
SET TALK OFF
SET CURSOR OFF

DEFINE  WINDOW menwin ;
       FROM 5, 10 ;
       TO   15, 34 ;
       DOUBLE ;
       COLOR +W/B

ACTIVATE WINDOW menwin

STORE 1 TO hi_opt, i
num_opts = 4
```

```
DO WHILE i <= num_opts
  DO men1_hilo WITH i, i=hi_opt
  i = i + 1
ENDDO

* keystroke loop
DO WHILE .T.
  last_key = INKEY(0)

  DO CASE

    CASE last_key = 17 .OR. ;
         last_key = 27 && ^Q or Esc
       EXIT

    CASE last_key = 13 .OR. ;
         last_key = 23 && Enter or ^W
       DO men1_action WITH hi_opt

    CASE last_key = 5 && Up arrow or ^E
       DO men1_hilo WITH hi_opt, .F.
       hi_opt = IIF( hi_opt = 1, num_opts, hi_opt-1 )
       DO men1_hilo WITH hi_opt, .T.

    CASE last_key = 24 && Down arrow or ^X
       DO men1_hilo WITH hi_opt, .F.
       hi_opt = IIF( hi_opt = num_opts, 1, hi_opt+1 )
       DO men1_hilo WITH hi_opt, .T.

    OTHERWISE
       * do nothing or ?? CHR(7) (beep) if you want

  ENDCASE
ENDDO

RELEASE WINDOW menwin

*************************************************************
*** men1_action — action code for menu 1
*************************************************************

PROCEDURE men1_action
PARAMETER opt_num
PRIVATE k

DEFINE  WINDOW fake_win ;
      FROM  8, 40 ;
      TO   12, 66 ;
      PANEL ;
      COLOR W/R
```

```
ACTIVATE WINDOW fake_win

DO CASE
  CASE opt_num = 1
    @ 1, 1 SAY "This is fake action # 1"
  CASE opt_num = 2
    @ 1, 1 SAY "This is fake action # 2"
  CASE opt_num = 3
    @ 1, 1 SAY "This is fake action # 3"
  CASE opt_num = 4
    @ 1, 1 SAY "This is fake action # 4"
ENDCASE

k = INKEY(0)
RELEASE WINDOW fake_win

RETURN                                    && end of men1_action


*************************************************************
*** men1_hilo — hilite/lolite for menu 1
*************************************************************

PROCEDURE men1_hilo
PARAMETER opt_num, is_hi

IF is_hi
  SET COLOR TO +W/BG
ELSE
  SET COLOR TO W/B
ENDIF

DO CASE
  CASE opt_num = 1
    @  1, 1 SAY " Everyone's option   "

  CASE opt_num = 2
    @  3, 1 SAY " Universal option    "

  CASE opt_num = 3
    @  5, 1 SAY " Private option      "

  CASE opt_num = 4
    @  7, 1 SAY " Very private option "
ENDCASE

RETURN                                    && end of men1_hilo


*************************************************************

* end of file MENU1.PRG
```

Writing a menu from scratch is a bit like baking a cake from scratch. It's not hard once you know how, but there are so many good mixes on the market that it's hard to justify the extra trouble.

Unlike cakes, though, you can do interesting things to make your menus function your own way if you write them yourself. Let's add first-letter sensitivity to this menu to see what it's like to add a feature.

First-Letter Sensitivity

Right now, our menu does not respond to the user pressing a letter that corresponds to a menu option. Let's add this feature, as a sample of the type of work involved in adding a feature. Listing 13–07 shows the new lines added to MENU1.PRG in a lighter shade. The rest of the program is unchanged.

Code Listing 13–07

```
STORE 1 TO hi_opt, i
num_opts = 4
first_lets = 'EUPV'

DO WHILE i <= num_opts
  DO men1_hilo WITH i, i=hi_opt
  i = i + 1
ENDDO

* keystroke loop
DO WHILE .T.
  last_key = INKEY(0)
  ltr = UPPER( CHR(last_key) )

  DO CASE

    CASE last_key = 17 .OR. ;
         last_key = 27 && ^Q or Esc
      EXIT

    CASE ltr$first_lets
      DO men1_hilo WITH hi_opt, .F.
      hi_opt = AT( ltr, first_lets )
      DO men1_hilo WITH hi_opt, .T.
      DO men1_action WITH hi_opt

    CASE last_key = 13 .OR. ;
```

As you see, there are three pieces needed. First, we add a string of the relevant letters. Next, we simplify the upcoming CASE by assigning the variable "ltr" the uppercase character version of the user's keystroke. Finally, a CASE is added to process the occurrences of these keys.

The CASE has to move the light bar and call the associated action routine. (For your purposes, it may be better not to immediately call the action routine. That's just a matter of leaving out the call to the men1_action() routine.)

In this case, I've used the first letters of each menu option. The code works just as well if you choose different letters for the "first_lets" variable. A similar technique handles Control "hot keys."

Writing a Menu Engine

It's a bit more work to write your own menuing engine, but once it's built, building custom menus is just as easy as using the dBASE built-in menu capabilities. Again, the dBASE built-in commands, such as DEFINE BAR, only provide the data with which the dBASE menu engine works.

Programmers who program engine-driven menus and other modules delight in making their code as tight as possible. Here, I'll do a menu engine that is not totally crunched, but is very small. First, you have to define a menu's parameters. This will be a combination of global variables (the menu colors are one good candidate) and individual variables for the menus.

I put the colors into globals and the menu into a string, as Listing 13–08 shows:

Code Listing 13–08

```
menu_clr = '+W/B'
hilit_clr = '+W/BG'
lolit_clr = 'W/B'

* menu structure is:
* top, left, bottom, right, ;
* num_opts, first_lets, ;
* options:
*   length (one byte), text
```

```
menu1 = CHR(5) + CHR(10) + CHR(15) + CHR(34) && coordinates
menu1 = menu1 + CHR(4) + 'EUPV' && num_opts + first_lets
menu1 = menu1 + CHR(17) + "Everyone's option"
menu1 = menu1 + CHR(16) + "Universal option"
menu1 = menu1 + CHR(14) + "Private option"
menu1 = menu1 + CHR(19) + "Very private option"

DO menu_eng WITH 'menu1', 'men1_action'
```

You can obviously create a lot of menus this way, at very little cost in RAM consumption. If you think about this string approach, you see that you can also store these strings in memvar files, or in .DBFs.

The menu engine looks very much like the code we wrote, except that it has to pick apart the menu string. The new setup code is in Listing 13–09.

Code Listing 13–09

```
****************************************************************
*** menu_eng — common menuing engine
****************************************************************

PROCEDURE menu_eng
PARAMETERS menu_str, action_name
PRIVATE menu, tp, lft, bttm, rght, num_opts, first_lets, ;
        opt_array, loc, i, prmpt_wdth, hi_opt

DECLARE opt_array[20]

menu = &menu_str
tp   = ASC( SUBSTR(menu,1,1) )
lft  = ASC( SUBSTR(menu,2,1) )
bttm = ASC( SUBSTR(menu,3,1) )
rght = ASC( SUBSTR(menu,4,1) )

num_opts = ASC( SUBSTR(menu,5,1) )
first_lets = SUBSTR( menu, 6, num_opts )

loc = 6 + num_opts

prmpt_wdth = 0

i = 1
DO WHILE i <= num_opts
  size = ASC( SUBSTR(menu,loc,1) )
```

```
  opt_array[i] = SUBSTR( menu, loc+1, size )
  prmpt_wdth = MAX( prmpt_wdth, LEN(opt_array[i]) )
  loc = loc + size + 1
  i = i + 1
ENDDO

DEFINE  WINDOW &menu_str ;
        FROM tp, lft ;
        TO  bttm, rght ;
        DOUBLE ;
        COLOR &menu_clr

ACTIVATE WINDOW &menu_str

STORE 1 TO hi_opt, i

DO WHILE i <= num_opts
  DO menu_hilo WITH i, i=hi_opt
  i = i + 1
ENDDO
```

Except for picking apart the compressed menu string, the work is very much what we had before.

If you have been reading the listings, you'll notice that there is no provision for a separate highlight/lowlight routine for each menu. We can get by with a single, generalized routine. This one uses double-spaced menu options. You might want one to do single-spaced options or add a byte to the menu string to specify the spacing.

Listing 13–10 shows a double-spacing version.

Code Listing 13–10

```
****************************************************************
*** menu_hilo — hilite/lolite for menu 1
****************************************************************

PROCEDURE menu_hilo
PARAMETER opt_num, is_hi
PRIVATE prompt

IF is_hi
  SET COLOR TO &hilit_clr
 ELSE
  SET COLOR TO &lolit_clr
ENDIF
```

```
prompt = opt_array[opt_num]
prompt = ' ' + prompt + SPACE( prmpt_wdth )

@ 2*opt_num-1, 1 SAY LEFT( prompt, prmpt_wdth+2 )

RETURN                                     && end of menu_hilo
```

The keystroke loop is unchanged, except that the calls to men1_hilo() become calls to the generalized menu_hilo() and the call to men1_action() becomes a call to "&action_name."

Listing 13–11 shows the full, engine-driven menu.

Code Listing 13–11

```
* MENU1.PRG — menu sample 1
* copyright 1993, Martin L. Rinehart

PRIVATE i, ltr, menu
SET TALK OFF
SET CURSOR OFF

menu_clr = '+W/B'
hilit_clr = '+W/BG'
lolit_clr = 'W/B'

* menu structure is:
* top, left, bottom, right, ;
* num_opts, first_lets, ;
* options:
*    length (one byte), text

menu1 = CHR(5) + CHR(10) + CHR(15) + CHR(34) && coordinates
menu1 = menu1 + CHR(4) + 'EUPV' && num_opts + first_lets
menu1 = menu1 + CHR(17) + "Everyone's option"
menu1 = menu1 + CHR(16) + "Universal option"
menu1 = menu1 + CHR(14) + "Private option"
menu1 = menu1 + CHR(19) + "Very private option"

DO menu_eng WITH 'menu1', 'men1_action'

**************************************************************
*** menu_eng — common menuing engine
**************************************************************

PROCEDURE menu_eng
PARAMETERS menu_str, action_name
PRIVATE menu, tp, lft, bttm, rght, num_opts, first_lets, ;
        opt_array, loc, i, prmpt_wdth, hi_opt
```

```
DECLARE opt_array[20]

menu = &menu_str
tp   = ASC( SUBSTR(menu,1,1) )
lft  = ASC( SUBSTR(menu,2,1) )
bttm = ASC( SUBSTR(menu,3,1) )
rght = ASC( SUBSTR(menu,4,1) )

num_opts = ASC( SUBSTR(menu,5,1) )
first_lets = SUBSTR( menu, 6, num_opts )

loc = 6 + num_opts

prmpt_wdth = 0

i = 1
DO WHILE i <= num_opts
   size = ASC( SUBSTR(menu,loc,1) )
   opt_array[i] = SUBSTR( menu, loc+1, size )
   prmpt_wdth = MAX( prmpt_wdth, LEN(opt_array[i]) )
   loc = loc + size + 1
   i = i + 1
ENDDO

DEFINE  WINDOW &menu_str ;
        FROM tp, lft ;
        TO  bttm, rght ;
        DOUBLE ;
        COLOR &menu_clr

ACTIVATE WINDOW &menu_str

STORE 1 TO hi_opt, i

DO WHILE i <= num_opts
   DO menu_hilo WITH i, i=hi_opt
   i = i + 1
ENDDO

* keystroke loop
DO WHILE .T.
   last_key = INKEY(0)
   ltr = UPPER( CHR(last_key) )

   DO CASE

      CASE last_key = 17 .OR. ;
           last_key = 27 && ^Q or Esc
         EXIT
```

```
        CASE ltr$first_lets
           DO menu_hilo WITH hi_opt, .F.
           hi_opt = AT( ltr, first_lets )
           DO menu_hilo WITH hi_opt, .T.
           DO &action_name WITH hi_opt

        CASE last_key = 13 .OR. ;
             last_key = 23 && Enter or ^W
           DO &action_name WITH hi_opt

        CASE last_key = 5 && Up arrow or ^E
           DO menu_hilo WITH hi_opt, .F.
           hi_opt = IIF( hi_opt = 1, num_opts, hi_opt-1 )
           DO menu_hilo WITH hi_opt, .T.

        CASE last_key = 24 && Down arrow or ^X
           DO menu_hilo WITH hi_opt, .F.
           hi_opt = IIF( hi_opt = num_opts, 1, hi_opt+1 )
           DO menu_hilo WITH hi_opt, .T.

        OTHERWISE
           * do nothing or ?? CHR(7) (beep) if you want

     ENDCASE
ENDDO

RELEASE WINDOW &menu_str

*****************************************************************
*** men1_action — action code for menu 1
*****************************************************************

PROCEDURE men1_action
PARAMETER opt_num
PRIVATE k

DEFINE  WINDOW fake_win ;
        FROM  8, 40 ;
        TO   12, 66 ;
        PANEL ;
        COLOR W/R

ACTIVATE WINDOW fake_win

DO CASE
  CASE opt_num = 1
    @ 1, 1 SAY "This is fake action # 1"
  CASE opt_num = 2
    @ 1, 1 SAY "This is fake action # 2"
```

```
   CASE opt_num = 3
      @ 1, 1 SAY "This is fake action # 3"
   CASE opt_num = 4
      @ 1, 1 SAY "This is fake action # 4"
ENDCASE

k = INKEY(0)
RELEASE WINDOW fake_win

RETURN                                     && end of men1_action


*****************************************************************
*** menu_hilo — hilite/lolite for menu 1
*****************************************************************

PROCEDURE menu_hilo
PARAMETER opt_num, is_hi
PRIVATE prompt

IF is_hi
  SET COLOR TO &hilit_clr
 ELSE
  SET COLOR TO &lolit_clr
ENDIF

prompt = opt_array[opt_num]
prompt = ' ' + prompt + SPACE( prmpt_wdth )

@ 2*opt_num-1, 1 SAY LEFT( prompt, prmpt_wdth+2 )

RETURN                                     && end of menu_hilo


*****************************************************************

* end of file MENU1.PRG
```

From now on, all you have to do to create a custom menu is create a new menu string and write the menu action routine. Listing 13–12 is the code for a second menu.

Code Listing 13–12

```
* MENU2.PRG — sample nested pulldown

menu2 = CHR(7) + CHR(30) + CHR(15) + CHR(43) && coordinates
menu2 = menu2 + CHR(3) + 'ABC' && num_opts + first_lets
```

```
menu2 = menu2 + CHR(8) + "Option A"
menu2 = menu2 + CHR(8) + "Option B"
menu2 = menu2 + CHR(8) + "Option C"

DO menu_eng WITH 'menu2', 'men2_action'

**************************************************************
*** men2_action — action code for menu 1
**************************************************************
PROCEDURE men2_action
PARAMETER opt_num
PRIVATE k

DEFINE  WINDOW fake2 ;
        FROM  8, 40 ;
        TO   12, 66 ;
        PANEL ;
        COLOR W/G

ACTIVATE WINDOW fake2

DO CASE
  CASE opt_num = 1
    @ 1, 1 SAY "This is fake action A"
  CASE opt_num = 2
    @ 1, 1 SAY "This is fake action B"
  CASE opt_num = 3
    @ 1, 1 SAY "This is fake action C"
ENDCASE

k = INKEY(0)
RELEASE WINDOW fake2

RETURN                              && end of men2_action

* end of file MENU2.PRG
```

Listing 13–13 highlights the simple change needed to call this second menu from the first option of our original menu.

Code Listing 13–13

```
DO CASE
  CASE opt_num = 1
    DO menu2

  CASE opt_num = 2
    @ 1, 1 SAY "This is fake action # 2"
```

If you like to compress things, there is really no reason to have a separate action routine for each menu. You can generalize that, and add the option action code as substrings in the menu. It's up to you.

Adding Security to the Menu Engine

Now that we have a general-purpose menu engine, our last job is to modify it so that it will only display the menu options our user is entitled to access.

First, we will need a routine that looks up the permissions granted to the user for this menu. It will return a string of "Y"s and "N"s, showing the Yes (access permitted) or No permissions granted this user.

In Chapter 16 we will discuss permissions in detail. For the moment, let's stub out a simple test routine. Listing 13–14 shows mine.

Code Listing 13–14

```
*******************************************************************
*** opt_perm – checks user's option permissions
*******************************************************************

FUNCTION opt_perm
PARAMETERS user, menu
PRIVATE perms

* Test code only. Ignores user.
* In practice this data comes from a table.

DO CASE
  CASE menu = 'menu1'
     perms = 'YYYN'

  CASE menu = 'menu2'
     perms = 'YNY'
ENDCASE

RETURN perms                              && end of opt_perm
```

In this test, our user is granted permissions for all options except "Very Private" on the first menu. On the second menu, the user can access options "A" and "C," but not "B."

The main job added to our menu engine is to adjust "first_lets," "num_opts," and "opt_array" based on the permissions granted. We also create a new array, "actions," to record action indexes.

The "actions" array is used when we call the action routine. We can't use "hi_opt" directly, since the second menu option may not be the second action item. In the menu2 case above, permissions are "YNY." The user will see a menu that has two prompts: "Option A" and "Option C." If the user chooses "Option C," "hi_opt" will be 2, but you actually want to execute the third action routine.

Listing 13–15 shows the working part of the new setup code in the menu engine routine.

Code Listing 13–15

```
ok_opts = opt_perm( user_name, menu_str )
old_num = num_opts
old_lets = first_lets

i = 1
num_opts = 0
first_lets = ''

DO WHILE i <= old_num

  IF SUBSTR( ok_opts, i, 1 ) = 'Y'
     num_opts = num_opts + 1
     first_lets = first_lets + SUBSTR( old_lets, i, 1 )
     opt_array[num_opts] = opt_array[i]
     actions[num_opts] = i
   ELSE
     bttm = bttm - 2
  ENDIF

  i = i + 1
ENDDO
```

Note that this code also brings the bottom line of the menu up for every option that has an "N" permission. This is so the user won't see a menu with "holes" where options disappeared.

Listing 13–16 highlights the two changed lines in the keystroke loop that call the action routine.

Code Listing 13–16

```
CASE ltr$first_lets
   DO menu_hilo WITH hi_opt, .F.
   hi_opt = AT( ltr, first_lets )
   DO menu_hilo WITH hi_opt, .T.
   DO &action_name WITH actions[ hi_opt ]

CASE last_key = 13 .OR. ;
     last_key = 23 && Enter or ^W
   DO &action_name WITH actions[ hi_opt ]

CASE last_key = 5 && Up arrow or ^E
```

Listing 13–17 shows the final version of MENU1.PRG. Note that there are no changes in MENU2.PRG and there will be no changes in any other menu routine. The part of MENU1.PRG that defines "menu1" is unchanged. The permission sub-system was fit neatly into the menu engine, without changing the other code in the system.

Code Listing 13–17

```
* MENU1.PRG — menu sample 1
* copyright 1993, Martin L. Rinehart

PRIVATE i, ltr, menu
SET TALK OFF
SET CURSOR OFF
user_name = 'USER1'

menu_clr = '+W/B'
hilit_clr = '+W/BG'
lolit_clr = 'W/B'

* menu structure is:
* top, left, bottom, right, ;
* num_opts, first_lets, ;
* options:
*    length (one byte), text

menu1 = CHR(5) + CHR(10) + CHR(15) + CHR(34) && coordinates
menu1 = menu1 + CHR(4) + 'EUPV' && num_opts + first_lets
menu1 = menu1 + CHR(17) + "Everyone's option"
menu1 = menu1 + CHR(16) + "Universal option"
menu1 = menu1 + CHR(14) + "Private option"
menu1 = menu1 + CHR(19) + "Very private option"
```

```
DO menu_eng WITH 'menu1', 'men1_action'

*************************************************************
*** menu_eng — common menuing engine
*************************************************************

PROCEDURE menu_eng
PARAMETERS menu_str, action_name
PRIVATE menu, tp, lft, bttm, rght, num_opts, first_lets, ;
       opt_array, loc, i, prmpt_wdth, hi_opt
PRIVATE ok_opts, old_num, old_lets, actions

DECLARE opt_array[20]
DECLARE actions[20]

menu = &menu_str
tp   = ASC( SUBSTR(menu,1,1) )
lft  = ASC( SUBSTR(menu,2,1) )
bttm = ASC( SUBSTR(menu,3,1) )
rght = ASC( SUBSTR(menu,4,1) )

num_opts = ASC( SUBSTR(menu,5,1) )
first_lets = SUBSTR( menu, 6, num_opts )

loc = 6 + num_opts

prmpt_wdth = 0

i = 1
DO WHILE i <= num_opts
  size = ASC( SUBSTR(menu,loc,1) )
  opt_array[i] = SUBSTR( menu, loc+1, size )
  prmpt_wdth = MAX( prmpt_wdth, LEN(opt_array[i]) )
  loc = loc + size + 1
  i = i + 1
ENDDO

ok_opts = opt_perm( user_name, menu_str )
old_num = num_opts
old_lets = first_lets

i = 1
num_opts = 0
first_lets = ''

DO WHILE i <= old_num

  IF SUBSTR( ok_opts, i, 1 ) = 'Y'
     num_opts = num_opts + 1
     first_lets = first_lets + SUBSTR( old_lets, i, 1 )
```

```
        opt_array[num_opts] = opt_array[i]
        actions[num_opts] = i
      ELSE
      bttm = bttm - 2
    ENDIF

  i = i + 1
ENDDO

DEFINE  WINDOW &menu_str ;
       FROM tp, lft ;
       TO  bttm, rght ;
       DOUBLE ;
       COLOR &menu_clr

ACTIVATE WINDOW &menu_str

STORE 1 TO hi_opt, i

DO WHILE i <= num_opts
  DO menu_hilo WITH i, i=hi_opt
  i = i + 1
ENDDO

* keystroke loop
DO WHILE .T.
  last_key = INKEY(0)
  ltr = UPPER( CHR(last_key) )

  DO CASE

     CASE last_key = 17 .OR. ;
          last_key = 27 && ^Q or Esc
        EXIT

     CASE ltr$first_lets
        DO menu_hilo WITH hi_opt, .F.
        hi_opt = AT( ltr, first_lets )
        DO menu_hilo WITH hi_opt, .T.
        DO &action_name WITH actions[ hi_opt ]

     CASE last_key = 13 .OR. ;
          last_key = 23 && Enter or ^W
        DO &action_name WITH actions[ hi_opt ]

     CASE last_key = 5 && Up arrow or ^E
        DO menu_hilo WITH hi_opt, .F.
        hi_opt = IIF( hi_opt = 1, num_opts, hi_opt-1 )
        DO menu_hilo WITH hi_opt, .T.
```

```
      CASE last_key = 24 && Down arrow or ^X
         DO menu_hilo WITH hi_opt, .F.
         hi_opt = IIF( hi_opt = num_opts, 1, hi_opt+1 )
         DO menu_hilo WITH hi_opt, .T.

      OTHERWISE
         * do nothing or ?? CHR(7) (beep) if you want

   ENDCASE
ENDDO

RELEASE WINDOW &menu_str

****************************************************************
*** men1_action — action code for menu 1
****************************************************************

PROCEDURE men1_action
PARAMETER opt_num
PRIVATE k

DEFINE  WINDOW fake_win ;
      FROM  8, 40 ;
      TO   12, 66 ;
      PANEL ;
      COLOR W/R

ACTIVATE WINDOW fake_win

DO CASE
   CASE opt_num = 1
      DO menu2

   CASE opt_num = 2
      @ 1, 1 SAY "This is fake action # 2"
   CASE opt_num = 3
      @ 1, 1 SAY "This is fake action # 3"
   CASE opt_num = 4
      @ 1, 1 SAY "This is fake action # 4"
ENDCASE

k = INKEY(0)
RELEASE WINDOW fake_win

RETURN                                  && end of men1_action


****************************************************************
*** menu_hilo — hilite/lolite for menu 1
****************************************************************
```

```
PROCEDURE menu_hilo
PARAMETER opt_num, is_hi
PRIVATE prompt

IF is_hi
   SET COLOR TO &hilit_clr
ELSE
   SET COLOR TO &lolit_clr
ENDIF

prompt = opt_array[opt_num]
prompt = ' ' + prompt + SPACE( prmpt_wdth )

@ 2*opt_num-1, 1 SAY LEFT( prompt, prmpt_wdth+2 )

RETURN                                    && end of menu_hilo


****************************************************************
*** opt_perm — checks user's option permissions
****************************************************************

FUNCTION opt_perm
PARAMETERS user, menu
PRIVATE perms

* Test code only. Ignores user.
* In practice this data comes from a table.

DO CASE
   CASE menu = 'menu1'
      perms = 'YYYN'

   CASE menu = 'menu2'
      perms = 'YNY'
ENDCASE

RETURN perms                              && end of opt_perm


****************************************************************

* end of file MENU1.PRG
```

When you build engine routines like this one, pay particular attention to the PRIVATE declarations. Remember that this engine is called by a main routine. The engine then calls an action routine. One of the common things for an action routine to do is another menu, which will call the engine again.

The engine code must be fully re-entrant. That means that it cannot modify any global variables, and that all its working data must be in PRIVATE variables. To see what happens when you do this wrong, remove "hi_opt" from the list of PRIVATEs and run the code again.

Summary

While dBASE includes many excellent tools for building menus without any programming (or, more accurately, with the programming being done for you by dBASE's template system), client-server systems demand additional security that is best provided by writing your own menuing system. Our basic goal is to have menus that will allow selected menu options to simply never appear on users' screens if they don't have permission to use the item.

We don't want to show an option that says "privileged data here!" and then, when the user tries to select that option respond "but not for you." We don't want the users to even see options to which they have not been granted privileges. This requires a custom menu capability, which is shown here.

All menu code shares a common structure. There is some setup code, a keystroke loop, and a highlight/lowlight system. The key-stroke-loop code shows menu activities by appropriately calling the highlight/lowlight system. The light bar is moved by lowlighting the current choice, then highlighting a new choice. Menu action code may either be in a separate subroutine, or built into the keystroke handler.

The setup code is simple. You establish variables that set the number of menu options and other menu facts. Then you define and activate a window that will hold the menu. Control is then passed to the keystoke controller. On return, you release the window.

The highlight/lowlight system is simple, too. It's called with an option number, and a logical flag specifying whether the color is to be high or low. After setting the color as directed by the flag, the routine picks the appropriate option with a DO CASE switch, and @ SAYs the option.

The keystroke handler is an infinite loop that gets keystrokes and processes them. Exit keystrokes, such as ESC, terminate the loop. Action keystrokes, such as Enter, call the menu action code. Movement keystrokes lowlight the current option, select a new current option, and highlight it.

The menu action code, whether separate or built into the keystroke loop, is a DO CASE switch. It has one CASE for each menu option. The code within the CASE executes whatever action should be registered when the user selects the associated menu option.

Professional menus should also have first-letter sensitivity. When an appropriate letter is pressed, the keystroke handler first moves the light bar by lowlighting the current option, selecting the new option, and highlighting it. Then it calls the action code for the newly highlighted option.

Some of this code sets up parameters that are unique to each menu, such as the number of options, their text, and their placement. Other parts of the code are common to all menus, such as processing arrow keys. I separate the common code into a general-purpose menu engine to drive all the menus. This saves program space, as well as your coding time. With this engine (plus your custom additions), it's no more trouble to program our custom menus than it was to use dBASEs' built-in features.

Finally, we looked at the security features that were the requirement that induced us to create our own menus. I showed you code that first asked the permission system for a list of legal options. Based on this list, it appropriately adjusted the menu so that only the permitted options were shown, with no "holes" left to indicate missing options. We ended up with a menu engine that would show different menus to different users, depending on their permissions.

With this engine, these flexible menus that change for each user are no more trouble to code than simple, fixed menus, using the dBASE built-in menuing commands.

In the next chapter, we'll use the same techniques to build our own scroller. Again, we'll need to abandon the dBASE built-ins (such as BROWSE) to get the level of precise control that good client-server systems require.

Chapter 14

Client-Server Scrolling

I build my applications around the .DBF scroller. Right now, you may use the BROWSE command as a quick scroller. In this chapter, I'll explain how I use the scroller, and how to build one that goes beyond BROWSE's capabilities. You'll see in Chapter 15 that this is key to maintaining data integrity.

Back in the early 1980s I wrote my first general-purpose dBASE data maintenance applications. They were built with a record-oriented view, and had a bottom-line menu with options like "Next" and "Previous," to let you scroll through the data.

I don't think those applications are up to today's standards. Some years back I changed to a scroller. The user interface built around scrollers requires much less training and provides more features. I let the user scroll with the standard PC navigation keys (arrows, PgUp/Dn, Home, and End). The Ins and Del keys provide the obvious record insert and delete functions.

The same scroller that lets a user look through the customer table, for example, can also serve as a point-and-shoot device when the user is entering an invoice and needs to pick a customer. With the record range appropriately restricted, the scroller works equally well when you want to let the user browse through the invoices attached to a particular customer.

There is one problem with the BROWSE-type view that is not associated with the record view. With the record view, you can see John Smith's name, full address, telephone numbers, and so on. With a typical BROWSE view, you are lucky if you can fit much more than a name and maybe another field or two.

I combine the best of both worlds by showing a BROWSE-type window and simultaneously showing a record-oriented view. The data in the record-oriented window changes as the user moves the highlight bar in the BROWSE window.

Of course, this means that you have to provide your own scroller since you will be going beyond the capabilities of dBASE's BROWSE. Don't be tempted to skip this step, since the extra work of providing the scroller lets you eliminate almost all of the problems normally associated with maintaining referential integrity, as we'll discuss in the next chapter.

You'll see that scrolling lets us neatly tie together what we've learned about keys, relationships, and indexes and filters. BROWSE code is, like many things in programming, not difficult once you know how it's done. But there is a significant problem we have to address before we can take advantage of our scroller.

Field Read Loop

Think about a typical invoicing sub-system, specifically the part that lets a user enter an invoice. We want the user to enter or confirm some preliminary information, such as date and perhaps an invoice number. Then we'll pop up the customer list, so the user can select one via point-and-shoot. Next we'll enter the invoice detail lines.

That could be another point-and-shoot where the user picks a product from the product table. Then the user types the quantity ordered and other detail items. Finally, the user enters or confirms some more data, such as shipping and tax information, to complete the invoice.

For maintaining invoices (corrections, additions, and deletions), we give the user a scroller that shows, perhaps, the customer's name, invoice date, and total amount.

Now we have a scroller for the invoice table. In the invoice entry process, we called the customer table scroller for point-and-shoot lookup (M*:1 from invoices to customers). These were parent record lookups.

Then we called another scroller for entering repeated invoice detail lines. (The scroller lets the user go back and forth to make corrections in the detail records.) There is a 1:M+ relationship from invoices to invoice detail items.

From the invoice details, we called another scroller for point-and-shoot lookup in the product table (1:M* from invoice details to products). In the point-and-shoot lookups, we have no problems other than routine coding tasks.

But when we changed from the invoice data entry to the invoice detail line scroller, we had to place a "hold" on the invoice fields while we entered invoice detail records. And, if we let the user enter a new customer into the database, we have another instance where we want to put one set of fields on hold to enter another set of fields.

To make effective use of our scrollers, we want to have a stack where we can push and pop complete sets of field reads. The convenience of dBASE's @ GET/READ commands has suddenly become a liability. What we really need is to read each field individually or we will have to do a great deal of coding to customize each table's data-entry process. Of course, we don't want to lose the convenience of the navigation keys for moving between fields, either.

This seeming contradiction is surprisingly simple to arrange.

GET/READ Pairs

First, we need to put a READ command after every @ GET. That will let us pop up a scroller into another data-entry form without worrying about pending GETs, since there won't be any. Unfortunately, it will also destroy our navigation capability, so we'll have to create a framework to rectify this.

This is a sample GET/READ routine that will let us use a custom controller to handle the navigation:

```
PROCEDURE cust_get
PARAMETER which_fld

DO CASE
    CASE which_fld = 1
        @ r1, c1 GET name PICTURE . . .

    CASE which_fld = 2
        @ r2, c2 GET address VALID . . .

    CASE which_fld = 3
        etc.

ENDCASE

READ

RETURN
```

If you keep a generic routine on file, with lots of CASEs but no @ GETs, you can just delete any extra CASEs and then type in your @ GETs. This is barely more trouble than just typing the @ GETs. The real trouble with this code is the same as with regular @ GETs—you have to carefully think through PICTURE, VALID, and other clauses.

As you can see, if you called this routine in a loop, it would GET all the fields from first to last. This is what that could look like:

```
fld_num = 1
DO WHILE fld_num <= max_flds

    DO cust_get WITH fld_num
    fld_num = fld_num + 1

ENDDO
```

Of course, this is not quite what you want. If the user presses the Up arrow to exit the third field, you don't want the cursor to calmly hop down to the fourth field. You want the cursor to hop up to the second field, of course.

Navigating in the Fields

Navigating in the fields is less trouble than it might first appear. The one line in the calling loop has to be a little bit smarter. Here, in pcode, is the general idea.

```
fld_num = 1
DO WHILE fld_num <= max_flds

   DO cust_get WITH fld_num

   IF LASTKEY() = Up_arrow
      fld_num = fld_num - 1
    ELSE
      fld_num = fld_num + 1
   ENDIF

ENDDO
```

This still does not handle all the possibilities, of course. If the user presses ^W, we want to write the new data to disk and leave the loop. On Esc or ^Q, we want to exit without writing the data, and so on. The code in Listing 14–01 is a typical field loop handler.

Code Listing 14–01

```
field_num = 1

DO WHILE field_num < max_flds

  DO &get_name WITH field_num

  last_key = LASTKEY()
  DO CASE

     CASE (last_key = 23) && ^W
        DO &rep_name
        EXIT

     CASE (last_key = 17) .OR. ;
          (last_key = 27) && ^Q or Esc
        EXIT

     CASE (last_key =  9) .OR. ;
          (last_key = 24) && Tab or down arrow
```

```
        IF field_num = max_flds
           field_num = 1
         ELSE
           field_num = field_num + 1
        ENDIF

    CASE (last_key=-400) .OR. ;
         (last_key=    5) && Shift-Tab or up

       IF field_num > 1
          field_num = field_num - 1
        ELSE
          field_num = max_flds
        ENDIF

    CASE fld_num = max_flds && completed last field
       DO &rep_name
       EXIT

    OTHERWISE
       field_num = field_num + 1

    ENDCASE

ENDDO
```

This code handles the inter-field navigation. It handles Up and Down arrows; ^E and ^X; Tab and Shift-Tab; ^Q, Esc, and ^W. It wraps nicely from bottom to top and vice-versa. It will also exit nicely when the user completes the last field either by filling it or pressing Enter.

A Basic Scroller

Moving a light bar up and down a scroll window is not much different from moving it in a menu. You write one display routine that handles both highlighted and regular displays. To move the light bar, you call that routine to display the current row in the regular color, move to the next record, and display it in the highlighted color. Of course, we need to SKIP through the database as we do this.

Here is the basic Up arrow and Down arrow code:

```
CASE last_key =  5 && Up arrow or ^E
   DO display WITH current_row, .F.
   SKIP -1
   current_row = current_row - 1
   DO display WITH current_row, .T.

CASE last_key = 24 && Down arrow or ^X
   DO display WITH current_row, .F.
   SKIP
   current_row = current_row + 1
   DO display WITH current_row, .T.
```

Unfortunately, your scroller has to handle a lot of conditions that this simple code ignores. For instance, the Down arrow has to check to see if it is already at the bottom of the window. It has to check for the end of the file, too.

In fact, our Up and Down arrow routines are additional DO CASE switches. None of the code in the scroller is particularly complicated, but there are lots of conditions to handle.

Tracking Facts

The trick to a good scroller is keeping continuous track of what's where. I start by checking the first and last records in the file. (Remember that you will be scrolling in index order, not in record number order.) Then I track the records that are at the top and bottom of the display window.

Next, I keep continuous track of which row holds the highlighted record. Finally, I always have the database positioned at the highlighted record, so RECNO() is also the number of the highlighted record.

As an estimate, perhaps 90% of your non-trivial bugs will come from not having one of these facts correct. You can forget to update something, or update it with the wrong value. Either way, from then on your scroller will be misbehaving. Remember that the bug you see is probably *not* in the code you are executing. It would be in the code for whatever you did when the scroller last worked.

The Structure

As with a menu, a scroller has a little setup code and a keystroke loop. There is a highlight/lowlight display routine. Finally, there is a critical routine to display a full page of data. Except for arrow keys when the highlight is not at the end of either the window or file, everything works by displaying a full page.

A short header creates a window and then calls a general-purpose scroll engine. The highlight/lowlight routine is a simple one, coded individually for each .DBF.

The keystroke handler (event handler, if you add a mouse) takes care of PgUp and PgDn, Home, End, and so on. Arrow keys at either end of the window also call the page display routine. There is no actual scrolling in the code I am going to show you. Scrolling is simulated by just redisplaying the full page. With modern equipment, this is completely smooth, but if you have to run on old, slow PCs, use small windows to improve the feel of the scroller.

All the variables in the scroller are private, to let you call another scroller within a scroller. As with the field handling, you need re-entrant code, which means that you cannot modify global variables.

Debugging Code

I always assume that I am not smart enough to write code that will work without debugging. So I take a little time to design the debugging process. Since experience has taught me that most scroller bugs occur in the fact set that should always be maintained, I build a display for the fact set and watch it carefully as I run the scroller.

If you start out with a scroll window that is wider than necessary, you'll have space to put these facts to the right of the scroll area. As you'll see, I leave this display code in comments until I need it.

The Page Display Routine

Let's begin looking at the setup code. The job of the display routine is simple, but it must be meticulous about maintaining these variables created in the scroll engine. Listing 14–02 shows the setup code.

Code Listing 14–02

```
* bof_rec - the record at the beginning of the file
* top_rec - the top visible record
* bot_rec - the bottom visible record
* eof_rec - the last actual record in the file

* hi_row  - the highlighted row
* the file is always positioned at the highlighted record

GO BOTTOM
eof_rec = RECNO()

GO TOP
bof_rec = RECNO()

STORE 0 to top_rec, bot_rec
seek_chrs = ''

hi_row = disp_page(0)
```

The rows we use are zero through "last_row," a parameter. The page display routine, disp_page(), is called with the row we want to highlight. It also returns the row that it highlighted.

This seems strange when you look at the first call. But it makes sense if you think about the possibility of short files that do not entirely fill the scroll window. Disp_page() could be called with a request that it highlight the fourth line, but might find that there are only three lines to display.

With that introduction, let's look at the routine. Disp_page() is shown in Listing 14–03.

Code Listing 14–03

```
*************************************************************
*** disp_page - display a full page of data
*************************************************************

FUNCTION disp_page
PARAMETER hi_line
PRIVATE i, r, hi, hi_rec

* Note: disp_page will highlight the last row of data if
* hi_line would be past the end of the file.
```

```
top_rec = RECNO()
hi_rec = 0
hi = hi_line

i = 0
DO WHILE ( i <= last_row )

  IF ( hi_rec = 0 ) .AND. ( RECNO() = eof_rec )
     hi = i
  ENDIF

  DO &ld_name WITH i, i = hi

  IF i = hi
     hi_rec = RECNO()
  ENDIF

  i = i + 1
  IF .NOT. EOF()
     SKIP
  ENDIF

ENDDO

SKIP -1

bot_rec = RECNO()

GO hi_rec

IF LEN(seek_chrs) = 0
  @ last_row+1, 1 SAY SPACE(12) COLOR &swin_clr
ENDIF

RETURN hi                              && end of disp_page
```

To use disp_page(), your calling routine first positions the rec-ord pointer to the first record to display. From there, disp_page() writes a full page of records into the scroll window.

Actually, disp_page writes a full page or less (if EOF() is encountered before the end of the page). The individual-line display routine is responsible for putting a blank line in place if the .DBF is at EOF(). This way, disp_page() always writes a window-full of lines. These will either be data or will clear the extra window lines.

Disp_page() carefully records "top_rec," "bot_rec," and "hi_rec." Note that it gets "hi_rec" right even if it comes to EOF() before it reaches the row that the calling routine wanted highlighted.

The Custom Display Routine

The hand-coded, .DBF-specific display routine is short and simple, as you can see in Listing 14–04.

Code Listing 14–04

```
**************************************************************
*** ld_people - line display for PEOPLE.DBF
**************************************************************

PROCEDURE ld_people
PARAMETER row, is_hi

IF is_hi
  SET COLOR TO +GR/BG
ELSE
  SET COLOR TO W/B
ENDIF

IF EOF()
  @ row, 0 SAY SPACE(34)
ELSE
  @ row, 0 SAY ' ' + people->name + ' '
ENDIF


RETURN                              && end of ld_people
```

There are two issues to bear in mind. First, you want to set the correct color. Next, your routine has to clear the window line if the .DBF is at EOF(). When you're not at EOF(), you display whatever data is appropriate.

The Calling Program

The calling program has to provide the window and a .DBF open in the current work-area. The order in which the contents of the .DBF is displayed has to be one that the user will find natural for scrolling.

Listing 14–05 shows a sample calling program.

Code Listing 14–05

```
USE people
SET ORDER TO name

swin_clr = 'W/B'

DEFINE WINDOW people_s ;
      FROM 10, 20 ;
      TO   21, 55 ;
      COLOR &swin_clr,,+W/B ;
      DOUBLE

ACTIVATE WINDOW people_s
DO scroll WITH 'ld_people', 8
RELEASE WINDOW people_s
```

With this code, we have seen everything except the keystroke loop.

The Keystroke Loop

The keystroke loop is not complicated, but it is not short. We have a lot of things to handle, and many of these things are simple but with lots of exceptions to handle. As with a menu, the superstructure is an infinite loop, with provisions to exit when the user orders it. It looks like this:

```
DO WHILE .T.
   last_key = INKEY(0)

   DO CASE
      CASE last_key = this,
         * code for "this"

      CASE last_key = that, or
         * code for "that"

      CASE last_key = the other
         * code for "the other"

   ENDCASE
ENDDO
```

Let's look at the keystroke loop code two pieces at a time. The keystrokes come in pairs, and the handlers are close to mirror images.

Up and Down Arrows

First, let's look at the Up and Down arrow keys. These each handle three conditions: being at the end of the file, being at the end of the page but not the end of the file, and being in the page.

Listing 14–06 shows the Up arrow code.

Code Listing 14–06

```
CASE last_key =  5 && Up arrow or ^E
   seek_chrs = ''

   DO CASE
      CASE RECNO() = bof_rec
         ?? CHR(7)

      CASE hi_row = 0
         GO top_rec
         SKIP -1
         hi_row = disp_page(0)

      OTHERWISE
         DO &ld_name WITH hi_row, .F.
         SKIP -1
         hi_row = hi_row - 1
         DO &ld_name WITH hi_row, .T.
   ENDCASE
```

If the current record is the first record in the file, this code emits a protest beep and does nothing. If the highlighted record is at the top of the window, but is not the first one in the file, we skip backward one record, and call the page display routine, specifying highlighting of row 0.

If neither of those conditions apply, we can move the highlight bar upward within the page. We do this by the standard process of writing the current record in the regular color, then backing up and highlighting the previous record.

The Down arrow code is similar, as you see in Listing 14–07.

Code Listing 14–07

```
CASE last_key = 24 && Down arrow or ^X
   seek_chrs = ''

   DO CASE
      CASE RECNO() = eof_rec
         ?? CHR(7)

      CASE hi_row = last_row
         SKIP -(last_row-1)
         hi_row = disp_page(last_row)

      OTHERWISE
         DO &ld_name WITH hi_row, .F.
         SKIP
         hi_row = hi_row + 1
         DO &ld_name WITH hi_row, .T.
   ENDCASE
```

Again, we beep if we are already at the last record in the file. If we are at the bottom of the window, we skip backward to the record that is now the second record in the display. Then we call the page display routine asking it to highlight the last row.

If neither of those conditions apply, we perform the basic light bar movement.

PgUp and PgDn

The PgUp and PgDn code is simpler than the Up and Down arrow code, as you can see in Listing 14–08.

Code Listing 14–08

```
CASE last_key = 18 && PgUp or ^R
   seek_chrs = ''
   IF top_rec <> bof_rec
      GO top_rec
      SKIP -( last_row+1 )
      hi_row = disp_page( hi_row )
   ENDIF
```

```
CASE last_key =  3 && PgDn or ^C
   seek_chrs = ''
   IF bot_rec <> eof_rec
      GO bot_rec
      SKIP
      IF EOF()
         SKIP -1
      ENDIF
      hi_row = disp_page( hi_row )
   ENDIF
```

You can see that both cases do nothing if the highlighted record is at the end of the file from which you cannot move in the specified direction. If you can move, the PgUp code goes to the top displayed record and then skips backward a full page. The PgDn code goes to the bottom displayed record and then skips just one record.

Both then call for a new page display. They ask the page display routine to leave the highlight bar wherever it was when the key was pressed.

Home and End

The Home key is very simple. Since redisplaying the page is harmless if you are already at the beginning, it doesn't even check. It just goes to the first record and calls for a new page display. This is shown in Listing 14–09.

Code Listing 14–09

```
CASE last_key = 26 && Home or ^Z
   seek_chrs = ''
   GO bof_rec
   hi_row = disp_page( 0 )
```

The End key first checks to see if the last displayed record is actually the end of the file. If not, it does a full page display, showing the last page of data, highlighting the last row.

If the last page of data is already showing (possibly without completely filling the window), the page display routine is called to redisplay the page with the highlight bar at the last row.

Listing 14–10 shows this algorithm.

Code Listing 14–10

```
CASE last_key =  2 && End  or ^B
   seek_chrs = ''
   IF bot_rec <> eof_rec
      GO eof_rec
      SKIP -last_row
   ELSE
      GO top_rec
   ENDIF
   hi_row = disp_page( last_row )
```

In each of these routines, I've not mentioned the "seek_chrs" variable. This gets explained in the next section.

"SMI" To Find Smith

For scrolling in a large file, the ability to press, for example, an "S" and get to the first record starting with "S" is vital. We want the user to be able to press two or three keys and move instantly to the record that starts with those keys.

To support this capability, we should also let the user press the backspace key to delete the last one of these characters. This routine displays any characters used this way at "last_row" plus one in the scroll window.

The variable "seek_chrs" holds any characters the user has entered to do this seeking. Listing 14–11 shows the backspace editing code.

Code Listing 14–11

```
CASE last_key = 127 && Backspace
   IF LEN(seek_chrs) > 0
      seek_chrs = LEFT( seek_chrs, LEN(seek_chrs)-1 )
      IF LEN(seek_chrs) > 0
         @ last_row+1, 1 SAY ' ' + ;
            LEFT( seek_chrs, 10 ) + ' ' ;
            COLOR N/W
      ELSE
         @ last_row+1, 1 SAY SPACE(12) COLOR &swin_clr
      ENDIF
   ENDIF
```

As you can see, there are three conditions to handle. First, the backspace is ignored if the "seek_chrs" buffer is empty. If "seek_chrs" is not empty, there are two possibilities.

If there is just one character in "seek_chrs," this buffer is emptied and the display area is cleared. If there is more than one character, "seek_chrs" is appropriately shortened and the buffer is redisplayed.

Listing 14–12 shows the OTHERWISE case that handles adding keys to the "seek_chrs" buffer.

Code Listing 14–12

```
OTHERWISE
   r = RECNO()
   s = seek_chrs + UPPER( CHR(last_key) )
   SEEK s
   IF FOUND()
      seek_chrs = s
      hi_row = disp_page(0)
      @ last_row+1, 1 SAY ' ' + ;
         LEFT( seek_chrs, 10 ) + ' ' ;
         COLOR N/W
   ELSE
      GO r
   ENDIF
```

This code adds the uppercase version of the letter (or other key), then SEEKs for the appropriate value. If it finds it, it calls the page display routine and displays the new "seek_chrs" buffer. If it doesn't find the specified value, it is careful to return to the original position in the file. You might want to add a beep to the not-found portion of this code.

The Full Program

Listing 14–13 shows the full SCROLLER.PRG. This is a stand-alone program including a scroll engine, a sample call, and a sample data-display routine.

Code Listing 14-13

```
* SCROLLER.PRG — database scrolling routine
* copyright 1993, Martin L. Rinehart

SET TALK OFF
SET CURSOR OFF

USE people
SET ORDER TO name

swin_clr = 'W/B'

DEFINE WINDOW people_s ;
      FROM 10, 20 ;
      TO   21, 55 ;
      COLOR &swin_clr,,+W/B ;
      DOUBLE

ACTIVATE WINDOW people_s
DO scroll WITH 'ld_people', 8
RELEASE WINDOW people_s

SET CURSOR ON

*****************************************************************
*** scroll — lets the user scroll through a database
*****************************************************************

PROCEDURE scroll
PARAMETER ld_name, last_row
PRIVATE bof_rec, top_rec, bot_rec, eof_rec, ;
      hi_row, seek_chrs

* bof_rec — the record at the beginning of the file
* top_rec — the top visible record
* bot_rec — the bottom visible record
* eof_rec — the last actual record in the file

* hi_row  — the highlighted row
* the file is always positioned at the highlighted record

GO BOTTOM
eof_rec = RECNO()

GO TOP
bof_rec = RECNO()
```

```
STORE 0 to top_rec, bot_rec
seek_chrs = ''

hi_row = disp_page(0)

DO WHILE .T.
   * debugging code (use with a widened window)
   * set color to w/n
   * @ 0, 35 say 'bof_rec:'+str(bof_rec,3)
   * @ 1, 35 say 'top_rec:'+str(top_rec,3)
   * @ 2, 35 say 'bot_rec:'+str(bot_rec,3)
   * @ 3, 35 say 'eof_rec:'+str(eof_rec,3)
   * @ 4, 35 say 'hi_row :'+str(hi_row ,3)
   * @ 5, 35 say 'recno():'+str(recno(),3)

   last_key = INKEY(0)
   DO CASE
      CASE last_key = 27 && Esc
         EXIT

      CASE last_key =  5 && Up arrow or ^E
         seek_chrs = ''

         DO CASE
            CASE RECNO() = bof_rec
               ?? CHR(7)

            CASE hi_row = 0
               GO top_rec
               SKIP -1
               hi_row = disp_page(0)

            OTHERWISE
               DO &ld_name WITH hi_row, .F.
               SKIP -1
               hi_row = hi_row - 1
               DO &ld_name WITH hi_row, .T.
         ENDCASE

      CASE last_key = 24 && Down arrow or ^X
         seek_chrs = ''

         DO CASE
            CASE RECNO() = eof_rec
               ?? CHR(7)

            CASE hi_row = last_row
               SKIP -(last_row-1)
               hi_row = disp_page(last_row)
```

```
            OTHERWISE
                DO &ld_name WITH hi_row, .F.
                SKIP
                hi_row = hi_row + 1
                DO &ld_name WITH hi_row, .T.
        ENDCASE

    CASE last_key = 18 && PgUp or ^R
        seek_chrs = ''
        IF top_rec <> bof_rec
            GO top_rec
            SKIP -( last_row+1 )
            hi_row = disp_page( hi_row )
        ENDIF

    CASE last_key =  3 && PgDn or ^C
        seek_chrs = ''
        IF bot_rec <> eof_rec
            GO bot_rec
            SKIP
            IF EOF()
                SKIP -1
            ENDIF
            hi_row = disp_page( hi_row )
        ENDIF

    CASE last_key = 26 && Home or ^Z
        seek_chrs = ''
        GO bof_rec
        hi_row = disp_page( 0 )

    CASE last_key =  2 && End  or ^B
        seek_chrs = ''
        IF bot_rec <> eof_rec
            GO eof_rec
            SKIP -last_row
        ELSE
            GO top_rec
        ENDIF
        hi_row = disp_page( last_row )

    CASE last_key = 127 && Backspace
        IF LEN(seek_chrs) > 0
            seek_chrs = LEFT( seek_chrs, LEN(seek_chrs)-1 )
            IF LEN(seek_chrs) > 0
                @ last_row+1, 1 SAY ' ' + ;
                    LEFT( seek_chrs, 10 ) + ' ' ;
                    COLOR N/W
```

```
            ELSE
               @ last_row+1, 1 SAY SPACE(12) COLOR &swin_clr
            ENDIF
         ENDIF

      OTHERWISE
         r = RECNO()
         s = seek_chrs + UPPER( CHR(last_key) )
         SEEK s
         IF FOUND()
            seek_chrs = s
            hi_row = disp_page(0)
            @ last_row+1, 1 SAY ' ' + ;
               LEFT( seek_chrs, 10 ) + ' ' ;
               COLOR N/W
          ELSE
            GO r
         ENDIF

   ENDCASE

ENDDO

RETURN                                    && end of scroll


*************************************************************
*** disp_page — display a full page of data
*************************************************************

FUNCTION disp_page
PARAMETER hi_line
PRIVATE i, r, hi, hi_rec

* Note: disp_page will highlight the last row of data if
* hi_line would be past the end of the file.

top_rec = RECNO()
hi_rec = 0
hi = hi_line

i = 0
DO WHILE ( i <= last_row )

  IF ( hi_rec = 0 ) .AND. ( RECNO() = eof_rec )
     hi = i
  ENDIF
```

```
    DO &ld_name WITH i, i = hi

    IF i = hi
       hi_rec = RECNO()
    ENDIF

    i = i + 1
    IF .NOT. EOF()
       SKIP
    ENDIF

ENDDO

SKIP -1

bot_rec = RECNO()

GO hi_rec

IF LEN(seek_chrs) = 0
   @ last_row+1, 1 SAY SPACE(12) COLOR &swin_clr
ENDIF

RETURN hi                                && end of disp_page


****************************************************************
*** ld_people — line display for PEOPLE.DBF
****************************************************************

PROCEDURE ld_people
PARAMETER row, is_hi

IF is_hi
   SET COLOR TO +GR/BG
 ELSE
   SET COLOR TO W/B
ENDIF

IF EOF()
   @ row, 0 SAY SPACE(34)
ELSE
   @ row, 0 SAY ' ' + people->name + ' '
ENDIF


RETURN                                   && end of ld_people


****************************************************************
* end of file SCROLLER.PRG
```

To test this program with your own .DBF, edit the .DBF-opening lines to USE your file and SET ORDER to the appropriate index tag. Then make sure that the window is wide enough to accommodate your data.

Finally, modify the ld_people() routine or replace it with your own routine. If you replace it, don't forget to change the "ld_people" string in the "DO scroll" call to whatever routine you create.

As you will see in the next section, this custom, .DBF-specific routine is the key to providing a record view simultaneously with the BROWSE-type view. It's the reason for using our own scroller.

Integrating the Record View

As with menus, our scrolling routine is a general-purpose engine. Using it is no more trouble than using a BROWSE. Providing a .DBF-specific display routine allows us to do anything we want. Showing a record-oriented view of a highlighted item, for example, is simple.

We'll need a window to write the data, and then we'll call a separate display routine when we write the highlighted record. Listing 14–14 shows the additions to the calling program.

Code Listing 14–14

```
swin_clr = 'W/B'
iwin_clr = '+W/B'

DEFINE WINDOW people_s ;
      FROM 10, 10 ;
      TO   21, 45 ;
      COLOR &swin_clr,,+W/B ;
      DOUBLE

DEFINE WINDOW people_i ;
      FROM  5, 45 ;
      TO   15, 75 ;
      COLOR &iwin_clr;
      PANEL
```

```
ACTIVATE WINDOW people_s
DO scroll WITH 'ld_people', 8

RELEASE WINDOW people_s
RELEASE WINDOW people_i

SET CURSOR ON
```

With the window available, the next change to make is in the ld_people() routine. It calls the new routine when it sets the highlighted color. This is shown in Listing 14–15.

Code Listing 14–15

```
PROCEDURE ld_people
PARAMETER row, is_hi

IF is_hi
  DO rd_people
  SET COLOR TO +GR/BG
ELSE
  SET COLOR TO W/B
ENDIF
```

Finally, you have to supply the record-oriented display routine. Listing 14–16 shows a sample display.

Code Listing 14–16

```
****************************************************************
*** rd_people — record-oriented display for PEOPLE.DBF
****************************************************************

PROCEDURE rd_people

ACTIVATE WINDOW people_i

SET COLOR TO &iwin_clr
@ 1, 1 SAY people->name
@ 2, 1 SAY people->addr1
@ 3, 1 SAY people->addr2
@ 4, 1 SAY people->city + ' ' + people->state + ' ' + ;
          people->zip

@ 6, 1 SAY people->phone PICTURE '@R (999) 999-9999'

ACTIVATE WINDOW people_s

RETURN && end of rd_people
```

The code in rd_people() is simple display code, but you could make it far more complex. Whatever you do, you must remember to restore everything that the calling program needs. For example, leave the same window activated and leave the .DBF positioned at the same record. Since the call to your routine immediately precedes a SET COLOR command, you don't need to preserve the color setting.

Improvements

The code shown here was written for this book. My own general-purpose scroller has too many years' worth of features and improvements added to see the basic structure of the code anymore. You'll want to begin improving your code right away, too.

First, you should replace the dBASE commands and functions, such as SKIP and EOF(), with the cover routines we developed in Chapter 9. That will support index-based filtering for efficient access.

Once that is done, you may want to consider adding a mouse capability. Chapter 3 showed you how to handle a mouse and keyboard event loop, with appropriate semaphore-based communication. It doesn't show you what to do when you are using INKEY() to get keystrokes.

The mouse is turned off during INKEY()s, for reasons that I do not understand. At any rate, it is simple enough to work around. @ GET a single-byte memvar in some out-of-the-way corner of the screen. (Row 1, column 78 is one of my favorites.) Set the color to 'W/W' or whatever will make it an invisible character. Then when you READ the mouse will be active and, if the cursor is off, the user will not see the dummy variable.

Summary

A scroller-based system provides a contemporary replacement for the old-style record views with "Previous" and "Next" menu options at the bottom of the screen. By building our own scroller, we can provide capabilities such as simultaneous scrolling and record views of the database.

Before we use our custom scroller to its fullest, we have to be able to nest our READ commands. For example, we want one scroller to pop up for point-and-shoot use during a data-entry screen input session. This scroller may pop up another data-entry screen, if the user elects.

The way to provide this capability is by doing a READ after every GET. This eliminates all nesting-related problems. It does mean, however, that we must provide our own inter-field navigation capability.

I've shown code here that does inter-field navigation, simulating all the usual dBASE control keys. This is done in a general-purpose field-control engine. Using this engine, you can build data-entry screens as easily as you could using dBASE's native multi-field GET/READ combinations.

Then we got into the code for a custom scroller. The first item we discussed is the key set of facts that this code must maintain. These facts constantly track which record is at the top and bottom of the visible window, which record is highlighted, and so on.

The scroller's overall code structure is similar to the menu's structure. There is setup code, a keystroke loop, and a highlight/lowlight system. Once again, we get the appearance of movement by lowlighting one item and then highlighting another.

Scrollers are, however, more complex than menus. I've learned to simplify their development by building debugging code *before* attempting to implement the scroller, not afterward. It is left in the scroller, commented out, for future use.

Next, we discussed the key routine of any scroller, the page display. Like the initial display of a menu, the page display calls the highlight/lowlight system to show a page of data, with one item highlighted. Unlike a menu, it handles SKIPping through the database and recording the key facts that we constantly maintain.

The page display calls a custom, table-specific highlight/lowlight routine that you write for each data table or .DBF. This is simple code that @ SAYs the scroller field or fields in the high or low color specified by a flag parameter.

The calling program that uses this scroller is similar to a menu's caller. It defines and activates a window, and handles other minor chores.

The largest part of the scroller code is in the keystroke loop. This loop contains far more code than a menu keystroke loop, since far more conditions must be tested. For example, a Down arrow must check that it is not already at the last record in the file. Then it tests that it is not at the last visible row in the window. Only then can it do the menu-like job of lowlighting the current record, then SKIPping and highlighting the next record.

As you've seen, the code for each condition is simple, but there are a large number of conditions to process. We discussed code for each keystroke pair, beginning with Up and Down arrows, continuing with PgUp and PgDn, and proceeding to Home and End. Finally, we looked at code for multiple-letter first-letter sensitivity, showing how the user can type "SMI" to find "Smith," for example.

The total code discussed and listed provides a complete scrolling engine. Once it is built, calling the engine takes about the same amount of setup work as you need for a BROWSE command.

Finally, we looked at a sample of a record view integrated with the scroller. This addition was almost trivially easy, since we had anticipated it and could fit it neatly into the custom routine.

Now you have your own scroller, and can use it as a front-end for data entry, or as a point-and-shoot lookup device. In Chapter 15, you'll see that being able to use scrollers this way is key to maintaining referential integrity.

Chapter 15

Complete Data Integrity

Every system builder has a vision of people sitting down at their computers, pressing a few keys and getting the right answer to a question. Perhaps they want the number of patients admitted last night, or the sales for the northeast territory last month, or the amount of money left in the software budget. Whatever it is, the answer is there and is easy to get.

In truth, our systems are making it easier to get answers such as these, but the hard part is making sure they are right answers to the right questions. Maybe the network went down last night and admissions were recorded manually. Perhaps your best salesperson changed territories and her accounts were credited to the wrong territory last month. Or the software budget looks well-stocked, but that's only because one supervisor hasn't signed a very large, disputed invoice.

To maintain data integrity, we use the software system to help insure that incorrect data does not get into the system. Both domain integrity and relational integrity must be continuously maintained.

What is the difference between them? Domain integrity makes sure that the night watchman's salary is within the range for night watchmen, not for sales VPs. Relational integrity guarantees that each invoice is attached to a customer and that nobody can delete a customer which has outstanding invoices.

Complete data integrity does not insure right answers. None of the three hypothetical problems noted above would be prevented by total data integrity. But it is the best prevention that the system builder can provide.

Domain Integrity

Domain integrity begins with having the right type of value in each field. If the field is numeric, it must contain a number. If it's a date, it must contain a date. Beyond that, domains can get even more restrictive.

We'll build a picklist function that lets the user point-and-shoot when there are a small number of choices. In our sample, our customers come from the six states of the New England region of the northeastern U.S. The value in the state portion of the address must be one of only six two-character postal state codes. (There are 676 possible combinations of two uppercase English-language letters. 670 of these are not in the "a state in New England" domain.)

Domains can also be complex calculations. For example, a salesperson's monthly commission check could range from zero up to a very large amount. Presumably, that amount is a function of sales made by that salesperson, overall company sales, funds received, and/or other factors. As system builders, we want to limit entries into any field to the smallest possible domain to guarantee the highest probability of data accuracy.

dBASE Features

From its beginning, dBASE has limited its field entries to values that meet the broadest domain checks. For example, you can only enter numbers in numeric fields. As dBASE has grown, its domain integrity tools have improved.

All the clauses of the @ GET command can come into play. Entering values into a field with PICTURE "@R (999) 999-9999" gets a North American telephone number. (Actually, other checks can be applied. The second digit, for example, must be a "0" or a "1." The first digit must not be a "0," and so on.)

RANGEs help maintain domain integrity, and VALID clauses are the most powerful of the domain integrity tools. The most powerful form of the VALID clause is the VALID User-Defined Function (UDF).

The telephone number checks suggested above could be done in a VALID UDF that augmented the PICTURE clause. VALID UDFs are often the location of all the business rules that your diligent searching uncovers.

In Chapter 14, we used a field-controlling keystroke loop to allow us to do a READ after each GET. Our structure for a typical GET routine was:

```
PROCEDURE cust_get
PARAMETER which_fld

DO CASE
   CASE which_fld = 1
      @ r1, c1 GET name PICTURE . . .

   CASE which_fld = 2
      @ r2, c2 GET address VALID . . .

   CASE which_fld = 3
      etc.

ENDCASE

READ

RETURN
```

We can make this an even more flexible structure, if we place a READ immediately after each @ GET command. That would look like this:

```
PROCEDURE cust_get
PARAMETER which_fld
```

```
DO CASE
   CASE which_fld = 1
      @ r1, c1 GET name PICTURE . . .
      READ

   CASE which_fld = 2
      @ r2, c2 GET address VALID . . .
      READ

   CASE which_fld = 3
      etc.

ENDCASE

RETURN
```

As shown here, this adds command lines without changing the functionality. But what it now lets us do is this:

```
PROCEDURE cust_get
PARAMETER which_fld

DO CASE
   CASE which_fld = 1
      DO WHILE .T.
         @ r1, c1 GET name PICTURE . . .
         READ

         * Here we can have any sort of checking
         * or calculating or whatever.

         * We can display messages for the user,
         * ask for additional values or whatever.

         IF we're happy with the result
            EXIT
         ENDIF

      ENDDO

   CASE which_fld = 2
      @ r2, c2 GET address VALID . . .
      READ
```

```
      CASE which_fld = 3
         etc.

ENDCASE

RETURN
```

As the above pseudo-code suggests, there is really no limit to the code you can create for any field in the database. For one example, let's consider a picklist that gets just one of six values. Our company sells products in the New England region of the U.S. The states and postal codes in this region are:

```
State              Postal Abbreviation
-----              ------ ------------
Maine              ME
New Hampshire      NH
Vermont            VT
Massachusetts      MA
Rhode Island       RI
Connecticut        CT
```

We've decided to use the two-letter abbreviation as the field in our database, but we want the user to pick from a list showing the full state names.

We want the calling code to be:

```
CASE which_fld = 5
   state = pick_state( state )

CASE which_fld = 6
   etc.
```

Alternatively, instead of using a pick_state() routine, we could put all the calling code (DECLARE and build the list of names and postal abbreviations, and so on) right here in our GET routine.

Array-Based Picklist

The code in this section provides you with a general-purpose, array-based picklist routine. We'll cover picking from .DBFs in the "Referential Integrity" section of this chapter. This capability was first introduced in Xbase in the Clipper dialect as the ACHOICE() built-in function.

I tried ACHOICE() and was impressed by what a good idea it was, and with the number of places where I thought it would be handy. Then, as usually happens with these tools, I started noticing things that weren't quite done my way. For example, I like to have a space on either side of the highlighted choice.

With a little thought, I decided to just add the extra spaces to the strings in the array of choices. But this didn't quite do it. Since every choice started with a space, I inadvertently killed a nice feature. The light bar should hop straight to the next choice that started with a given letter if the user pressed a letter key. If three items started with "M," pressing "M" three times should hop to each one in turn. But with my extra spaces, every choice started with the space character.

Finally I gave up and wrote my own version of ACHOICE(). It does everything exactly the way I want it to, of course. I'll discuss the code here since I'm pretty sure that my way is not exactly your way. You can tweak this one to meet your own specifications.

Listing 15–01 shows the setup and calling code.

Code Listing 15–01

```
DECLARE choices[6]
DECLARE answers[6]

choices[1] = 'Maine         '
choices[2] = 'New Hampshire'
choices[3] = 'Vermont       '
choices[4] = 'Massachusetts'
choices[5] = 'Rhode Island '
choices[6] = 'Connecticut   '


answers[1] = 'ME'
answers[2] = 'NH'
answers[3] = 'VT'
answers[4] = 'MA'
answers[5] = 'RI'
answers[6] = 'CT'

achc_loclr = 'W/B'
achc_hiclr = '+GR/BG'
```

```
DEFINE WINDOW achc_win ;
      FROM 5, 10 ;
      TO  12, 26 ;
      DOUBLE ;
      COLOR &achc loclr,,&achc loclr

ACTIVATE WINDOW achc win

ans = my_achc( 2, 6 )
RELEASE WINDOW achc win

@ 24, 0 SAY '*** ' + ans + '  ***'
                                          && end of mainline
```

As you see, you set up two arrays. Choices[] holds the choices that you show to the user, and answers[] holds the answers that you put in your database. You also DEFINE and ACTIVATE an appropriately sized window before calling the my_achc() routine.

The actual call specifies both the default choice and the total number of choices. After the call you RELEASE the window. The line "@ 24, 0 SAY . . ." is purely for debugging.

This version of my_achc() is simple. It does not scroll an array larger than the window. You can add that feature if you need it using the logic from our file-based scroller.

My_achc() hops the light bar, just like our menus and file-based scrollers. The key is the simple display routine shown in Listing 15–02.

Code Listing 15–02

```
*************************************************************
*** my_acdsp — line display for my_achc()
*************************************************************

PROCEDURE my_acdsp
PARAMETERS chc_num, is_hi

IF is_hi
  SET COLOR TO &achc_hiclr
ELSE
  SET COLOR TO &achc_loclr
ENDIF

@ chc_num-1, 0 SAY ' ' + choices[chc_num] + ' '

RETURN                                  && end of my_acdsp
```

This should be pretty familiar to you by now. As always, we use this routine to move the light bar. The movement is controlled from the keystroke loop. Listing 15–03 shows the main keystroke loop's CASEs.

Code Listing 15–03

```
CASE last_key = 27 .OR. ;
     last_key = 13 .OR. ;
     last_key = 17 .OR. ;
     last_key = 23 && Esc, Enter, ^Q or ^W
   EXIT

CASE last_key =  5 && ^E or Up arrow
   DO my_acdsp WITH choice, .F.
   choice = IIF( choice = 1, num_chcs, choice-1 )
   DO my_acdsp WITH choice, .T.

CASE last_key = 24 && ^X or Down arrow
   DO my_acdsp WITH choice, .F.
   choice = IIF( choice = num_chcs, 1, choice+1 )
   DO my_acdsp WITH choice, .T.

CASE last_key = 26 && ^Z or Home
   DO my_acdsp WITH choice, .F.
   choice = 1
   DO my_acdsp WITH choice, .T.

CASE last_key =  2 && ^B or End
   DO my_acdsp WITH choice, .F.
   choice = num_chcs
   DO my_acdsp WITH choice, .T.
```

These CASEs are all straightforward, and are considerably simplified by not having to worry about scrolling.

The last CASE is the one that handles character keypresses. It uses a find function that searches the choices[] array. It first searches from the choice following the highlighted one through the end. If it doesn't find the letter there, it searches from the beginning of the array up to the highlighted choice. It hops the light bar to the first matching choice it encounters.

This is different from the .DBF-based scroller in Chapter 14. That one searches for one or more characters, and allows primitive editing of the character buffer. This one only searches for a single letter and does not maintain a character buffer. This one is a better choice for a routine built purely for small arrays. Remember, our .DBF scroller was searching an alpha-sorted file. This one does not depend on the array being sorted. Listing 15–04 shows the CASE that does the first-letter searching.

Code Listing 15–04

```
CASE last_key > 31
   loc = 0
   IF choice < num_chcs
      loc = find_chc( CHR(last_key), num_chcs, ;
                      choice+1 )
   ENDIF

   IF loc = 0 .AND. choice > 1
      loc = find_chc( CHR(last_key), num_chcs, ;
                      1, choice-1 )
   ENDIF

   IF loc <> 0
      DO my_acdsp WITH choice, .F.
      choice = loc
      DO my_acdsp WITH choice, .T.
    ELSE
      @ 0, 0 SAY CHR(7)
   ENDIF
```

You can, of course, adopt the logic from the .DBF-based scroller in Chapter 14 if you prefer.

Listing 15–05 shows the find_chc() function that does the actual searching.

Code Listing 15–05

```
************************************************************
*** find_chc — find a value in the choices[] array
************************************************************

FUNCTION find_chc
PARAMETERS val, array_len, start_loc, stop_loc
PRIVATE i

IF PCOUNT() < 4
  stop_loc = array_len
ENDIF
```

```
IF PCOUNT() < 3
  start_loc = 1
ENDIF

i = start_loc
DO WHILE i <= stop_loc
  IF UPPER( choices[i] ) = UPPER( val )
     RETURN i
  ENDIF
  i = i + 1
ENDDO

* If "val" is found, RETURNs # from inside the loop

RETURN 0                                && end of find_chc
```

The entire program is shown in Listing 15–06. The small set of test data used here checks all of the possibilities for the single-letter search capability. Make sure you have *at least* one matching pair of choices if you want to test this engine with your own data.

Code Listing 15–06

```
* A_CHOICE.PRG — choose from an array
* copyright 1993, Martin L. Rinehart

DECLARE choices[6]
DECLARE answers[6]

choices[1] = 'Maine          '
choices[2] = 'New Hampshire'
choices[3] = 'Vermont        '
choices[4] = 'Massachusetts'
choices[5] = 'Rhode Island '
choices[6] = 'Connecticut  '


answers[1] = 'ME'
answers[2] = 'NH'
answers[3] = 'VT'
answers[4] = 'MA'
answers[5] = 'RI'
answers[6] = 'CT'

achc_loclr = 'W/B'
achc_hiclr = '+GR/BG'

DEFINE WINDOW achc_win ;
      FROM 5, 10 ;
```

```
        TO  12, 26 ;
        DOUBLE ;
        COLOR &achc_loclr,,&achc_loclr

ACTIVATE WINDOW achc_win

ans = my_achc( 2, 6 )
RELEASE WINDOW achc_win

@ 24, 0 SAY '***  ' + ans + '  ***'
                                            && end of mainline



************************************************************
*** my_achc — my version of Clipper's ACHOICE
************************************************************

FUNCTION my_achc
PARAMETER hi_chc, num_chcs
PRIVATE i, choice

* called with:
* a window ACTIVATEd
* a global array choices[] that the user sees
* a global array answers[] of the values to return
* hi_chc — the number of the default choice
* num_chcs — the total number of choices

* returns:
* the number of the users choice
* the keystroke variable is last_key, not PRIVATE

i = 1
DO WHILE i <= num_chcs

 DO my_acdsp WITH i, i=hi_chc

 i = i + 1
ENDDO

choice = hi_chc

DO WHILE .T.

  last_key = INKEY(0)

  DO CASE
    CASE last_key = 27 .OR. ;
         last_key = 13 .OR. ;
         last_key = 17 .OR. ;
```

```
            last_key = 23 && Esc, Enter, ^Q or ^W
         EXIT

      CASE last_key =  5 && ^E or Up arrow
         DO my_acdsp WITH choice, .F.
         choice = IIF( choice = 1, num_chcs, choice-1 )
         DO my_acdsp WITH choice, .T.

      CASE last_key = 24 && ^X or Down arrow
         DO my_acdsp WITH choice, .F.
         choice = IIF( choice = num_chcs, 1, choice+1 )
         DO my_acdsp WITH choice, .T.

      CASE last_key = 26 && ^Z or Home
         DO my_acdsp WITH choice, .F.
         choice = 1
         DO my_acdsp WITH choice, .T.

      CASE last_key =  2 && ^B or End
         DO my_acdsp WITH choice, .F.
         choice = num_chcs
         DO my_acdsp WITH choice, .T.

      CASE last_key > 31
         loc = 0
         IF choice < num_chcs
            loc = find_chc( CHR(last_key), num_chcs, ;
                        choice+1 )
         ENDIF

         IF loc = 0 .AND. choice > 1
            loc = find_chc( CHR(last_key), num_chcs, ;
                        1, choice-1 )
         ENDIF

         IF loc <> 0
            DO my_acdsp WITH choice, .F.
            choice = loc
            DO my_acdsp WITH choice, .T.
          ELSE
            @ 0, 0 SAY CHR(7)
         ENDIF

      OTHERWISE
         * do nothing (or ?? CHR(7), if you like)

   ENDCASE

ENDDO

RETURN answers[ choice ]                    && end of my_achc
```

```
***************************************************************
*** my_acdsp - line display for my_achc()
***************************************************************

PROCEDURE my_acdsp
PARAMETERS chc_num, is_hi

IF is_hi
  SET COLOR TO &achc_hiclr
ELSE
  SET COLOR TO &achc_loclr
ENDIF

@ chc_num-1, 0 SAY ' ' + choices[chc_num] + ' '

RETURN                                    && end of my_acdsp



***************************************************************
*** find_chc - find a value in the choices[] array
***************************************************************

FUNCTION find_chc
PARAMETERS val, array_len, start_loc, stop_loc
PRIVATE i

IF PCOUNT() < 4
  stop_loc = array_len
ENDIF

IF PCOUNT() < 3
  start_loc = 1
ENDIF

i = start_loc
DO WHILE i <= stop_loc
  IF UPPER( choices[i] ) = UPPER( val )
    RETURN i
  ENDIF
  i = i + 1
ENDDO

* If "val" is found, RETURNs # from inside the loop

RETURN 0                                  && end of find_chc



***************************************************************
* end of file A_CHOICE.PRG
```

When you build this into your systems, make sure that you call it with the current value in the database as the default value. This means that the user who simply presses Enter when the picklist pops up will leave the current value intact. This is consistent with the treatment of all of your other fields.

My_achc() is a routine that is very commonly used in the systems I build. It guarantees that the database value will be in a tightly restricted domain. But just as important, it shows how our GET routine structure lends itself to custom routines that are not limited to @ GET code.

Referential Integrity

Referential integrity is achieved when every foreign key matches exactly one primary key. This means that every invoice is "attached" to exactly one customer; every invoice detail record is attached to exactly one invoice and refers to exactly one product.

With the exception of deletes, where some special checking is required, you can build referential integrity into the front-end. This requires an intelligent implementation of the Enter keystroke in our scroller.

You may call the scroller in two modes: as a data-browsing and data-entry tool, or as a point-and-shoot lookup tool. The difference is that in the former mode (I'll call it "standard" mode) an Enter keystroke pops up the data-entry window on the highlighted record. In point-and-shoot mode, Enter selects the highlighted record, returning to a calling program.

There are two ways to call the scroller in standard mode. First, you can use it to let the user browse the database. You can also call it to browse just the children of a parent record by setting a logical filter prior to calling the scroller. For example, you may be in a customer record and call the invoice scroller to examine only the invoices related to that customer.

The set_filter() routine described in Chapter 9 handles this job. With the scroller modified to use the other routines developed in Chapter 9, no additional work is needed. Different treatment is needed in the handling of the Ins keystroke.

Add

In standard mode, pressing Ins appends a blank record and then lets you add data to it. In my systems, I usually have Ins trigger insert mode, where you keep appending records until an Esc key signals that you are finished. Having Ins trigger a single-record insert may be a better choice in some circumstances.

When filtered() is True (see Chapter 9, Listing 9–03) your code varies slightly. If you are in the invoice scroller with a filter setting that limits access to the invoices related to the current customer, your data-entry routine will automatically supply that customer's primary key as the customer foreign key (attaching the new invoice to the current customer).

If filtered() was False, you call the customer scroller in point-and-shoot mode. The user selects a customer. You then transfer the customer primary key into your foreign key field.

In pcode, the Ins treatment looks like this:

```
CASE fld_num = the customer foreign key
              in the invoice table
   IF filtered()
      REPLACE invoic->cust_k WITH cust->cust_k
    ELSE
      DO customer scroller
      REPLACE invoic->cust_k WITH cust->cust_k
   ENDIF
```

Of course, in your working code you will not REPLACE directly into the fields, but will assign the input to a memvar or array element. REPLACE is only shown here to clarify the main point.

You could make this a bit tighter by rewriting it this way:

```
CASE fld_num = the customer foreign key
              in the invoice table
   IF .NOT. filtered()
      DO customer scroller
   ENDIF
   REPLACE invoic->cust_k WITH cust->cust_k
```

Resist the temptation to tighten it that way to save one line. You'll need that line. The full code when you are not filtered() is more like this:

```
IF filtered()
. . .
 ELSE && .not. filtered()
   DO customer scroller WITH point_and_shoot_mode

   IF the user did not exit via Esc or ^Q
      REPLACE invoic->cust_k WITH cust->cust_k
    ELSE
      dont_do_it_flag = .T.
      EXIT && from the field entry loop
   ENDIF
ENDIF
```

Again, the REPLACE is only shown here to illustrate the point. Your system will save the value in memory, and do the REPLACEs as discussed in Chapter 10.

What we have are two possibilities. One way, the customer was selected before we got into the invoices. The other way, the user picks a customer after we get into invoices. In both methods, the user is looking at data such as the customer's name and address. But underneath the visible portion, your software is transferring the primary key from the parent file, cust->cust_k, into the foreign key field, invoic->cust_k.

The foreign key will match the primary key at the time the record is added.

Edit

Edits work similarly. If the invoice is accessed from an individual customer, the customer key is not changed. If the invoice data is accessed directly, the user is given point-and-shoot access to the customer data.

Any change in the customer key is made by the same transfer of cust->cust_k into invoic->cust_k after the user has made a selection. Again, the visible point-and-shoot process shows the user the name and address of the customer. The underlying transfer uses the keys we introduced in Chapter 4 to tie the tables together.

There is at least a theoretical possibility that one user could delete a customer while another user is adding an invoice for that customer. In many systems, this is a problem that delete management will avoid. If it is a practical problem, the same sema-phore system discussed in Chapter 8 can detect this. You would just check the revision number of the parent record immediately before the REPLACEs to make sure that it matches the revision number that you read when you got the primary key.

Delete

Deletes are handled in one of two ways. If there are records attached to the record you want to delete (invoices for a customer, for example) you can refuse the delete or cascade the delete. But be aware that most auditors oppose cascading deletes in most situations.

In a cascaded delete, you would delete the customer, delete any invoices attached to the customer, and delete invoice detail rec-ords attached to those invoices. There is no theoretical depth limit attached to a cascading delete. You go from each parent to each child, deleting until the whole branch of the tree is gone.

On the other hand, you could simply refuse the delete. If there are any children attached to a parent record, your system just dis-plays a "sorry about that" message if you attempt to delete the par-ent record.

In my scrollers, I use the Del key to delete the highlighted rec-ord. (If the scroller is called for point-and-shoot selection, the Del key is disabled.) Direct access is provided from parents to their chil-dren. For example, the invoices for a customer are all available from the individual customer record. Within each invoice, the user has direct access to the invoice detail records.

If there are only a few attached records, it is only a matter of a few seconds with the Delete key to clear child records. Once the children are gone, the delete that was refused becomes an accept-able delete.

Cascaded deletes are only necessary when there are a lot of records attached to a parent. In many cases, such as a customer who has many outstanding invoices, this sort of delete poses some seri-ous management questions. Why, for example, are you deleting all the data about a customer with many open invoices? There are few honest situations where this is desirable. This is one of the reasons that cascaded deletes make auditors very nervous.

Cascaded deletes also pose problems with permissions, as we will discuss in Chapter 16. The user needs "write" access to a record to delete it. (Some systems have separate "write" and "delete" permissions. But since "write" gives users the ability to blank out a record, little seems gained by separating them.) But write access to a record does not imply write access to all the related child records.

For example, the sales people may add and update customer name and address information. However, the sales people normally do *not* have write access to invoice data.

A cascaded delete requires that the user initiating the delete have write access to all the records (children, grandchildren, and so on) attached to the parent record.

Using the seek_ctl() routine (Chapter 9, Listing 9–10) it is easy to check for records in related child files. In the customer table, for example:

```
SEEK for invoic->cust_k matching cust_cust_k
```

If you find any invoices whose foreign keys match the primary key of the customer you want to delete, refuse the delete with an appropriate message. More generally:

```
delete_ok = .T.
FOR each child table with possible attached records
   SEEK foreign_key matching primary_key
   IF FOUND()
      delete_ok = .F.
      EXIT
   ENDIF
ENDFOR

IF delete_ok = .T.
   DELETE the record
 ELSE
    politely refuse
    * log the refusal?
ENDIF
```

Your auditor will advise you whether refusals are items that you want to log. Logging refusals or other non-update behaviors is normally done in files other than the regular audit trail files. You can use .DBFs or low-level text files to record these events.

With DELETEs handled this way, none of the three data-updating transactions can violate referential integrity.

I put the delete-checking code in a single routine, where it is easy to examine and change as the system design evolves. This is a typical example:

```
FUNCTION del_ok

DO CASE
    CASE sele_area = 5 && cstmer
       * SEEK cstmer->cstmer_k in invoic->cstmer_k
       RETURN .NOT. FOUND()

    CASE sele_area = 6 && invoic
       * SEEK invoic->invoic_k in invdtl->invoic_k
       RETURN .NOT. FOUND()

    CASE sele_area = 7 && invdtl
       RETURN .T.
       * this table has no child records

    CASE sele_area = 8 && prduct
       * SEEK prduct->prduct_k in invdtl->prduct_k
       RETURN .NOT. FOUND()

    OTHERWISE
       * fatal error on call to del_ok

ENDCASE
```

If there is a table with multiple children, you can return .F. (deleting is not OK) as soon as a SEEK finds the first attached child. You can only return .T. if all the SEEKs fail. The code looks like this:

```
CASE sele_area = multiple child record types
    SEEK parent->parent_k in child1->parent_k
    ok = .NOT. FOUND()
    IF ok
       SEEK parent->parent_k in child2->parent_k
       ok = .NOT. FOUND()
       IF ok
          SEEK parent->parent_k in child3->parent_k
          ok = .NOT. FOUND()
       ENDIF
    ENDIF
    RETURN ok
```

Summary

You can have your system help with data integrity. If you maintain domain and referential integrity you will avoid a large class of errors. You will not, however, be assured that your data is correct.

Domain integrity ensures that only acceptable values are placed in each field. In its simplest form, it means that you cannot enter a name into a numeric field. The acceptable domain of a field may be a simple specification, such as a positive integer, or it may be a sophisticated calculation, such as sales commissions as a function of sales and other factors.

dBASE itself provides you with many controls on domain integrity. At its simplest, for example, only dates can be entered into date-type fields. Many additional dBASE features also help ensure domain integrity.

These include PICTURE clauses, RANGEs, and VALID clauses. With user-defined functions available in VALID clauses, there is no technical reason for not modelling even the most complex business rules.

One of the most common types of domain integrity is the list of acceptable values. I showed you subroutines that use point-and-shoot picklists to enter values into the database. These show the user a set of acceptable answers, entering a code (not necessarily the same one you show to the user) into the field.

Referential integrity ensures that each foreign key matches the corresponding primary key. Each invoice is "attached" to one and only one customer, for example. In the software we discussed, scrollers are used to position the database, and the actual assignment of foreign keys goes on a level below the user's actions.

On adding an invoice, for example, there are two possibilities. If the user has already selected a customer, you transfer that customer's primary key into the new invoice record automatically. If no customer is selected, you call the customer scroller in point-and-shoot mode, allowing the user to choose a customer. Again, after the user selects your system transfers the appropriate primary key into the foreign key field.

We handle data edits the same way, using scrollers to show the user a "natural" view of the database, handling keys in response to point-and-shoot user actions. For example, an invoice that has an attached customer will pop up the customer scoller, already positioned to the selected customer. The user can accept that choice by pressing Enter, or can use the scroller to change the selection. Again, our system transfers keys in response to the users' actions with the scrollers.

Deletes cause us special concens. You cannot delete a customer, for example, who has invoices outstanding. Of the two methods of handling deletes, cascading and refusing, cascading (automatically deleting attached invoices when a customer is deleted) is seldom acceptable or auditable data. Deletes can be made a convenient substitute if we can show the user a scroller limited to, for example, just the open menus for one customer. Using the index-based filtering discussed in Chapter 9, this is simple.

Our final chapter considers the password and permission subsystems. As always, systems are integrated affairs that don't have clear, linear paths. In Chapter 13, for example, we built our menu engine to use permissions that we hadn't yet discussed. Chapter 16 closes this final loop.

Chapter 16

Passwords and Permissions

This chapter would be more accurately called "user-name authentication and permissions"—passwords are really just one piece of the procedure for identifying your user. But everyone calls the user-name authentication sub-system a password system. We all understand that the topic is letting authorized users have the access rights that they have been granted, while preventing unauthorized access and use.

Passwords and permissions are a client-side sub-system. The server software is normally protected with physical mechanisms. I recommend storing the server programs on removable media and bringing them to the server as needed, for complete security. For mild security, you can, of course, adopt any of the techniques discussed here.

Passwords

We'll begin with the user-name authentication software. Separately, you have granted users permissions to read or write various parts of your database. The front-end process that we're calling a password system is the process of asking your user for a name, and then verifying that the name is legitimate.

Names

Your network software probably has a name and password subsystem that identifies the user when he or she logs in. In some systems, this name data can be made available to your dBASE program, so no additional work is needed. In many systems, you'll need to write a short program in C or Assembler and use dBASE's LOAD and CALL facilities to access the user name.

There are several good reasons to add a name and password system to your dBASE client code, even if it duplicates the network facility. One is that it is much easier to implement if you are not a C or Assembler programmer experienced with dBASE's LOAD requirements.

A more important reason is that even if you are an old hand at LOAD routines, this software needs regular maintenance, which should be within the capabilities of a typical dBASE programmer. You should change the password encryption/decryption routines regularly. You will also need to change the network access code whenever you change or upgrade networks.

Even if you are not planning a network change, there is every possibility that your employer will merge with another company, be combined with another government agency, or something similar. Murphy's Law guarantees that the other folks will not be using the same network operating system that you are using.

Even if the software maintenance problem did not exist, there remains the network security problem. Many users log into their network at the start of the day and stay logged in. They stay logged in when they go to a meeting, or to lunch, or any number of other places away from their computers. You cannot be sure that the person seated in front of the computer is really the person who logged into the network.

The simple solution is to ask the user for his or her name when your client software begins. Then follow up the name with a request for a hidden password.

Passwords

Names are often public, but passwords never are. You may also wish to treat the name entry the same way you treat the password entry—as a hidden item known only to the authorized user. The software shown here can be used with any character field.

When the user enters a password, you want to disguise the entry from prying eyes. Many people do this by setting the color to something invisible, such as "N/N" and doing a normal dBASE @ GET and READ. That is a poor solution compared to showing a visible character, such as an asterisk, for each character typed.

If you display asterisks, users can make typical mistakes and use the backspace key to delete mistakes, just as if they were entering a normal text field. The routine in Listing 16–01 provides this facility.

Code Listing 16–01

```
*****************************************************************
*** pass_enter - password entry
*****************************************************************

FUNCTION pass_enter
PARAMETER row, col, pw
PRIVATE k, ptr, l, pdisp

l = LEN(pw)
@ row, col SAY SPACE(l)
ptr = 1                    && points to current char in buffer
pdisp = ''                 && the '*'s to display

DO WHILE .T.

   @ row, col SAY pdisp + SPACE(l-LEN(pdisp))
   @ row, col+ptr-1 SAY ''          && position the cursor
   k = INKEY(0)                     && get a keystroke

   DO CASE

      CASE k = 13 && Enter
         EXIT

      CASE k = 27 && Esc
         pdisp = ''
```

```
   pw = SPACE(1)
   ptr = 1

CASE k > 31 .AND. k < 127 && any non-control character
   pw = STUFF(pw,ptr,1,CHR(k))
   pdisp = pdisp + IIF(ptr > LEN(pdisp), '*', '')
   IF ptr < 1
      ptr = ptr + 1
   ELSE
      ?? CHR(7)
   ENDIF

CASE k = 127 && Backspace
   IF ptr = 1
      ?? CHR(7)
    ELSE
      ptr = ptr - 1
      pw = STUFF(pw,ptr,1,'')+' '
      pdisp = REPLICATE('*',LEN(pdisp)-1)
   ENDIF

CASE k = 19 && Left arrow or ^S
   IF ptr > 1
      ptr = ptr - 1
    ELSE
      ?? CHR(7)
   ENDIF

CASE k = 4  && Right arrow or ^D
   IF ptr < MIN(1, LEN(pdisp)+1 )
      ptr = ptr + 1
    ELSE
      ?? CHR(7)
   ENDIF

CASE k = 7  && Delete or ^G
   IF ptr <= LEN(pdisp)
      pdisp = REPLICATE('*',LEN(pdisp)-1)
      pw = STUFF(pw,ptr,1,'')+' '
   ELSE
      ?? CHR(7)
   ENDIF

CASE k = 26 && Home or ^Z
   IF ptr > 1
      ptr = 1
    ELSE
      ?? CHR(7)
   ENDIF
```

```
        CASE k = 2 && End or ^B
            IF ptr < MIN(LEN(pdisp)+1,1)
                ptr = MIN(LEN(pdisp)+1,1)
            ELSE
                ?? CHR(7)
            ENDIF


        OTHERWISE
            ?? CHR(7)

    ENDCASE

ENDDO

RETURN pw                              && end of pass_enter
```

As you can see, this provides all the keys that a typical user might think reasonable for entering a password. It displays asterisks in each place the user enters a character. The code in Listing 16–02 is a short driver that you can use to test this code.

Code Listing 16–02

```
set talk off
set color to w/n
clear
@ 10, 10 say 'password: '
set color to n/w
pw = pass_enter( 10, 20, space(12) )

@ 12, 10 say pw
k = inkey(0)
```

As you can see from the lowercase style, this is throwaway code, but it illustrates the calling logic. You set your color for the password, then call pass_enter() with the display coordinates and a string set to the size you want.

Auditors usually recommend that the password be at least 5 characters long. Most recommend that users pick passwords near the lower limit of password size. Passwords that are easy to remember and easy to type get used as intended. Passwords that are difficult to type can be stuck in keyboard macros, for example. This is a bit of cleverness you don't want to see.

Passwords should be updated regularly. Monthly updates are commonly recommended, but this is a matter that varies from system to system. Password changes should also be mandated whenever an employee leaves.

Listing 16–04 will show the code that gets and verifies a new password. Meanwhile, Listing 16–03 is a general-purpose message routine used in the new password code.

Code Listing 16–03

```
*****************************************************************
*** pop_say — pop up a message box
*****************************************************************

PROCEDURE pop_say
PARAMETERS s, s0, s1, s2, s3, s4, s5, s6, s7, s8, s9
PRIVATE buf, c, i, mac, ml, r, rows, temp

ml = LEN(s)
rows = PCOUNT()+1
IF rows > 2
 i = 0
 DO WHILE i <= rows-3
   mac = 's'+STR(i,1)
   ml = MAX( ml, LEN(&mac) )
   i = i + 1
 ENDDO
ENDIF


DEFINE WINDOW popsay_win ;
       FROM 0, 76-ml ;
       TO rows+2, 79 ;
       DOUBLE
ACTIVATE WINDOW popsay_win

@ 1, 1 SAY s

IF PCOUNT() > 1
 i = 0
 DO WHILE i <= rows-3
   mac = 's'+STR(i,1)
   @ i+2, 1 SAY &mac
   i = i + i + 1
 ENDDO
ENDIF
```

```
temp = INKEY(0)
RELEASE WINDOW popsay_win

RETURN                                          && end of pop_say
```

The pop_say() routine is a handy tool for displaying temporary messages. It pops up a message box showing as many lines as you passed it parameters, up to 11. You may, if you need to, set a color and cursor status before calling pop_say(). In practice, I generally just call it and don't worry about these items.

Listing 16–04 shows the pass_new() function. This gets a new password from the user, and requests a confirming repeat of the password. It handles failures to correctly repeat the password, and ensures that the password is at least five characters long. You may want to add a check that the new password is not the same as the old one.

Code Listing 16–04

```
*****************************************************************
*** pass_new — enter a new password
*****************************************************************

FUNCTION pass_new
PARAMETER pw
PRIVATE top, left, newpass, newpassc

top = 6
left = 25
width = LEN(pw)+20

* display entry box
DEFINE WINDOW newpasswin ;
       FROM top, left ;
       TO top+5, left+width ;
       COLOR +W/B,,+W/B
ACTIVATE WINDOW newpasswin

DO WHILE .T.
   @ 0, 1 SAY 'Enter new password            '

   DO WHILE .T.
      newpass = SPACE(LEN(pw))
      newpass = pass_enter( 2, (width-LEN(pw))/2, newpass )
```

```
     IF LEN( RTRIM(newpass)) < 5
        DO pop_say WITH ;
        'Password must be at least 5 characters long','', ;
        'Press Enter, then choose another password'
      ELSE
         EXIT
      ENDIF
   ENDDO


   * get confirming password
   @ 0, 1 SAY 'Please repeat this password '
   newpassc = pass_enter( 2, (width-LEN(pw))/2, ;
                          SPACE(LEN(pw))  )
   IF newpassc = newpass
     pw = newpass
     EXIT
    ELSE
     DO pop_say WITH ;
     'This does not match your first entry','', ;
     'Press Enter, then repeat from the beginning'
    ENDIF

 ENDDO

 RELEASE WINDOW newpasswin

 RETURN newpass                        && end of pass_new
```

With these routines, you can build a sub-system that asks your user for a name and password, and validates these against a name and password file. Have the database administrator assign user names (possibly the same as those assigned for network access), leave the passwords blank, and put a field in for the date the password was assigned. When the database administrator first enters the user name, also enter a password date that is obsolete.

The routine that reads this file to check the name and password should call pass_new() to get a new password whenever the password date is obsolete. It should store only encrypted passwords in the database.

Password Encryption

By storing encrypted passwords, the only decrypted version exists momentarily in the client machine. The next two routines are ones that I give every client with the direction: "Replace this code!"

Don't use them. They are included here to get you thinking about your own encryption and decryption routines. Listing 16–05 is code you should not use.

Code Listing 16–05

```
*************************************************************
*** encrypt — returns coded form of string
*************************************************************

FUNCTION encrypt
PARAMETER string
PRIVATE s, i

s = ''
i = 1
DO WHILE i <= LEN(string)
 s = s + CHR(255 - ASC( SUBSTR(string,i,1) ) )
 i = i + 1
ENDDO

RETURN s                                    && end of encrypt


*************************************************************
*** decrypt — reverses encrypt
*************************************************************
FUNCTION decrypt
PARAMETER string

RETURN encrypt(string)                       && end of decrypt
```

As you can see, encrypt() changes a CHR(1) to a CHR(254), a CHR(2) to CHR(253) and so on, up to changing CHR(254) to CHR(1). (Remember that dBASE won't work on a CHR(0), but the pass_enter() routine ensures that the only characters used are between CHR(33) and CHR(126).) Decrypt isn't really a function at all. It's just another way of calling encrypt.

The reason for decrypt is to remind you that you need a reverse operation. It just happens that this encrypt() is so simple that it is its own reverse operation, as well. You want decrypt(encrypt(x)) to be equal to x, of course. In this case, encrypt(encrypt(x)) is also the same as x.

Use something trickier than this. By all means, make the encrypted form a string of high-bit characters (128 and up) so a person stumbling into the password file can't read it. But rotate the letters, or write the last one, then the first one, then the next to last and so on. Make the encryption a function of the password date.

None of this will slow down a determined cryptographer, but that is not the point. You don't want the password file to allow a person (a person who shouldn't have this file in the first place!) to gain easy access to your database. Once a month, write a new encryption algorithm.

File-Based Passwords

Of course, when you replace the encryption algorithm, reset all the password dates to an obsolete time, so the system will request new passwords. For other changes, and for additional server security, you can use file-based passwords.

These aren't really passwords at all. Put any distinctive nonsense you like in a low-level file. Then put the same nonsense in a character string in the program. Have your system read the file to make sure that its nonsense matches the file nonsense. If there is no match, take some appropriate action, like denying access.

Why use file-based passwords? One common use is to ensure that the executable in the client machine is the latest version. On a lightly used network, you may simply have the client download the executable from the server every time they start the program. That is slow and an unreasonable burden for a heavily used network, however.

A better solution is to have the executable start by checking a file-based password. If there is no match, the executable knows it is obsolete. It can display a message and fail politely, or it can automatically initiate a new download for the user.

Logging Security Violations

In all password systems, the routine that reads the password and attempts to match it against the filed password should log all attempted security violations. Ask your auditors for their suggestions for this log.

A typical logging system is triggered when the user fails to provide the correct password after two or three attempts. At this point, a log entry is written and the executable shuts down. A more security-oriented system may also invalidate the user name after this kind of breach.

You must balance the ability of this mechanism to prevent unauthorized access against the ability of users to make simple typing mistakes. This is another reason for using the pass_enter() routine, and not just READ the password in a field colored "N/N."

Permissions

Once you have logged users on with their names, you check their permissions, as determined by the database administrator. My systems allow Yes and No permissions for each menu item, and Read, Write, or No permissions for each .DBF, field, and record.

Individually assigning each user permission for each field is a tedious, and normally unnecessary task. I classify users into groups, and classify system components into groups, too.

Typical users get access to the names, titles, telephone numbers, and so on in the company's personnel records. They have no access to salary or benefits information, of course. The benefits information, such as medical claims, is another data group, to which Read and Write permissions are granted only to the small number of people responsible for those things. Salary information is handled similarly.

Menu Permissions

The most effective permissions (or exclusions) are menu-based. We discussed the menuing software in Chapter 13. It is based on a general-purpose menu engine (as shown in Listing 13–17). This engine calls a system-specific routine that you supply, which returns a string of "Y"s and "N"s, showing permission for each menu option.

If there is an "N" permission, the menu option simply disappears. The remaining options close in to avoid leaving a hole in the menu. The user has no reason to even notice that something is missing. He or she wouldn't see, for example, that medical benefits would have been accessible if they had access to additional menu choices.

.DBF Permissions

.DBF permissions are seldom used, since menu-based permissions can perform the same service more gracefully. If your system has field-level permissions, the .DBF-based permission is not needed. To grant Read access to a .DBF, for instance, you simply grant Read access to all the fields in the .DBF.

Field Permissions

Many dBASE programmers do not grant permissions down to the field level. This is unfortunate, since it means that your system design will need to split object and other tables according to the different access classes. With our individual field reads, as shown in Chapter 14, field permissions are simple enough to add.

This is a sample GET/READ CASE, from Chapter 14:

```
PROCEDURE cust_get
PARAMETER which_fld

DO CASE
   CASE which_fld = 1
      @ r1, c1 GET name PICTURE . . .

   CASE which_fld = 2
      @ r2, c2 GET address VALID . . .

   CASE which_fld = 3
      etc.
```

This is the same fragment, with a permission check:

```
PROCEDURE cust_get
PARAMETERS which_fld, permit

DO CASE
   CASE which_fld = 1
      IF permit = 'W'
         @ r1, c1 GET name PICTURE . . .
```

```
        ELSE
          IF permit = 'R'
             @ r1, c1 SAY name PICTURE . . .
          ENDIF
      ENDIF

   CASE which_fld = 2
      IF permit = 'W'
          @ r2, c2 GET address VALID . . .
        ELSE
          IF permit = 'R'
             @ r2, c2 SAY address
          ENDIF
      ENDIF

   CASE which_fld = 3
        etc.
```

Note that this code does not let users with "N" permission see any field. You will not need to modify your GET keystroke-control loop to pass over "N" fields.

Another consideration is that the typical data-entry screen shows field labels, as well as fields. For those fields that you want to hide completely, move the @ SAY of the label into the field's CASE in the GET routine. The next sample shows this.

```
PROCEDURE cust_get
PARAMETERS which_fld, permit

 DO CASE
    CASE which_fld = 1
       IF permit = 'W'
          @ r1, c1-6 SAY "Name: "
          @ r1, c1 GET name PICTURE . . .
        ELSE
          IF permit = 'R'
             @ r1, c1-6 SAY "Name: "
             @ r1, c1 SAY name PICTURE . . .
          ENDIF
      ENDIF

    CASE which_fld = 2
       IF permit = 'W'
          @ r2, c2-9 SAY "Address: "
          @ r2, c2 GET address VALID . . .
```

```
              ELSE
                IF permit = 'R'
                   @ r2, c2-9 SAY "Address: "
                   @ r2, c2 SAY address
                ENDIF
              ENDIF

          CASE which_fld = 3
              etc.
```

With that addition, the fields with 'N' permission also disappear from the data-entry screen. You can make the same adjustment in the record-oriented display boxes discussed in Chapter 14.

Record Permissions

Finally, there are some permissions which should be based on the value in the individual records. For example, you may give each salesperson 'W' access to records for his or her own accounts, but 'N' access to records for anyone else's accounts. The sales manager might have 'R' access to all of the records.

This situation is handled in the software discussed in Chapter 9. You place the logic in your dBASE cover functions SKIP, GO TOP, and others.

Summary

There are two components to the software part of the overall security system: a password sub-system and a permission sub-system. The password sub-system is more accurately referred to as a username authentication sub-system. The permission sub-system provides only authorized system activities to each user.

The "password" system begins with the assignment of user names. These can be the names used during network login, but many systems will benefit from an additional, system-specific set of names.

Passwords are picked by the authorized users and revised at regular intervals. Passwords of less than five characters are generally too easy to decipher, but going as long as ten or more characters can make passwords difficult to remember and enter accurately. Software is discussed that allows entry into a simulated text field, appropriately responding to the Left and Right arrows, Del, and Backspace keys, while displaying an appropriate number of asterisks on the user screen.

Passwords are encrypted and decrypted at the client machine, so that unencrypted passwords are not sent over the network. Sample software for password encryption and decryption is shown with the firm recommendation that you write, and regularly rewrite, your own. The sample shows how this can be done in dBASE.

File-based passwords are suggested for applications such as ensuring that only the latest version of the client software is run. Small files at the server can be read by the client software and compared to embedded patterns. If there is no match, corrective action, such as downloading a new version of the client software, can be taken.

Simple or elaborate systems can be embedded to log attempted security violations. These should be discussed in advance with your auditors. A typical example is logging any occurrence of three successive attempts to log in with an invalid password.

Permissions are read from a permissions file once the user's name and password have been validated. The menuing software discussed in Chapter 13 shows how you can use this information to prevent unauthorized menu choices from appearing on the user's screen.

Less frequently, Read, Write, or No access permissions can be granted to selected .DBFs, when menu-based permissions do not handle this chore. Read, Write, and No access permissions are simple to add on a field-by-field basis, using the inter-field navigation engine shown in Chapter 14.

Record-level permissions are accomplished by setting appropriate filters. Record-level permissions could be used, for example, to grant Read access to the sales supervisor for all client records. The individual sales people could be granted Write access to their own client records, but No access to all other salespersons' records.

This completes our tour of the design and building of dBASE client-server systems. If you follow the techniques you've seen here, and employ the software I've presented, you'll be able to build your own mission-critical, auditable, client-server systems.

Index

124239 002401 610200